FAULKS

ON

FICTION

FAULKS

ON

FICTION

GREAT BRITISH CHARACTERS
AND THE SECRET LIFE OF THE NOVEL

SEBASTIAN

FAULKS

BBC
BOOKS

This book is published to accompany the television series
entitled *Faulks on Fiction*, first broadcast on BBC2 in 2011.

Executive Producer: Basil Comely
Series Producer: Mary Sackville-West

1 3 5 7 9 10 8 6 4 2

Published in 2011 by BBC Books, an imprint of Ebury Publishing.
A Random House Group Company

The Random House Group Limited Reg. No. 954009

Addresses for companies within the Random House Group can be found at
www.randomhouse.co.uk

A CIP catalogue record for this book is available from the British Library.

Hardback ISBN 978 184 607959 7
Export ISBN 978 184 990002 7

Mixed Sources
Product group from well-managed
forests and other controlled sources
www.fsc.org Cert no. TT-COC-2139
© 1996 Forest Stewardship Council

FSC

The Random House Group Limited supports the Forest Stewardship Council (FSC),
the leading international forest certification organisation. All our titles that are
printed on Greenpeace approved FSC certified paper carry the FSC logo.
Our paper procurement policy can be found at www.rbooks.co.uk/environment

Commissioning editor: Albert DePetrillo
Project editor: Laura Higginson
Copy-editor: David Milner
Production: David Brimble

Designed and set by seagulls.net
Printed and bound in UK by Clays Ltd

To buy books by your favourite authors and register for offers, visit www.rbooks.co.uk

CONTENTS

SNOBS

VILLAINS

'L'homme n'est rien, l'oeuvre tout.'

'The author's life is nothing; it's the work that matters.'

Gustave Flaubert in a letter to George Sand, December 1875.

INTRODUCTION

The way people think and write about books is always changing. I was raised on the 'New Criticism' (though it was pretty old by the time I got to it), which insisted that a work of literature is a self-contained entity and discouraged the student from trying to make connections between the text and the real world – particularly with any personal details of the author's life. You just wrote about the poem or the book, and how it achieved what it did. Although, like all schools of criticism, it was eventually pushed too far, it offered an essentially sound way of approaching a novel. It was replaced in the 1970s and 80s by critical theories that drew on other disciplines, notably Marxism and psychoanalysis. The most fruitful of these were those based on linguistics; they at least had a basis in neuroscience, and it was a scientific rigour that many literary critics felt ashamed of lacking. Few if any of these critical theories, however, made an impact on the reading public. This was partly because in the world of 'theory', returns diminish rapidly; the ratio of insight to verbiage is discouraging after a page or two.

The broader movement of criticism over the last twenty years has been biographical. Far from being banned from comment, the author's life and its bearing on the work became the major field of discussion. The advantage of this new emphasis was that it re-humanised the way that people looked at books: it made novels appear once again to be about people and experience, not structural linguistics. The bad news was that it opened the door to speculation and gossip. By assuming that all works of art are an expression of their authors' personality, the biographical critics reduced the act of creation to a sideshow. It has now reached such a pass that the only topic some literary journalists seem able to approach with confidence is the question of whom or what people and events in novels are 'based on'. Biographical criticism may have begun as a healthy reaction to extremes of New Criticism with its 'closed systems' and puritanical exclusion of facts; but it may now have reached its own terminal stage.

When I went round the country doing readings after my fourth novel *Birdsong* came out in 1993, most people could not conceal their disappointment. They had expected me to be 105 years old, French and – in some odd way – female. One man asked me how I knew what it was like to fight at the Battle of the Somme. I told him I'd read a lot of documents, visited the site, then made it up. 'You made it up?!' he almost spat at me. He didn't believe me, and neither did anyone else there. They thought I'd found a pile of old papers and passed them off as mine. When the politician Vince Cable recommended *Birdsong* in a magazine, he assured readers that I had based it on letters of my grandfather that I'd found in an attic. But there were no letters and no attic.

A subsequent novel, *Human Traces*, was concerned with the early days of psychiatry. When I spoke to a lunchtime gathering as part of the promotion for the book it seemed to me that the people present found it impossible to grasp the concept of fiction. They assumed that everything in a novel is based on personal experience, which is then lightly, or perhaps not at all, rewritten. In trying to persuade them otherwise, I despairingly recounted the story of the *Birdsong* sceptic and concluded with a heavy jest: 'So now I've given up and just admit that yes, I'm really a 105-year-old French woman, that I was parachuted into France for SOE in 1942 to write *Charlotte Gray* and wrote *Human Traces* only because my great-aunt was in a lunatic asylum in 1895.'

There was some sympathetic laughter; but when I was leaving, a woman stopped me, all concern, and asked: 'Which asylum was your aunt in?'

How did we come to this? It's not, after all, the natural state of affairs. A child first marvels at the invention of a story; he doesn't ask who Rumpelstiltskin was modelled on; he just loves it that a wishing chair can fly or animals can talk. In adult fiction, the element of wonder has somehow been lost; some readers seem to find it frightening to think a writer can conjure people, scenes and feelings from a void. Yet to me that is a novelist's single saleable skill, his USP.

Many novelists, I concede, haven't helped themselves. In the 1960s and 70s there was a movement in fiction against invention and towards semi-autobiographical writing (I go into this in more detail in the section on *The Golden Notebook*). And the separation between fact and fiction is not as clear-cut as purists, including me, would like it to be. Unless a novelist is psychotic, inhabiting a delusional universe, the fictional characters he creates and the thoughts he attributes to them are doubly connected to reality, first by his locating them in a recognisable world and, second, by the fact that they have passed, several times, through his own mind, which itself has been formed by millions of experiences in reality. I can honestly say that all the characters in all my novels are un-autobiographical in conception; none of them 'is' me; but at certain moments I am sure that details have been drawn from things that I have seen or felt and then – after double-checking their aptness – allowed to be attached to an imagined character as his own. The sensation of a hot bath, for instance, or of driving rain on the skin – many such small things have doubtless been experienced by my characters in a way so similar to that in which I experienced them as to be indistinguishable. But they are only details; and I take the line that, whatever the eighteenth-century philosophers may have argued, there are common human experiences of the phenomenal world. When Mike Engleby feels happy to be released from the hell of carsickness even into a place that resembles Broadmoor, it was not my experience of nausea that was being invoked, but yours.

While it is inevitable that parts of reality will thus seep through into fiction in more or less unchanged form, that does not alter the fact that most parts of most of the best novels ever written are either just invented, torn from a void, or represent aspects of reality so radically reshaped and recombined that they in essence become something new: not mixtures, but compounds with their own living properties. To me, this is the line beyond which there can be no more concessions to biographical reductionism.

Gore Vidal summed up the wearying nature of 'based on' critics in an essay on Ford Madox Ford: 'I must confess to a lifelong boredom with the main purpose of literary biography: the Life as opposed to the Work, which is, after all, all. I have also never had the slightest interest in knowing on whom a writer has based the character of Jeff, say; and should Jeff's affair with Jane be just like a real-life one with Gladys, I feel gravity tugging at the volume in my hand … It is not the sort of game that an English teacher ought to encourage his students to play. It is enough that they learn how to read and understand fiction *tout court*, to perceive what it is on the page that makes, as the Master said with unusual hard preciseness, *Interest*.'

And here is perhaps a major reason for the predicament we are now in. Just as in the 1980s British novelists, many of them graduates of the University of East Anglia creative writing course, were admirably turning their backs on the semi-autobiographical fictions of the 1960s and 70s and reasserting the novelist's ability to invent, so at the same time a large industry in literary biography had grown up, attracting some of the most gifted writers of that generation. Clearly it is legitimate for a scholarly biographer to mention *in passing* in the course of a full critical consideration of, say, *Vanity Fair*, that Thackeray had so much admired a young dragoon's side whiskers that he gave some similar ones to his imagined character, George Osborne; not interesting, admittedly, but legitimate. And while there is far more to the best of such biographies than merely identifying sources for this or that character, it may be that some of the lustre these distinguished biographers brought to the genre legitimised the efforts of less gifted Jeff-and-Gladys merchants. It's not then so hard to understand why a journalist reading an admiring review of a biography that revealed that X was 'based on' Y would feel he had been given the go-ahead to indulge exactly that sort of speculation in his own reviews or reporting. And if you think I am being unfair to the great biographers of the generation above mine, consider the words of one of the best, Sir Michael Holroyd: 'Biography is at the shallow end of history … The essential truth is simple. Flaubert was born. Flaubert wrote his novel. Flaubert died. It is his work which is unique, that matters, not the ordinary experience he shared with so many others.'

From the best biographers, however, via lesser ones, sideways into newspapers and out into the real world, 'based on' has become the default mode in which many readers now approach a novel. There are monthly book groups that meet to discuss a novel but end up talking about only two things: the extent to which the contents are drawn from the author's life and the extent to which these in turn tally with the readers' own experience of such matters. The 'success' or otherwise of the novel is calculated by how close a fit the author has managed between his or her presumably autobiographical narrative and the reader's own experience of similar events. It is difficult to explain how dispiriting such conversations would appear if overheard by a novelist who has tried, by invention, to reshape reality into something new, and more satisfying.

This book does not purport to be a work of literary criticism, still less of scholarship; it began life, after all, as a companion to a television series. I have looked at all these characters as though they were real people and tried to understand what makes them work without reference to their authors' lives. This is undoubtedly, and deliberately, an unfashionable approach, but I hope it might prove to be a touch on the brake of the runaway truck of biographical reductionism and an encouragement to others to think on these lines. If some of those so persuaded were sixth-formers, so much the better.

The choice of characters was restricted to books that the viewing public might reasonably have been expected to have heard of, if not actually read. It seemed a good idea to group them into the four character types that British novelists have returned to most often and, in addition to looking at the individual examples, to ask why these four have been so useful. These are not necessarily my all-time favourite writers or characters (though many are); they are ones that worked for television purposes.

However, as this book went along, it did seem to gather an identity of its own. It's meant to be a book of enthusiasm; it tries to celebrate the ability of novelists to create – from nothing, or from the imagination. Following Gore Vidal's advice, I have tried to read and understand twenty-eight works of fiction *tout court*, to perceive what it is on the page that makes, as Henry James said with unusual hard preciseness, *Interest*. Without the stimulus of this book, I would probably never again have opened *Tess of the d'Urbervilles* or *Great Expectations*, believing that I had 'done' them in my student days. Of the twenty-eight books here, twenty-three were re-reads; and of these my enjoyment was greater the second time in most cases. As to why I had never actually read the Raj Quartet or *The Woman in White* before, I can't imagine, but I can only say how happy I am to have done so.

Occasionally the pleasure of my reading was touched by sadness, and that was when it was necessary to think about 'posterity', or the chances of these novels still being read a hundred years from now. A university lecturer I talked to while writing this book laughed when I asked if *Vanity Fair* was popular with her students. She told me that *Vanity Fair* and *Middlemarch* will never again be read by undergraduates because they are 'too long'. One or two brave souls will tackle bantamweight *Silas Marner*, but most will go no further, she said, than a single photocopied chapter. Evidence from this world is inconsistent, however. Two graduate researchers who worked on the programme wrote excellent background notes on the characters' historical reception that showed every indication that they had read most of the books in question; and *Middlemarch* is a set book at A level for one exam board at least in 2011.

However, the idea that the intrinsic value of a book will 'keep it alive' seems absurd, when the thrust of tertiary education for the last fifty years has been to do away with the idea that there is any such thing as one book being 'better' than another. Part of the collateral damage of the 'theory' years of criticism in the 1970s and 80s was that in their search for a new scientific rigour many English literature teachers accepted that they could not 'prove' that *Middlemarch* was 'better' than the *Beano*, because 'better' was too imprecise and unscientific a word. This is logically true; but pundits proceeded to push logic beyond reason: I remember, with intense embarrassment, hearing people with the rare privilege of a good education arguing on Radio Four that you could never suppose that the *Divina Commedia* was *in any way* superior to the lyrics of Girls Aloud ...

So there will probably be no posterity of achievement, no survival for the fittest, because the culture can no longer accept that such things as 'fitness' exist; the sociopolitical damage of admitting that some things are better than others has become unendurable.[1] But that is too sad a thought to end on. The characters who appear in the following pages are still alive to me and to thousands, probably millions, of other readers. It's too much to imagine my enthusiasm for them and for the books they appear in will have any effect on their viability, but I hope that what follows can at least be read as a prolonged and heartfelt thank-you letter from a reader for all that he has learned from living people created in the minds of others.

----

[1] But publishers abhor a vacuum. While the academic world declared nothing was better than anything else, the consumer sector decided the exact opposite. Every coffee bar, hedge fund or mobile-phone group that sponsors a literary prize issues a list of books they have chosen or rejected; an indiscreet judge usually reveals which of the finalists 'really' came second or third. Literature festivals and newspapers pour out tables and rankings; in 2010, several published the order of precedence that novels published forty years earlier might have finished in, *had there been a prize* that year for them to enter... In *The Big Read* programme in 2003, BBC television invited viewers to list their favourite novels from any period, and ranked them in order from one to a hundred.

PART ONE

HEROES

It's a while now since anyone referred to the main character of a novel as the 'hero'. Yet for a word that was at best a misnomer and at worst a category error, it enjoyed a long life. I suspect that for nearly 200 years the misuse influenced the way that even the best novelists thought about their books and what they put into them.

Anthony Trollope seemed to think so, when he wrote in 1866: 'Perhaps no terms have been so injurious to the profession of the novelist as those two words hero and heroine. In spite of the latitude which is allowed to the writer in putting his own interpretation upon these words, something heroic is still expected: whereas if he attempts to paint from Nature, how little that is heroic should he describe!'

So even after the novel in its currently recognisable form had been around for 150 years Trollope still felt he was 'expected' to have a main character who displayed extraordinary qualities. Wouldn't it have been as sensible to expect him always to have red hair or be left-handed?

The explanation of how it happened is quite simple, though. The word 'hero' developed, as many words do; it changed its meaning over time through a semantic shift. The definition evolved roughly like this: (1) The offspring of a god and a human – someone like Achilles, who was the son of Peleus, a man, and Thetis, a nymph; (2) Someone of great distinction in battle (but could be wholly human); (3) Someone of great bravery in any field; (4) The main character in an epic poem, then, more loosely, in a play or story.

These things happen,[2] but the shift is seldom laid out as clearly as it is for 'hero' in the full *Oxford English Dictionary*. The first time it is used in our sense (4) is in 1697, in Dryden's *Life of Virgil*: 'His Heroe falls into an … ill-tim'd Deliberation'. Dryden was actually referring to Aeneas, literally a half-god hero; but one can see how the slightly playful use of the word here could be misread. This is how semantic shifts often occur: someone uses a word out of context or with a little spin; a reader fails to see the irony or tension; others follow.

By 1711, Richard Steele is using the word 'hero' in its new sense: 'The Youth who is the Hero of my story'. And so it goes on. But why could 'hero' not just *change* its meaning and come to mean 'main character of this exciting new genre', and forget about demigods? Why in 1866 were readers still half-expecting that the central figure in a Trollope novel should be the offspring of a nymph?

The answer again is not complicated. The evolution of meaning is no more clear-cut than the evolution of species; vestiges of previous incarnations can remain before a new species become discrete, unable to breed with its progenitors. So it was with the word 'hero' for most of the history of the novel, where for 200 years or more the old idea of admirable super-being lay behind the new meaning of 'main character'.

*

---

[2] Compare the word 'buxom', which went roughly: supine, obedient, compliant, pleasing, wifely, womanly, large-breasted.

You can see why the reading public in the early eighteenth century would like a word that promised something exciting in this new – novel – kind of book. And one can see, too, why the practitioners of an untried, irreligious form might at first have enjoyed the idea of inbuilt grandeur: it bestowed respectability by at least suggesting that their books would have a moral shape. Unlike poetry, novels didn't at first have much of a critical vocabulary in which to be discussed, and it was quicker to say 'hero' than 'principal character'. Like most shifts, it began as a mistake but caught on because it met a need.

To begin with, all went well. *Robinson Crusoe* is the first[3] novel and its main character is, as luck would have it, a hero. He has unusual, almost supernatural gifts. He succeeds in imposing 'civilised' values and order on a primitive world. He is a hero in both the primary (ultra-human) and the secondary (main character) senses. But perhaps he sets the novel off up a blind alley. Defoe may himself have thought so, if the character of Moll Flanders is anything to go by.

In the person of Tom Jones, Fielding has another try. His proposition is that a good heart is the best of possessions. It is a simple and sometimes simplistic view of the world. Crusoe prevails by means of his inner resources; Tom survives by means, one feels, of his author's interventions. He has a natural decency; he is passionate in love, lust and righteous anger. He 'works' as a hero because he is fortunate enough to be the protagonist of a well-crafted adventure and the brainchild of an avuncular providence.

---

[3] First for these purposes, viz. recent British. There is really no such thing, and there will always be people who can think of an earlier one than you can – Petronius, Gunadhya, Zhang Zhuo – or will change the definition to include poets.

By the time we reach Becky Sharp in *Vanity Fair*, the novel has revised its ideas of heroism. Becky is a cold-hearted, mercenary adventuress and a cruelly negligent mother. So what are her heroic qualities? Well, for a start, she is daring: she throws out Dr Johnson's dictionary and all the patriarchal lore it represents; she backs herself against the world, where even Achilles relied on divine help. She is honest; or at least, while she is duplicitous with others she is quite candid with herself. Third, she is the most interesting character. In the person of Becky Sharp, Thackeray makes explicit for the first time the rift between real-life and literary morals by showing that the highest virtue a fictional character can possess is *interest*. John Updike called it 'vitality', but it's the same thing. These qualities combine to make a fourth, and clinching one: we back her; this negligent mother, this selfish seductress is our representative at Vanity Fair. We select her over all the others – even good old Dobbin; and thus Becky clinches what will become the hero's most enduring quality: being the reader's point of identification.

In *Vanity Fair*, Thackeray successfully deconstructed the idea of novel 'heroism'. That he was concerned to do this is shown by the book's sub-title: 'A Novel Without a Hero'. Dickens, incidentally, was as concerned as Trollope with the word, though in *David Copperfield*'s opening page he puts his anxiety to comic effect: 'Whether I shall turn out to be the hero of my own life, or whether that station will be held by anybody else, these pages must show.'

Sherlock Holmes was perhaps the purest example of a hero-as-main-character that a British writer had contrived. Holmes has aspects of the demigod; he looks back to Achilles and forwards to Superman. We don't know if he was held by his heel in a river of immortality or formed on the planet Krypton, but he behaves as though something of the kind had happened in his youth. His feats seem devilish or supernatural to his enemies. But he is also a cocaine addict and a depressive; he is incapable of forming emotional attachments; he is afflicted by anomie and is addicted to violent crime – or at least to solving it. Over his super-rationalism seems to hang a *fin de siècle* premonition of some awful conflict in which the forces of reason will be annihilated.

And after 1918, it became increasingly difficult for the hero to find a place in serious novels. The Great War taught people that they were part of a murderous species that was not, after all, very clever. Individual acts counted for little on the Western Front in the face of a mechanised slaughter; Dobbin and George Osborne were arguably heroes of Waterloo, but to call any single man a hero of the Somme would seem to be missing the point.

What was hard to reignite after 1918 was the idea that individuals themselves counted for anything. Some post-war 'stream-of-consciousness' novels look with hindsight like a desperate attempt to locate value internally, because to claim significance in one's outer life was to overlook or, worse, dishonour, the fact that whole factory floors, football elevens and years of college freshmen were buried entire, side by side, in the mud.

In the twentieth century, the hero lost his freedom. He became a prisoner – of circumstance or of the state. One of the better novels to emerge from the Great War was Richard Aldington's *Death of a Hero*, though he could almost have called it *Death of the Hero*. After a period of absence from the serious novel, however, the hero re-emerged in 1949 – or rather, in *Nineteen Eighty-Four*. Winston Smith is a reluctant and improbable hero. He betrays his love and his conscience, and is crushed by the political forces that have grown like poison spores in the shell holes of Flanders and the ovens of Auschwitz. The novel is more concerned with politics than with characterisation, yet Winston does work as a character. That is because there is a tension between what he is – reduced, wheezy – and the role of heroic rebel that the state assigns him. We back Winston, as we back Becky Sharp, but we back him because, frankly, he's the only game in town.

Mainland Europe dealt with the mid-century in a different way. From Kafka via Camus to Sartre, through a climate of intellectual revolt and nihilism there emerged the doubtful figure of the 'anti-hero' – a short-lived and not very interesting concept. What does it mean? The main character of a book, yes, and one perversely without 'heroic' qualities; but the heroes of serious fiction, as we have seen, almost never did have 'heroic' qualities. To have had long-term traction, the idea of the anti-hero would have had to come at a time when main characters were all highly virtuous, but it had been many years since that had – if ever – been the case. Alternatively, you could define the 'anti-hero' as a character whose vocation is failure and trace him through Don Quixote, Bloom in *Ulysses*, Meursault in *L'Etranger* and Lucky Jim to Yossarian in *Catch-22*. But Lucky Jim gets the girl, Quixote is more comic hero than anti-hero, Meursault is heroic by his own lights and so on. It is interesting that the term died out – unlike the word 'hero' which may have owed its birth to a misunderstanding but did serve a purpose.

Jim Dixon in *Lucky Jim* doesn't smoke Gauloises and drink pastis in boulevard cafés; he doesn't reflect, like Meursault, that he could kill or not kill and that in the end it would come to exactly the same thing. No; he makes rude faces behind his boss's back; he gets drunk and burns the sheets. He has a pretty good job – rather pukka, really, being a university lecturer. But he is imprisoned by it, by the need to be polite to his absurd professor, by the need for money, security, tenure ... England of the 1950s has him in its grip as strongly as Oceania had Winston Smith. Jim's gestures of revolt are infantile, but he has something new – he is the first hero without dignity. Even Winston with his varicose ulcer is involved in a *noble* fight, while Jim's battles are petty. But although his world is exotically drab, we can identify with him. We back him not because he is the only game in town (Crusoe, Smith) or because the author tells us to (Tom Jones), but because (as with Becky) we like what we see.

By the time we get to *Money* and John Self, the idea of the hero as someone of positive distinction is quite dead. What is heroic about John Self is his excess. This rolling, belching Caliban is frank about something else: carnal greed. There is a little Self in every little self. We have all enjoyed Blastfurters and booze. And sex with Selina? We could all use a little of that. Yes, but could we use a *lot* of that? That is the question. That is the great thing about John Self – his world has one axis only: quantity. He is a very twentieth-century hero in that, as we shall see, he is also imprisoned. It is like watching a fat porpoise in a net, beached and thrashing. The most heroic thing about John Self is the extent of his self-abuse. The hero has become a tramp.

In Marvel comics and their spin-off films, the hero lives on frantically – leaping off computer-generated skyscrapers and gunning down armies of goons. To a lesser extent he is alive in fictional genres, where Sherlock Holmes found a path for him. The most widely known character of the last twenty years world-wide is an old-fashioned hero of magical, Achillean qualities and quiet virtue: Harry Potter. And the main character of *The Da Vinci Code*, Robert Langdon, also has heroic qualities. But Harry Potter is a children's book and *The Da Vinci Code* is ... Something else. For the mainstream novel, the hero is no more.

'SINGLED OUT'

ROBINSON CRUSOE

The first great hero in the British novel is a German called Kreutznaer. His father is from Bremen, but his mother is a Yorkshire woman from a family called Robinson, and it's not long before the people of York anglicise the family surname to Crusoe. The Teutonic and the West Riding strains are dominant in the headstrong and resourceful Robinson Crusoe. His 'ancient' father wants him to be a lawyer, but the eighteen-year-old Crusoe longs only for the sea. He is an adventurer by nature, but also a merchant; his idea of seafaring is not to serve in the King's Navy but to make money by trading – tobacco, gold, slaves, anything. Daniel Defoe's *Robinson Crusoe* (first published in 1719) is extraordinary in that its main character passes most of his life alone, thus forfeiting the world of 'personal relationships' that was to form the staple subject matter of the novel as it developed. Yet its main character offered a sort of gold standard of what the new form could do in terms of giving the reader privileged access to a developing state of mind; it was as though the novel was in this way fully formed at birth.

Crusoe's father is like a parent in a Philip Roth novel, full of émigré caution, urging his young son to find a steady job, to stick to the 'middle path' and not over-reach himself; he has already lost two sons. From the start, Crusoe shows a mixture of determination and cunning. He decides to ignore his father's advice, but enlists his mother to break the news to the old man; he cannily waits to engage her until she is in a good mood – 'a time when I thought her a little pleasanter than ordinary'. These humorous touches are vital in a story that will soon cease to contain any human intercourse. No sooner is Crusoe out of the Humber estuary on his first voyage than the wind blows a storm and he is so seasick that he vows to do his father's bidding. The next day, he is made drunk on punch by his fellow crewmen, and with a calm sea and a skinful of liquor all his good intentions are forgotten. A worse storm sinks the ship off Yarmouth, and although the crew are saved, the master's son tells Crusoe he should take it as a sign that the sea is not for him. Crusoe, though aware of the hand of Providence in all things, is a cussed fellow. He is a man who tempts Providence – 'tempts' in the sense of 'tests'. 'Providence' to his northern Protestant mind is the movement of chance in the world, guided by the hand of God; it is not as rigid as Fate, nor as flexible as something that stems from direct divine intervention; it lies somewhere between the two, but is something you 'tempt' at your peril. His attitudes to Providence and to God change as the plot unfolds; the older Crusoe who narrates the story has learned from the experiences of the young hero and is able to see his life as a Christian narrative in which the many 'strange' and 'surprising' events are actually instances of God choosing natural means to work out his providential plans for both humankind and for Crusoe himself.

The narrative is plain yet exotic. Like many of the greatest novels, it is set (beginning in 1651) many years before it was written[4] (1719) and it seems to offer a direct route into the past. This, you feel, is a quasi-journalistic account of what life was like in those days, not dollied up with fine phrases, but told in merchant seaman's prose. The effect is undoubtedly thrilling, like time travel, but is made more so by the fact there is something modern about Crusoe's attitudes. His brash entrepreneurial spirit seems familiar, and only the religious qualms with which it is – intermittently – restrained seem especially of their era.

After a rewarding voyage to the African coast, Crusoe sets sail again, only to be taken captive by Moorish pirates and made a personal slave to the master of the privateer. He escapes with a Muslim boy and is rescued at sea by a Portuguese ship to whose captain he sells the boy as a slave on the condition that he will be converted to Christianity. He goes with the Portuguese ship to Brazil where he sets up a successful tobacco plantation, but then sets off again for Africa in the hope of taking and trading more slaves. It is shocking to read of such things mentioned in the same terms as any other commerce ('few Negroes were bought, and those excessive dear'), but bracing to read of them unmediated by anachronistic judgement. The ship does not get far before a storm wrecks it somewhere in the Caribbean. Crusoe, the only survivor, is washed up on an uninhabited island, where begins his life of solitude.

---

[4] The idea that a novel not set at the time of publication is part of a genre called 'historical fiction' is a relatively recent one. The novel has always been historical in its mainstream, even when – as in *Robinson Crusoe* or *Wuthering Heights* (published 1847, set mostly in the 1770s) – most readers imagine it to be contemporary because the reason for its being 'historical' is not immediately clear.

What the novel deals with, as everyone knows, is survival. The drama springs partly from the physical demands – the adventure story, which Defoe handles with skill and humour – but more importantly from the spiritual torment of solitude. There are questions of religious faith, of the values of Christian civilisation in a world that includes cannibals, and then there is the overriding test that Crusoe must answer: is humankind sufficiently developed and self-reliant that, with no other of his species on hand, he will continue to behave as a man. I think the book is, at its most interesting level, a consideration of the extent to which the speciating elements of *Homo sapiens* hold up under pressure and enable Crusoe to maintain his separateness from the rest of creation. One of the crucial points in the evolution of human consciousness came when an individual was first able to function apart from the group – to go out hunting or fishing alone and to carry in his head the idea of others continuing to exist without his presence.[5] Crusoe does more than this; his heroic belief not only in humanity but in the narrower virtues of Protestant Europe is triumphantly vindicated.

The ship is conveniently stranded on a sand bar, allowing Crusoe to swim out, rig up a raft from broken timbers and bring ashore as much as he can, most importantly some 'fowling pieces' (guns) and a carpenter's chest of tools. He is tempted by the large quantity of European and Brazilian coins on board, but comes to his senses when he recognises the money is of no use to him and would be better off at the bottom of the sea, like a 'creature whose life is not worth saving'. What is engaging about Crusoe, however, is the tension, often comic, between the pious, Low Church

---

[5] For a fascinating discussion of this hypothetical moment, see Part I, chapter 6, 'The Origin of Civilization', in Julian Jaynes: *The Origin of Consciousness in the Breakdown of the Bicameral Mind*. (N. Y. Houghton Mifflin, 1976)

German and the striving small businessman with a knowledge of the value of brass. And so, he tells us, 'Upon second thoughts, I took [the coins] away.' Retaining the money also shows an optimistic belief that his life will one day give him back a chance to spend it.

Among his first kills is a suckling she-goat. He hopes to bring up the orphaned kid as a pet, but 'it would not eat so I was forc'd to kill it and eat it myself'. This is a characteristic Crusoe sequence: knowledge of right and wrong, qualm, practical despatch. The other repeating pattern of thought is to bewail his wretched lot – being cut off from his fellow man for all time in desolate loneliness – and to ask why 'Providence should thus compleatly ruin its creatures'; then, just before giving way to despair, to wonder at his good fortune in being the only man saved from the wreck. 'Why were not they sav'd and you lost?' he asks himself in Calvinist terms; 'Why were you singled out?'

His spiritual project is to convince himself that he is not desolate but chosen, not abandoned but fortunate. Although he claims that 'I had very few notions of religion in my head', he seems to have absorbed a great deal; a whole vein of Protestantism is summed up in his reminder to himself that in the 'most miserable of all conditions in this world … we may always find something to comfort ourselves'. And no one who had not absorbed the rhythms, at least, of the King James Bible could have written this meditation: 'In a word as my life was a life of sorrow one way, so it was a life of mercy another; and I wanted nothing to make it a life of comfort, but to be able to make my sence of God's goodness to me, and care over me in this condition, be my daily consolation; and after I did make a just improvement of these things, I went away and was no more sad.'

And was no more sad … What intensifies his interest in the divine, however, is something that seems to him a miracle. He chucks out some dried corn husks from a bag he has salvaged from the ship and some time later sees that a small crop of barley has grown up where he threw them. A tiny crop of rice appears from the same unlikely source. It is one thing to recognise the different plants, another to know how to make bread. Crusoe is by no means a natural smallholder, still less a cook; like most of us, his ideas of how grain is harvested, winnowed, milled or whatever are rather sketchy. There is something touchingly ham-fisted and believable in his struggles to make this simplest of human foods. And as for his attempts at crockery ...

The pace and character of the narrative are varied by some pages from a journal. These also serve to give an impression of the passing of time – the days, the seasons, the years ... The philosophical debate in Crusoe's mind takes on a sharper outline. The concession that the previously un-regarded God has been merciful means He must be omnipotent and has therefore brought Crusoe to this pass. Again, despair beckons; and again he saves himself from it by reflecting on his 'mis-spent life', and asking why he was not drowned in previous shipwrecks, or killed by beasts in Africa or murdered by the pirates. None of these escapes, lucky though they were, really constitutes a 'mis-spent' youth. The things he might regret – slave-trading and avarice – do not occur to him as faults. However, he progresses from thinking rarely about God to giving 'hearty thanks' for allowing him this island solitude in which he may be happier than he would have been in society; and when in his salvaged Bible he comes across the words 'I will never, never leave thee, nor forsake thee', he believes they are written to him personally. Whatever one's own religious beliefs, it is hard not to feel a pricking of the eyes at this moment.

Most narratives of despair and imprisonment contain a moment of transcendence, at which the castaway or prisoner is able to see himself as part of a larger creation and is able somehow not only to accept his fate but to bless his fellow creatures, even his persecutors. One thinks of the Ancient Mariner, who has violated the natural order by shooting the albatross, so bringing death on his shipmates, but is able finally to save himself when he blesses the sea snakes he sees writhe below the surface of the endless ocean. *In God's Underground*, the account of a Rumanian pastor, Richard Wurmbrand, persecuted and imprisoned by the Communist government in the 1960s, contains a scene in which Wurmbrand, in the darkness of his torture and solitary confinement, stood up and danced because he remembered that the Psalms had commanded joy. More recently, Brian Keenan's moving account of his imprisonment in Lebanon, *An Evil Cradling*, has a moment of grace when he imaginatively reaches out and extends his sympathy to those who have so wronged him. For a precursor, Defoe had *Pilgrim's Progress*, written by Bunyan in Bedford jail.

The reader need neither be a believer nor be convinced that Robinson Crusoe is a sincere believer to be moved by the ardour of his hope. The crux of the novel, and the reason that it seems to have a resonance for all of us despite the outlandish nature of its central situation, is that Crusoe's total solitude and his intense hope for connection in this life or the next are in essence the conditions of every human being at nightfall.

While the spiritual aspect of *Robinson Crusoe* gives it depth of field, the foreground story of practical survival gives it charm. The hero's efforts to make himself clothes are clownish and have led to many famous depictions of a bearded man in animal-hide breeches with a goatskin umbrella. 'For if I was a bad *carpenter*,' Crusoe admits, 'I was a worse *tayler*' – where his italics provide the modest service of today's inverted commas. Yet he never really 'goes native'. He is always a northern European in his tropi-cal world: practical, grounded and, with whatever spasms of despair, self-confident. He makes a grindstone for his hatchets by rigging up a pedal and a piece of rope to turn it; when out at sea in his improvised canoe he finds a 'current like the sluice of a mill'. He never loses sight of European domestic invention as his yardstick and comparator. This rigour makes his efforts look ham-fisted, but makes the reader quietly proud of all the things we take for granted. The use of river energy to mill corn, for instance: how much more elegant and 'green' an invention could there be? And all of these things were newer 350 years ago, so more forcefully a source of pride to Crusoe.

There is more than pride and practicality, however, in the way he cleaves to the standards of the world he has left. There is a battle going on in him to remain human, to maintain a distinction between himself and the animals, both domesticated and wild, that are the other inhabitants of the island. I think it is significant that Crusoe does not become vegetarian. To begin with, when meat is his only source of food, he has no choice; but once, in addition to the available fruit, he has established cereal crops for bread and a dairy operation that produces butter and cheese, meat becomes optional. The instinct of most people in his isolated situation, I think, would be to try to draw comfort, succour, fellow feeling from the other living crea-tures in the environment. This would mean trying to commune with them on their level, as Crusoe does to a limited extent with a feral cat, a parrot and a dog; but for most people it would mean one thing before all others: not killing one's only source of companionship. Crusoe, however, sees no need to – as it were – get on all fours with nature. He is a man, the play-thing perhaps of Providence, but a man for all that and a European man to boot. He has a higher consciousness than the beasts; he can carry in his

'I was a worse *tayler*' – Robinson Crusoe depicted in animal hide (1719 edition)

memory not only the knowledge of what he did the day before, but of his entire life; furthermore he can carry a verbal memory of things done by others of his species – grinding, milling, planting, sowing, sewing – and by his cognitive power and the dexterity derived from opposable thumbs can make real belly-filling bread from little more than a half-understood idea. There is no need for him to crawl.

Crusoe has passed the test of his species. With whatever help he may have enlisted from his god, the genetic factors that made him human have continued to keep him separate from, and superior to, his fellow creatures. He is ready now to meet a man. He sees a footprint in the sand, and his response surprises him – or at least it surprises the older man who is recounting the story. He, like us, would have expected this to be 'a raising me from death to life, and the greatest blessing that Heaven itself ... could bestow; I say that I should now tremble at the very apprehensions of seeing a man, and was ready to sink into the ground at but the shadow, or silent appearance of a man's having set his foot in the island.'

Be careful what you wish for; and when it comes, Crusoe feels only fear and disorientation. Part of this is the natural colonist's caution, without which Europe would never have conquered vast areas of the other continents; but part is the personal panic of a man institutionalised in his own solitude: he cannot face the thought of violence; but nor can he face the thought of friendship. After consulting his Bible for comfort, Crusoe goes about fortifying his dwelling, making it safe against intruders. The storytelling Crusoe is a little ashamed of the young castaway's reaction; Crusoe is no hero to himself – though this is perhaps what makes him a hero to the reader.

It emerges that people from a nearby island, or mainland for all he knows, are using Crusoe's island as a destination for cannibalistic ritual. A captive is brought, killed and eaten, raising doubts in Crusoe's mind about whether he should intervene – though his firepower would mean murder. It works out that he does not at first need to act, and he gives thanks that God has delivered him from 'blood-guiltiness'. For a time Crusoe lives in fear, baking his bread in an improvised smokeless oven to give no sign of his presence. Eventually, he believes himself alone again. More than twenty-three years have passed since his shipwreck but he can't stop thinking about how much money he could have made from his tobacco plantation and from slave-trading if he had stayed in Brazil. He continues to blame his 'original sin' of disobeying his father, though still, oddly, does not admit that it was only by disobeying him and going to sea that he put himself in the way of the riches he now misses. He also begins to form a plan: next time the 'savages' come with a prisoner, he will free the individual, make him his servant, then use his services as a pilot to steer his, by now, sturdy canoe to civilisation. The first problem is that he will need to kill the captors, and he feels uneasy about this, 'tho' it was for my deliverance'; the second is that his yearning for escape shows insufficient gratitude to the Providence that has given him a comfortable life within his reinforced stockade.

Soon, Providence works to his advantage. A captive due to be eaten escapes his captors, two of whom pursue him. It occurs to Crusoe that if he can dispose of the two pursuers, the rest of the savages need never know what has happened to them and he can turn the surviving fugitive into his servant. Not a 'friend': a servant. And so it happens. One of the pursuers makes to fire his bow and arrow at Crusoe, so that his pre-emptive gunfire is justifiable as self-defence. The fugitive himself obligingly kills the other pursuer by borrowing Crusoe's sword and lopping his head off at a single blow. The bad deed is done by the non-Christian Caribbean, and Crusoe's conscience is clear.

Crusoe clothes his man ('Friday', as we know, is the name he chooses for him) and gives him a hare-skin cap, 'very convenient and fashionable enough'. He prevents him from eating the flesh of his former pursuers and soon finds him a very faithful servant, of almost filial devotion. He teaches him to speak English, and 'I began to really love the creature; and on his side, I believe he lov'd me more than it was possible for him ever to love any thing before.' Friday's increasing education gives rise to one or two ticklish theological questions – such as why does the all-powerful God not kill the Devil – but Crusoe's attitude to religion is nothing if not practical, and 'I pretended not to hear him.' The comedy of the Crusoe–Friday friendship is all the more effective for the fact that Crusoe never seems enraptured by the release from solitude that Friday has miraculously provided; he always sees him as servant and a means to an end.

When Crusoe leaves his island after twenty-eight years, two months and nineteen days, he takes his goatskin cap, his parrot, his umbrella – and the coins he had rescued from the wreck. The ordeal he has endured is something he will put behind him – a nuisance in the continuing merchant life he now intends to resume. This is the measure of the man and his triumph. He has conquered wild animals, seen off cannibals and manipulated foreign sailors into starting a small and peaceful colony on his island. He has looked into the void of time and the emptiness of the human heart, and if he has occasionally blinked, it has not been long before he has resumed his level gaze. He has shown himself to be the master of all that Providence has set before him and has called on his unseen Maker as much as he needed him, but no more. He has prostrated himself before neither God nor beast. He has trusted to the acquired knowledge of his species, of his family and his nation.

Crusoe's rescue from the island comes after hectic complications involving Friday's father, more cannibals, an English ship, a Spanish captain and a mutiny. It is a strange reflection on the nature of narrative that rather than seize on all this as relief, the reader feels wistful for the quieter sections when Crusoe was learning how to make a watertight ceramic pot for his goat broth. It is eloquent of the interest that Defoe packs into the inner life of his hero that the adventurous action seems an anticlimax by comparison. It may also be that this first great English novel thus signposted the way for future writers by showing that in the new form the inner life would always trump the outer.

'A THOUGHTLESS, GIDDY YOUTH'

TOM JONES

'Good-hearted' seems to be the word for Tom Jones, the hero of Henry Fielding's 1747 novel. Fielding had the fortune, good or otherwise, to be writing at the same time as Samuel Richardson, and tidy-minded readers have tended to see them as two weathermen. On the one hand, Richardson is all Puritanical seriousness, and his books are massively extended homilies on the necessity of Christian virtue, particularly in the female of the species. *Pamela* and *Clarissa* both show young women under siege from lustful males and there is no doubt of Richardson's didactic intent; indeed with *Clarissa* he revised the text extensively to make its moral clearer and to remove any possibility of the reader's sympathising with Clarissa's would-be seducer, Robert Lovelace. And against narrow, dried-up Richardson there is Fielding – rubicund, generous, clasping a pint of wine, blessed with a far more forgiving and realistic view of human virtue. He is the sort of beak that Bertie Wooster would want to be up in front of after Boat Race night; Richardson would put him behind bars, but Fielding would send him on his way with a ten-bob donation to a charity. Henry Fielding's very name seems to breathe a sort of National Trust benevolence.

Luckily for us, there is more to it than that. It's true that Fielding wrote *Joseph Andrews*, which starts as a parody of Richardson's *Pamela*. The main character is Pamela's brother and is subject to similar attempts on his virtue. Fielding had put his finger on a weakness in *Pamela*: like many readers he was not convinced that Pamela's 'virtue' was based entirely on religious scruples; it seemed to have an element of calculation about it, since a young servant woman knows the price at which to sell her most valuable possession; and Pamela eventually succeeds in persuading her pursuer into marriage. Fielding was also the author of *Shamela*, an even more ribald satire of Richardson's book. However, Fielding admired *Clarissa* and had no doubt that its psychological insight had taken the novel into territory that few other writers would ever reach. And, as we shall see (in the discussion of *Clarissa*'s Robert Lovelace), Richardson's writing could be lively, allusive, witty, seductive – and flexible enough to go deeper into human motivation than Fielding's.

I pretended to have read *Tom Jones* at the age of seventeen and it was quite easy to write a convincing schoolboy essay, because the colours (so far as I had glimpsed them through a couple of critical essays) seemed bright and primary. I did finally read it at university, where my college had been founded by Puritans so Richardsonian that they had built the chapel on a north–south axis to avoid any taint of symbolism (the Son rising above the altar in the east). And at the age of nineteen I found *Tom Jones* to be everything I had confidently called it in my entrance exam. Tom was the sort of

hero a student could identify with. He
starts with the disadvantage of being
a foundling; he is misunderstood
and not particularly devoted to his
studies; he is vigorous, lustful and
impulsively good-hearted – that
word already. Of course the 'morality' that governed him was more
flexible than the ecclesiastical
dogma that brought Clarissa to an
early death. It was fine by me that
Tom should have an affair with
Lady Bellaston in London and live off
her bounty while trying to find his true
love, Sophia Western. Lady B was
'Establishment' and rich, while Tom

Our first sighting of Tom Jones,
the foundling (1749 edition)

was an adventurer – and the lords of misrule are entitled to exploit the stew-
ards of the house, just as the have-nots are always to be backed against the
haves. It was terrific that his teachers, Thwackum and Square, one religious
and one philosophical, should both be revealed to be scheming hypocrites.
Ah, the stuffy older generation of pedagogues with their black gowns and
chalk dust! Fielding knew as well as I did that they were in denial of life and
lust. I loved the fact that promiscuous Tom was so modern in his free-love
outlook and that he befriended people not for 'who' they were – worthy,
respectable – but 'what' they were: basically good and basically good fun.
Oh yes, Tom Jones – now that I had finally read his story – Tom Jones,
c'était moi.

*

I was looking forward to encountering Tom again, and through him perhaps a younger self; when I reopened the book I half-expected an aroma of Double Diamond and Number 6 to rise from its long-closed pages. The first person you meet, however, is not Tom, but Henry Fielding; and he is to be an ever-present guide through the adventures that lie ahead; Chapter 7 has the subtitle 'Containing such grave matter, that the reader cannot laugh once through the whole chapter, unless peradventure he should laugh at the author'; I had forgotten quite how large he loomed. Yet there is confidence in Fielding's narrative; without too much detail, he has what Henry James would call 'solidity of specification' in his descriptions of Squire Allworthy's Somerset house, where Tom will spend his childhood. Some of the character names have a Jonsonian flag attached to them – decent Allworthy; Thwackum, the flogger – but they are filled in with defter touches. The jocular voice of the author, meanwhile, which will be with us for 912 pages in the Vintage Classics edition, carries an interesting edge of the experimental as it reminds us, by its constant presence, that this is a new form, unsettled as yet. Richardson absents himself completely from his novels by simply printing (and he was a professional printer) letters between the protagonists; Fielding, in utter contrast, mingles with his creations, puts an avuncular arm about their shoulders; you sometimes wonder whether Tom could get out of bed without the author there to rouse him. Either method is workable in the user-friendly, demotic form that the novel turned out to be, and many others would be discovered. It is easy to forget how rapidly the early practitioners of the novel – most famously Laurence Sterne in *Tristram Shandy* – took it to pieces or 'deconstructed' it, like children with a fascinating new mechanical toy; so that not the smallest part of Jane Austen's achievement, when the British novel had been alive for about a hundred years, was to establish a pattern of absentee narration through different character view-points that others could use as a template.

Fielding, meanwhile, gives the engaging sense that he is seeing what he can do with the new form, as well as making up the story as he goes along. The bluff, Johnsonian nature of his evident beliefs, the longish classical sentences and copious Latin quotation should not deflect us from the adventurous nature of his construction – nor from the quite revolutionary concept of goodness as something separate from religious doctrine that lies at the heart of his book. Fielding's idea of 'goodness' is still Christian, but it is looser than Richardson's more pious idea of 'virtue'. So when Tom is finally introduced in Book III Chapter 2, it is like this: 'We are obliged to bring our Heroe on the Stage in a much more disadvantageous Manner than we could wish; and to declare … that it was the universal Opinion of all Mr. Allworthy's Family, that he was certainly born to be hanged.' He spends much of his time stealing apples and poaching game to give to Black George, a gamekeeper on Allworthy's estate. 'He was indeed a thoughtless, giddy youth, with little sobriety in his manners, and less in his countenance'.

Tom is viewed unfavourably in comparison with Blifil, the son of Bridget Allworthy, the squire's sister. Blifil, the companion of Tom's youth, is also the favourite of his mother, who reproves her brother for his kindness towards the foundling, Tom. However, as Tom grows older and 'gave tokens of the gallantry of temper which greatly recommends men to women', Bridget Allworthy is won round and begins to favour Tom over Blifil; and her change of heart is much more significant than the reader can know at this stage.

Allworthy's neighbour, Squire Western, has a daughter called Sophia, the heroine of Tom Jones and one of the most successful characters Fielding created – a credibly unsophisticated country girl of good family, red-blooded, flirtatious but with a fine intelligence and a proper – though not mercenary – sense of her own worth. The excellent Sophia Western is Fielding's conclusive riposte to Richardson's Pamela Andrews. And what's more, 'she honoured Tom Jones and scorned Master Blifil almost as soon as she knew the meaning of those two words'. Tom, however, is not quite ready for Sophia, but is sowing some wild oats with Black George's willing daughter. Luckily a riding accident gives him a chance to be gallant towards Sophia; the citadel of his heart soon falls 'and the god of love marched in, triumphant'.

Fielding's interest in what he called 'imperfect heroes' gives *Tom Jones* its distinctive character and also caused a scandal when the book was published. The reading public still expected novels to be edifying in a religious sense and found Fielding's flexible, humanistic scheme of right and wrong to be shocking. The outrage was a gratifying measure of the power the new form seemed to have. I don't think I have ever read a social history in which the historian did not say that one of the defining aspects of his period was the 'emergence of a new and powerful middle class'; but in the era of Richardson and Fielding this really does seem to have been the case. Rising literacy among a mercantile class swollen by empire trade and serviced by a vigorous bookselling industry meant that novels might reach an audience untouched by poetry, history or sermons. The novel was, from the start, a popular and middle-class art form. The masses who could not read relied on Bible lessons in church or some oral folk traditions for literary entertainment: literature and 'improvement' were, for most people, indivisible; so the thought that a new form might not only lack an orthodox didactic position but might also have the power to reach tens of thousands of readers was alarming – though presumably thrilling to the writer.

I think it is really in this context that the character of Tom Jones has to be seen. In this book, I talk about fictional characters as though they were real people; the focus is deliberately narrow and psychological. There is a polemical aspect to the way I have tried to rehabilitate the simple idea of creating character from nothing – a sort of magic, and the gift that the novelist is selling to the public. I do recognise, however, that there are other ways of writing about novels; and in the case of *Tom Jones*, I think that trying to put the book in a literary–historical context is likely to be more rewarding than shining a tightly focussed beam on to the psychological make-up of its hero – for the simple reason that while *Tom Jones* the book is significant, there is not that much to Tom Jones the man.

Fielding successfully creates a sense of jeopardy around him, a real possibility that the grown-ups of the Allworthy and Western households will conspire to make Sophia marry the sneaking, hypocritical Blifil. Tension derives from whether Sophia can resist them. Tom has a further and more insidious enemy: himself. When Allworthy recovers from what appeared to have been a life-threatening illness, Tom is so overjoyed that he becomes drunk. This is misrepresented to Allworthy by Blifil as Tom showing loutish indifference to his benefactor's health, and Allworthy sadly banishes Tom, telling him to leave the country. Tom decides to go to sea, and makes for Bristol.

On his way, he is detained in an inn, at Upton, where he misbehaves with a Mrs Waters. Sophia, as luck would have it, passes by the same inn on her way to London to escape from her father's insistence that she marry Blifil. She discovers Tom's dalliance, and at this point we see that Tom's inability to keep his trousers on may be more damaging than all the wiles of age and money ranged against him. The reader, too, is detained at the inn at Upton – for almost 200 pages of only modestly entertaining incident. If there is a longer pub scene in English literature, I haven't read it, and if I ever come across one, I may have to plead a headache.

The sexual impulsiveness of Tom, which seemed so anarchic and so right to me at the age of nineteen, seemed a little trying this time round. Soon (by the standards of this leisurely narrative) he is in bed with Lady Bellaston, a prowling society cougar in London. And poor Sophia will discover this as well. Much though one likes and admires her, one does slightly wonder at what point her devotion to Tom and her belief in him might begin to waver.

Tom Jones, however, does work as a hero because, with whatever reservations, we do identify with him. He fights the adversity of his illegitimate birth and the false witness brought against him by Blifil. He is our representative in the story, as heroes are, and he flatters us by being better with the duellist's sword than we might be and more attractive to the opposite sex than we would dare believe ourselves. The way he treats people less well off than himself shows that he has intuitive, if not intellectual, access to a well-grounded value system; even strangers hail him as a 'gentleman'.

It is the 'intuitive' aspect that is limiting. While it's true to say that the morality that guides him is a sophisticated one, arguably more so than the religiously based precepts by which Richardson's heroines live because it is to some extent improvised and draws on Fielding's wider philosophical reading, Tom's understanding of it seems almost entirely instinctive. He is not a thinker; compared even to the practical trader Robinson Crusoe, Tom Jones seems to have no intellectual life. Such conflicts as arise in his existence are not solved by him. It is not only that he does not have the brain to outwit his enemies, he seems also to lack the moral courage to make any sort of self-sacrifice: of restraint, or chastity, for instance. He is always generous after the event, but seldom self-aware enough to be generous – or anything else – before it.

Misfortunes accumulate towards the end of the book. Tom appears stuck with the scheming Lady Bellaston, who has it in her power to ruin him. Later, at the nadir, he finds himself in prison, having fought an illegal duel with a man called Fitzpatrick. While there, he learns from Partridge, the Latin-prone teacher who has been his Sancho Panza on the road, that the Mrs Waters he slept with in the inn at Upton is none other than Jenny Jones, the village girl from Somerset who is Tom's … mother.

He badly needs help, but can he help himself? Not once. Tom is extricated from the Lady Bellaston tangle by a friend called Nightingale, who suggests he propose marriage to her in order to scare her away. This works. Mrs Waters, his pub amour, gets him out of prison by telling Squire Allworthy that Mr Fitzpatrick did not die as a result of the duel, and furthermore now admits to having started it. Mrs Waters then tells Allworthy that a lawyer, acting on behalf of an unnamed gentleman, tried to persuade her to conspire against Tom. Allworthy guesses that the unnamed gentleman is Blifil and decides never to speak to him again. Next, Mrs Waters reveals that Tom's mother was not herself, née Jenny Jones, but none other than Bridget Allworthy, the squire's sister. Help then comes from a most unlikely quarter – Mr Square, Tom's old tutor and tormentor, who writes to Allworthy to say that in fact Tom behaved honourably during the squire's illness and became drunk only in relief at Allworthy's recovery. The next good fairy is Tom's London landlady, Mrs Miller, who explains to Sophia the reasons for Tom's proposal to Lady Bellaston. And the final manumission is provided by the sorely tried Sophia, who grants Tom her loving forgiveness.

It is a triumph for Fielding's plotting – and he playfully points us to all the clues about Tom's parentage we have overlooked – but less so for Tom's character. It says something for the fecklessness of this 'thoughtless, giddy youth' that he needs not one but *five* other characters – Nightingale, Mrs Waters, Mr Square, Mrs Miller and Sophia – to swoop like *dei ex machinis* and free him from the troubles he has brought on his own head. Tom's inability to help himself does not seem to me to threaten Fielding's moral scheme, but it diminishes him as a character. First, we are inclined to think less of someone who relies so much on providence and on the kindness and enterprise of others to supply what he lacks. More importantly, though, Tom's passivity makes him much less interesting as a fictional character because he has no internal struggles; there is no sense of conflict or growth. He is a jolly cork upon a choppy sea, and not much more.

Some readers think that a hypothetical Tom Jones today, in middle age, would be active in public life, bringing light to bear on social issues. They may be right; but I have an unwelcome feeling that Tom at fifty would be a red-faced Somerset squire, given to referring to Sophia as 'the management'; that she would glance at him with tolerant indulgence when he made nudging reference, yet again, to his 'adventures on the road'; and that she would look out over the Mendips a little wistfully, wondering about the wisdom of her youthful ardour.

'THE LITTLE MINX'

BECKY SHARP

Jane Eyre is a heroine; Becky Sharp, the main character of Thackeray's *Vanity Fair* (1847–8), is a hero. No one seems to question the distinction: it's obvious. Rather harder is to say quite why. In the end, I think, it's a question of independence. Jane Eyre is a resilient woman, of higher moral calibre than Becky Sharp, but her happiness, and her psychological 'completion', seem to depend on her securing the love and companionship of another, Mr Rochester. All her battles from the orphanage onwards, with whatever doughty and feminist intelligence they are fought, are presented as leading to this one end. Becky can't be a heroine because she is not a 'good' enough person; while Jane Eyre's fine qualities see her through against the world, Becky is too much *of* that world. Her resourcefulness and skill at dealing with it, however, qualify her first for our interest, then for our backing and finally for something like heroic status.

A hero may well have a lover; the chase and the affair give opportunities for displaying qualities of romance and constancy. Ultimately, though, a hero can be disappointed or defeated in love and it will not matter, because pairing off is not the goal or completion of the heroic trajectory. The hero imprints his or her qualities on society, and by doing so overcomes false or smothering social restrictions. Crusoe's project is to retain the world of European 'civilisation' in his head while marooned for twenty-eight years. Does he even have a wife? He does, actually; he marries on his return to England, but she quickly dies before his next voyage. Tom Jones's task is to embody his author's philosophical ideas of a moral scheme more flexible than that embodied in the teaching of the Church. Tom will do battle with the social structures of both countryside and town and will triumph over them by his individual qualities. If Sophia had eventually tired of his sexual incontinence and married someone else, it would not have been fatal to Tom's role as heroic individual *contra mundum*. Marriage, or 'success' in love, is the prerequisite of the heroine; for the hero it is an optional extra.

While she has an undoubted fascination for men, Becky Sharp is magnificently indifferent to them. The thought of 'settling down' or 'finding the right man' would be risible to her, though from childhood she enjoys male company. She marries Rawdon Crawley because he is an affable, though temporary, associate in the business of her life: getting on in high society without working. He is no more, Thackeray says bluntly, than her 'upper servant and maitre d'hotel'. Men, sex and marriage constitute an important, but by no means dominant, element of the lifelong survival game that Becky plays. Thackeray never suggests that Becky's emotional life is such that it would influence her worldly actions. Most women in fiction cling at some stage to their feelings for a man as a fixed point or priority; it is at least one known star by which to steer. Becky never reaches such a stage of surrender, and would regard it as a weakness to admit that her progress in life had become dependent on something as unmarketable as 'feelings'.

This is a radical conception of female character in the mid-Victorian period and it is what gives Becky her enduring interest. Like Tom Jones, she has disreputable beginnings; she is the daughter of a French chorus girl and an alcoholic drawing master who abuses his wife and daughter. But from the first moment we see her, she is on the make, not inclined to 'rehabilitate' the memory of parents and to prove that 'society' disdain for them is snobbish or unkind, but to make a path for herself despite her disadvantages. Becky's world is all about *her*, and her challenge is to keep the faith with her own egotistical drive in a social world that is more venal, corrupt and smothering than anything portrayed in Fielding's London. Thackeray's London is literally pre-Victorian, belonging to the Regency period in which the story is set, but also, through the biblical reference of the title and the generic names such as Lady Bareacres, purporting to be timeless.

Becky begins what Thackeray aptly calls her 'campaign' in the company of the pleasant but silly Amelia Sedley. Becky is pale, slight and sandy-haired, but with enormous eyes that seem to fascinate men – including Amelia's fat, shy and absurd brother Joseph, or Jos, who is an Indian colonial administrator (the Collector, indeed, of Boggley Wollah), on home leave chez Sedley, where Becky temporarily lodges. Becky at once wins Jos's affections and has high hopes of coaxing a proposal from him; but Jos is at first too drunk to propose and is then teased about his feelings by George Osborne, a young dragoon with terrific side whiskers, who becomes Becky's next potential prey. She sees George admiring himself in the mirror and does not feel disappointed at his vanity but pleased that she has already got his measure. The drawback is that George is the object of

Amelia's uncritical devotion, and they are expected to marry – though for Becky this is not a serious problem: she would think little of pushing Amelia to one side if she wanted George, but for the time being she wants to see if she could do better. She has self-belief, this penniless girl.

Becky finds a post as governess to a family called Crawley, whose head, Sir Pitt, is MP for a Hampshire rotten borough. Sir Pitt is so rough in his manners that Becky mistakes him for the footman when he takes her luggage inside, but in her bedroom she sees a picture of his sons, 'one in a college gown, the other [Rawdon] in a red jacket like a solider. When she went to sleep, Rebecca chose that one to dream about.' Here is a young woman so focussed on self-betterment that she can control her unconscious mind and perhaps even sow in it, while sleeping, the seeds of love – or something that will pass for it. At this stage of the book, which was published serially, Thackeray is clearly enjoying himself with Becky. He is trying to shock the reader, a little, and to nudge us into disapproval. Of course, the high spirits of the narrative are such that every tut-tut from Thackeray – 'the little minx' – just draws us a little closer to her. We are novel-readers, not Stoic philosophers, and we already know which character holds the key to our amusement.

Soon Becky, Crawley's favourite, is behaving like the mistress of the house, though being careful not to offend the old retainers, because 'though young in years, our heroine was old in life and experience, and we have written to no purpose if [our readers] have not discovered that she was a very clever woman'. It is interesting that Thackeray is ready to grant the title of 'heroine' to Becky, since he has curtly denied it to the more morally upright Amelia ('As she was not a heroine, there was no need to describe her person'). In Thackeray's mind the word appears to signify 'main protagonist', and he has used the feminine form for Becky because in the idiom of the day, which had not yet been overhauled on gender lines, it would have been a solecism to use the masculine. When he called *Vanity Fair* in its subtitle 'a novel without a hero', he meant to indicate, I think, that none of the male characters fulfilled the heroic role, viz. coming from a disadvantaged beginning; giving a point of identification, however flattering, to the reader; being equipped with at least one quality to admire; overcoming obstacles set before him, often unfairly; imprinting personal values on a hostile social world and vindicating a liberal–individual morality against agreed norms. Dobbin, the worthy soldier who is Amelia's lifelong admirer, is a candidate for hero; he has qualities of honesty and faithfulness that the other men lack, but moral qualities are, oddly enough, beginning to seem the one dispensable aspect of the fictional hero as he evolves. As his name suggests, Dobbin is a bit of a carthorse, and not one who will kick over the traces.

Becky uses her experience; she gathers more cards to her hand, but is canny about playing them. Back in London, she meets George Osborne again and is able to condescend to him, pulling his leg about his recently rich family. Osborne *père* is a hard-faced financier who was given an early break by Amelia's father, a stockbroker, but in his new wealth is unwilling to repay any kindness to the now struggling Mr Sedley.

Becky Sharp's real problem lies not in her intelligence, education, beauty or cunning – on all of which she scores highly – but in the lack of liquidity in capital markets. It was simply very difficult for a clever middle-class girl with no money to acquire enough of it to live well. In the years between 1980 and 2008, by contrast, Becky might have found a job in finance and would have proved a cool-headed judge of deals and markets.

But women did not do that in Regency London. And while Lord Steyne, a persistent admirer, has accumulated huge riches through gambling, even winning his title at the table, and while Osborne senior has chiselled out his speculative profits while turning his back on old Sedley, there is little to suggest in *Vanity Fair* – or from bankers such as Dickens's Merdle in *Little Dorrit* or Melmotte in Trollope's *The Way We Live Now* – that, outside straightforward usury, there were quick and easy profits to be made in finance. There were bubbles, crazes and flotations, but they were risky. Markets were not international, there were few open exchanges and no price differentials to arbitrage, while derivatives and other lucrative trading options existed only as wagers struck between individuals after dinner – not as billion-dollar leveraged bets with multiple interlocking parts. Had Becky and Rawdon lived at some time in the last thirty years, Rawdon could conceivably have found himself a position in finance. He is an unflappable and not entirely straight gambler; he would seem to have the qualifications to work on the proprietary desk of an investment bank.

As it is, Becky is debarred by convention from working and has enough scruple, we think, not merely to sell her body for cash. Whether she actually sleeps with Lord Steyne in order to keep his flow of expensive presents coming her way, we do not know – because Thackeray tells us he does not know either. Acquiring straight cash by marriage into the Crawley family is made difficult, as so often in Victorian law and fiction, by a disputed will. Becky's access to money is therefore sporadic, and securing it is the main occupation of her life.

Her best opportunity seems to lie in war profiteering. The regiment is despatched to Brussels on the eve of the Battle of Waterloo, and Thackeray's relish for the 'campaign' is evident – both for the fighting itself and for the personal struggle of Becky, who is 'seen in the pretti-est and tightest of riding habits, mounted on a beautiful little Arab ... by the side of the gallant General Tufto'. The Brussels scenes are to the majority of readers the most successful in the book. Thackeray's social message that 'all is vanity' can elsewhere appear narrow and monoto-nous, while his authorial mockery of his characters often prevents them acquiring depth and shadow. His comprehensive itemisation of all their small vanities becomes stifling because it leaves no room in the narrative for readers to flex their own judgements. In war, however, this is not the case. The pre-battle finery and parties – fashion and champagne in the face of death – make a natural target for the theme of vanity, and the coming slaughter gives an unprecedented sense of urgency. For the first time, the vain George Osborne (by now half-heartedly married to Amelia), the simple spiv Rawdon Crawley, the fat coward Jos Sedley and the glitteringly opportunistic Becky Sharp seem to have real flesh on their wooden puppet bones; for the first time in the novel our emotions are engaged with them. After a dissolute evening, George's guilt-stricken farewell to Amelia, when he goes softly into her bedroom on the night before battle, provides one of those fictional moments when time seems to stop, as the whole plan of human life, and all its pitiful connections, are laid bare.

Becky prepares her husband Rawdon for battle, having kept George Osborne's approaches at arm's length, without completely discouraging him; she books her escape from Brussels, should it be necessary, by reheating Jos Sedley's interest in her. '"If the worst comes to the worst," Becky thought, "my retreat is secure; and I have a right-hand seat in the barouche."' These editorial stings no longer seem arch or perfunctory, but sink home with a bite as deep and damaging as Jane Austen's. In the event, Becky is able to sell her horses to Jos Sedley for a sum so great that she calculates that, with her widow's pension and the sale of Rawdon's effects, she will have enough to live on for the rest of her life. Unfortunately for Becky, it is not her husband who is killed in battle, but Amelia's, George Osborne, 'who was lying on his face, dead, with a bullet through his heart'.

Becky and Rawdon move to Paris where they are able to live for a year on the money Becky was paid by Jos for her horses. This is the high point of their life. Few Parisians seem to understand that Becky is an upstart – or to care. For Rawdon, there is plentiful gaming and 'his luck was good'. Back in Mayfair, they have a house in Curzon Street, and in a chapter called 'How to live well on Nothing a Year', Thackeray hints that 'some foul play must have taken place in order to account for the continued success of Colonel Crawley' at the gaming tables. Becky has a child, young Rawdon, and is a shockingly indifferent mother to him. Using charm and a simple Ponzi scheme, Becky is able to parlay Rawdon's £1,500 army cash into ten times that amount. London society, or at least a louche section of it, agrees that 'if the husband was rather stupid, the wife was charming'.

The narrative interest of *Vanity Fair* derives from the fact that by the halfway point it is clear that with all her considerable skills, Becky is not going to pull off a definitive coup. The financial and social restrictions of the world are too great even for such an adventuress, and her story then becomes one of endurance and variation. While she is the most conniving hero in Victorian literature, Becky retains an odd kind of innocence. When she stays at her in-laws' house in Hampshire she thinks she could be quite happy as a country gentleman's wife, counting the apricots on the wall, dishing out soup to the poor and dressing in the fashions 'of the year before last' – if only she had £5,000 a year. It is that simple lack that 'made the difference between her and an honest woman', Thackeray suggests. 'And who knows but Rebecca was right in her speculations?'

The other path to contentment – the following of the heart's affections – is not one that Becky ever contemplates. She seems to have no deep feelings. While she is fond enough of Rawdon as a business partner and 'upper servant', she does not love him. She dislikes her son. She views Amelia with sentimental compassion mingled with contempt. She sees the shallows of George Osborne from the first day. She enjoys the flattery, and perhaps even the company, of Lord Steyne, but there is no suggestion that she actually likes him. This emotional *froideur* seems psychologically plausible in someone who has undergone the childhood experiences that Becky has – abused, poor and ill-treated. Affection – and love even more so – need a basis of trust from which to proceed, and nothing in Becky's life up to the point at which the book opens has given her reason to trust anyone. However, what makes Becky fascinating is not the plausibility of environmental influence, but Thackeray's stronger suggestion that this is the way she is naturally made: a clever and attractive woman who cannot be won. This seems almost as thrilling a conception of character now as it must have seemed shocking then.

For Becky, though, it means not just independence, but discontent and a sort of bearable isolation. She comforts herself with trivialities – with the thought that her sister-in-law is the daughter of an earl, that she is a figure in London society and married to a colonel, himself the brother of a baronet; and all this is much better than the scrounging life she had as the child of a drunken father when she was sent to wheedle sugar and tea on tick from the grocer. Or at least it would be better, if only she had a private income. She tries unsuccessfully to extract money from her brother-in-law and finally resorts to 'looking after' the handsome legacy left to a servant.

The sticking point with Becky – the point at which many readers have parted company with her – is her dislike of her son, little Rawdon. She has no maternal feeling. She ignores him or bullies him, and is scornful of his father's fondness. She makes him eat in the kitchen or with the servants and despatches him to boarding school as soon as possible. Once, on 'seeing that tenderness was the fashion', she kisses the boy in public, only for him to point out, loudly, that she never does so at home. Rawdon the father, meanwhile, is a Samson shorn of strength, dependent on the wiles of his Delilah to extract money from the men she flirts with, while he, once a handsome dragoon, becomes an occasional billiard-table hustler and card sharp. When he finds himself detained by a creditor, under a sort of civilian arrest, Becky makes no hurry to bail him out. Freed eventually by his sister-in-law, Rawdon returns home to find Becky canoodling with Lord Steyne. She pleads her innocence, but Rawdon has seen enough and Steyne angrily questions what 'innocence' has allowed her to keep her husband on the fruits of the presents he, Steyne, has given her. Rawdon finds a banknote for £1,000 in Becky's purse and in the view of the world she is now 'a wicked woman, a heartless mother and a false wife'.

This is the end of Becky's hope of living respectably on nothing. From now on she becomes an exile, a drifter and a person of clearly disreputable character. Thackeray's way of portraying her becomes unstable, veering between his previously playful and half-approving stance and something more distancing. His narrative interest, meanwhile, shifts to the long-standing love of Dobbin for Amelia, and it is here that he provides the great emotional moment of his novel. Amelia is unable to see the value of the faithful Dobbin because she is still fixated on the memory of the self-seeking George. Thackeray, like Tolstoy, allows us to revisit characters after the passage of years and to see them subtly, and sadly, changed. Amelia, who was at first all sweetness by comparison with Becky, has suffered widowhood, poverty and the agony of seeing her beloved son brought up by the Osbornes, who were so ruthless towards her father, because she herself has no money. But Thackeray has worse in store for her. When Dobbin comes back and declares his love for her after so many hopeless years, she turns him down; and Thackeray lets us see how shallow and unworthy of Dobbin's long devotion Amelia has become.

Dobbin, for so long the doormat, rises to the occasion in a magnificent speech, which ends, 'I withdraw. I find no fault with you. You are very good-natured, and have done your best; but you couldn't – you couldn't reach up to the height of the attachment which I bore you, and which a loftier soul than yours might have been proud to share. Good-bye, Amelia! I have watched your struggle. Let it end. We are both weary of it.' This is one of the great speeches of Victorian fiction, and it is the entirely characteristic good manners and generosity of the majority that makes the dagger thrust – 'a loftier soul than yours' – so unbearably conclusive.

The novel's narrative coup is then to recall Becky and have her disclose to Amelia, for no selfish reason, that George asked her to run away with him on the night before Waterloo. With the icon of George now shattered, Amelia can recall Dobbin. But Dobbin and we know that Amelia, after all this time, is barely worth having. This is the Tolstoyan moment of the novel, and a great one – though it is not enough, despite what some critics have urged, to elevate *Vanity Fair* as a whole to the level of *War and Peace*, in the course of which Natasha, Prince Andrei, and Sonya, in particular, offer many more, and more penetrating, examples of how the passage of time can reveal a different aspect of a human personality; how that disclosure can alter our opinion of the character in question; and how that change casts a long mocking shadow on all the years that have gone before.

The further irony of Becky's intervention is that it turns out that Amelia has already written to Dobbin to summon him back – so Becky's one selfless act turns out to have been irrelevant. She herself has come full circle and fastens on to the very first man she fascinated: Amelia's capon of a brother, Jos. They live together in France, and when Jos dies mysteriously in Aix-en-Provence, Becky – or Lady Crawley, as she styles herself – is the beneficiary of the life insurance policy. She can at last live if not well, at least comfortably. Whether Becky is responsible for Jos's death is not something we feel we need to know; though Dobbin sends back his and Amelia's share of the insurance money and never speaks to Becky again.

The interest of Becky Sharp lies in the fact that she is a hero with no morally good qualities. She fulfils all the narrative requirements of the hero, but Thackeray has jettisoned the idea that such a person must be 'good'. The strange thing is, that it seems to work. Function trumps goodness. The novel is a user-friendly machine.

'SWEETER FOR MY PRESENCE'

SHERLOCK HOLMES

Sherlock Holmes reinvigorated the idea of what a fictional hero could be. Despite the realism problem that Thackeray, Trollope and other mid-century novelists had experienced – the improbable idea that the main character should be 'heroic' rather than just interesting – Conan Doyle created a hero who was morally good and exceptionally gifted, but also fascinating and believable. Significantly, however, he did so outside the mainstream novel and in what had not yet developed as such but would shortly become a genre of its own: the crime story.

So saturated were the bookshops by the end of the twentieth century with sleuths and detectives of all kinds – drunk, 'hard-boiled', depressed, divorced and so on – that it's hard to remember that there were none of any significance before Sherlock Holmes at the end of the nineteenth century. There were detectives of a kind in *Bleak House* and *The Moonstone*, but Holmes's only real antecedent was Edgar Allan Poe's C. Auguste Dupin, the main character of 'The Murders in the Rue Morgue' (1841), which established many features of the genre: the 'eccentric' amateur detective, the less brilliant friend as narrator, the plodding police and the final dramatic revelation to the gathered cast; it was also a 'locked-room mystery' of the kind Conan Doyle and later Agatha Christie viewed as a supreme test of plotting. Unfortunately, 'The Murders in the Rue Morgue' was, as a story, little short of idiotic: it was not the butler but an orang-utan that did it.

The glory of Holmes is that Conan Doyle took story-making seriously, and his plots are generally in that agreeable borderland between hokum and believability. They usually have two or three neatly interlocking turns or twists; they generally play fair with the reader by making important evidence available – though sometimes we have not seen Holmes discover vital facts. Most important of all is the character of Holmes himself. His powers of deduction are freakish and sometimes used by him as a circus trick to entertain or impress; his enemies consider his gifts 'devilish', and they do seem to border on the supernatural. Holmes draws on areas of darkness: cocaine, melancholy, dismal violin scraping. He is a city man, and, unlike Watson, immune to the attractions of the country air or the bracing seaside. In 'The Resident Patient', Watson says of a hot August in London, 'I yearned for the glades of the New Forest or the shingle of Southsea', but 'neither the country nor the sea presented the slightest attraction to [Holmes]. He loved to lie in the very centre of five millions of people, with his filaments stretching out and running through them, responsive to every little rumour or suspicion of unsolved crime.' He is unorthodox, operating outside the official police framework, though on cordial terms with it. He has no softer feelings, it seems, except on a handful of occasions when he betrays a fondness for Watson after having exposed him to unnecessary risk. He has never loved a woman – and not, it is suggested, because he is 'not that way inclined', but because all his processes are rational or intellectual. In Holmes's oddly unscientific idea of what a mind is (an attic with very limited storage space: be careful what you put in it) there is simply no room for emotion. He admires Irene Adler in 'A Scandal in Bohemia', but 'it was not that he felt any emotion akin to love for [her] … He never spoke of the softer passions, save with a gibe and a sneer.'

It was acute of Conan Doyle to reckon that Holmes needed this much darkness to make his heroic qualities attractive. We never find him sentimental, or too good, though perhaps we should. He tells Watson in 'The Final Problem': 'The air of London is the sweeter for my presence. In over a thousand cases I am not aware that I have ever used my powers on the wrong side.' He is brave, unselfish, honourable and frugal in his tastes; he has little interest in revenge or in enabling the retribution of law against even the worst criminals; he prefers to let them take their chances with the police. He declines knighthoods and honours, yet will turn his mind to helping the government of the day on patriotic grounds. When we finally leave him he is keeping bees on the Sussex Downs while advising his country as the Great War approaches.

Even the terrain in which Holmes operates is generally dark. London, we are told in the opening pages of the first story, *A Study in Scarlet*, is a 'great cesspool into which all the loungers and idlers of the Empire are irresistibly drained'; Holmes is given to 'long walks, which appeared to take him into the lowest portions of the city'. The stories are journalistically a very good snapshot of their time, in a way that Conan Doyle may himself not have appreciated. What they show is what Watson announces at the start: the meeting of Empire and Home – of Peshawar and Purley;

of New South Wales and Wandsworth Common; of Tanganyika and Toot-ing.[6] The wistaria-covered suburban villas disclose people who have died the most terrible deaths, their skulls smashed in and their faces frequently frozen in rictuses of such horror that others can't bear to look at them. Yet the passions that lie behind such violence have seldom been fomented in Epsom or Redhill; they owe their fire to a rivalry in the Veld, treachery in the Bush or adultery in the Punjab. The brilliance of Conan Doyle's conception was to see what drama lurked behind laburnum borders and rhododendron avenues when the mind filled in the gaps with palms and fever trees. There is a wistfulness in Watson (discharged wounded from the British Army Medical Corps in the second Afghan War), in the athletic Holmes – expert in unarmed combat and a traveller as far as Odessa on the Black Sea and Trincomalee in Ceylon – and perhaps in the rugby-playing medic Conan Doyle himself, for a virile empire that is starting to contract. The desperate deeds of men as they return from gold mines and tea plan-tations, from big-game hunting and East India trading, are granted a small indulgence: murder and violence are always wrong, but empire builders have lived an extraordinary existence, risking their one short life on foreign venture, far from domestic comfort and often to the economic advantage of their fellow countrymen at home; resettlement is always difficult, and a degree of understanding is extended even to the most hot-headed or vengeful. The poem that might provide the background music to all the Sherlock Holmes stories is Kipling's 'Recessional', written for the Diamond Jubilee of 1897:

---

[6] It is perhaps worth noting that Conan Doyle, a Scot, was able to write with a straight face about English suburbia. Most English writers cannot frame the word 'Esher' with-out a spasm of self-consciousness.

God of our fathers, known of old—
  Lord of our far-flung battle line
Beneath whose awful hand we hold
  Dominion over palm and pine—
Lord God of Hosts, be with us yet,
Lest we forget – lest we forget!

The tumult and the shouting dies;
  The captains and the kings depart:
Still stands Thine ancient sacrifice,
  An humble and a contrite heart.
Lord God of Hosts, be with us yet,
Lest we forget – lest we forget!

Far-called, our navies melt away;
  On dune and headland sinks the fire:
Lo, all our pomp of yesterday
  Is one with Nineveh and Tyre!
Judge of the Nations, spare us yet,
Lest we forget – lest we forget!

Many readers have viewed Conan Doyle as the supreme storyteller of British fiction, and I would not dispute this claim, except in one way. Too much of the action is given in speech. It is admittedly a convention of ghost stories, including *Wuthering Heights*, and of some plot-heavy novels such as Conrad's *Heart of Darkness*, to have a baffled narrator to 'frame' the ghastly events; but the danger is that it can put the action at arm's length. With Holmes, it is necessary for the client who comes panting up the stairs at Baker Street to give a summary of his or her problem, but it seems to me there are too many pages in which the paragraphs begin with inverted commas. Watson, you feel, could easily have summarised the salient points. Holmes often then relates to Watson what happens on a preliminary solo expedition; sometimes this contains a second lengthy testimony, so that we have inverted commas within Holmes's inverted commas. This obviously has a distancing effect and it is odd that a narrative craftsman of Conan Doyle's ability was happy to let it pass. The best stories tend to be those in which the majority of the action is witnessed, not related.

Sherlock Holmes may be immortal. When he apparently tumbled off the edge of the Reichenbach Falls at the end of the *Memoirs*, the public were so outraged that Conan Doyle was compelled to bring him back. Holmes is a formally educated man whose knowledge nevertheless shows the patchiness of the autodidact. Watson marvels at his utter ignorance of astronomy, literature and philosophy; even on scientific subjects, Holmes is unsound. In 'The Empty House', his ideas on heredity are fanciful, though some principles of inheritance had started to be understood by the time the volume was published in 1905.[7] It is only in chemistry, with a speciality in poisons, that Holmes convinces academically.

He is impractical and uninterested in money, with one notable exception. In 'The Priory School', he extracts a reward of £6,000 from the Duke

---

[7] Mendel's pioneering 1865 work on hybridisation was being 'rediscovered' and rapidly developed in the first decade of the twentieth century into a plausible genetic theory by de Vries, Bateson, Thomas Hunt Morgan and others. Even if Holmes was primarily a chemist he might have been expected to have some knowledge of what was going on in this exciting area of biology.

of Holdernesse for finding his missing son. At one point the duke tries to buy his silence with twice that figure. I am not sure how much the final cheque is for – £6,000 or £12,000 – but Holmes 'placed it carefully in his notebook. "I am a poor man," said he, as he patted it affectionately, and thrust it into the depths of his inner pocket.' The sum of £6,000 in 1895 is the equivalent of £516,000 in 2011, using the retail price index as a measure; or, if you use average earnings, it comes to £2,890,000. It is not surprising that Holmes can be carefree about money in his other cases.

He drinks little alcohol and eats sparingly, though in 'The Adventure of the Veiled Lodger' he points Watson to a pleasant-sounding supper that consists of 'a cold partridge on the sideboard … and a bottle of Montrachet'. Holmes's ancestors, he tells Watson in 'The Greek Interpreter', were country squires, though his grandmother was the sister of 'Vernet, the French artist' – a fact that leads him to some more unscientific speculation about heredity: 'Art in the blood is liable to take the strangest forms.' He believes his powers of observation to be 'hereditary' and offers his even more gifted brother Mycroft as proof. When, in 'The Sussex Vampire', Watson, for once in his life, comes up with a piece of information not already captured by Holmes, he is not gracious about it; Watson comes as close as he ever does to criticising his friend: 'It was one of the peculiarities of his proud, self-contained nature that, though he docketed any fresh information very quickly and accurately in his brain, he seldom made acknowledgment to the giver.'

Watson's role, as we all know, is to question, to come to the obvious but wrong conclusion, and to express his wonder and surprise at Holmes's genius. This leads him to a great number of ejaculatory remarks. '"My dear Holmes!" I ejaculated,' he recalls in 'The Resident Patient'. Watson ejaculates frequently in the pages of the early *Adventures* and the *Memoirs*, nowhere more inconveniently than during an all-night vigil with Holmes in 'The Man With the Twisted Lip'. 'In the dim light of the lamp I saw him sitting there, an old brier pipe between his lips, his eyes fixed vacantly upon the corner of the ceiling, the blue smoke curling up from him, silent, motionless, with the light shining upon his strong-set aquiline features. So he sat as I dropped off to sleep, and so he sat when a sudden ejaculation caused me to wake up.' In the *Return* and *His Last Bow*, Watson ejaculates less often, and by the time of the final *Case-Book* he seems to have stopped altogether. Whether this is due to a word having been whispered in Conan Doyle's ear or to a gradual weakening of the life force in an Afghan veteran seems beyond the scope of this essay to inquire.

Holmes's life force, meanwhile, remains unstoppable. He offers solutions, understanding and redemption in situations that at first sight seem impossibly tangled. I am not the first reader to have noticed that Conan Doyle was bringing out the Holmes stories at the same time that Freud was publishing his early case histories. Both are masterly narrators; both have an air of magic about them as they bring comfort to a modern world so badly strained by urbanisation and the loss of religious faith to scientific advance. At the end of a Freud case history you sometimes curse yourself for not having picked up the obvious 'clues' to the 'real' cause of some young woman's stomach ache or stammer. Freud was himself aware of this literary quality, commenting, 'It still strikes me myself as strange that the case histories I write should read like short stories and that, as one might say, they lack the serious stamp of science.'[8] It would not be stretching the point too far to say that in the

---

[8] *Studies in Hysteria*, Standard Edition Vol 2, p. 160.

Holmes stories the Empire represents the Unconscious. It is in these dark regions, where violent passions are left forgotten or suppressed, that the investigator must look for the cause of the present symptoms. The body in the suburban villa, the missing horse or the league of redheads are the equivalents of the symptoms that present at first consultation – bizarre and distressing, certainly, but of interest to the magus principally for their representative or symbolic value.

The difference between Holmes and Freud is that Holmes's solutions are more scientific. They were also more varied in diagnosis. Freud viewed all his early patients as suffering from 'hysteria', a condition whose aetiology neither he nor his professor in Paris, Jean-Martin Charcot, had ever been able to establish. This led him to misdiagnose numerous young women who would today be seen to be suffering from types of epilepsy or, in one case, Tourette's syndrome. It is rather as if Holmes had given a triumphantly convincing account of what had 'really' happened – but fingered the wrong culprit.

Freud's great work, of course, came when he dropped his opportunistic attempts at neurology and became a psychologist of commanding insight. Head to head with Holmes, however, there is no doubt whose work of this period has better stood the test of time. I suppose that is one of the advantages of being a fictional character.

Holmes is a hero who transcended the stories that gave him birth and lives now, as Conan Doyle rather dreaded, 'in some fantastic limbo of the children of the imagination, some strange impossible place where the beaux of Fielding may still make love to the belles of Richardson, where Scott's heroes may strut, Dickens's delightful Cockneys still raise a laugh, and Thackeray's worldlings continue to carry on their reprehensible careers'.

Sherlock Holmes would not have had such an impact had Conan Doyle not seen the need to balance the Christian redemptive qualities of his super-hero with some *fin de siècle* drugs and darkness. He would never have lived at all had Conan Doyle not seen both the huge entertainment potential of the detective puzzle and the drama that lay about him in the return of empire to the suburbs and the Home Counties.

Conan Doyle's wish that 'some more astute sleuth with some even less astute comrade may fill the stage which they have vacated' has not been granted. Many sharp-eyed solvers and plodding sidekicks have followed, but the mould that Sherlock Holmes set proved both too alluring and too inflexible for his epigones. After more than a century, Sherlock Holmes remains indispensable to the public imagination, capable of surviving the most witless portrayal on film. He was the first and the best, and he gave a new direction to the literary hero: away from the mainstream and into a territory to which he was in any case more suited – that of genre fiction, with its thrillers and horror and children's stories and sci-fi, in a world where the Good can be good, yet still retain the whorish reader's interest.

Sherlock Holmes as depicted in 'The Man with the Twisted Lip' (1891 edition)

(WARNING. The following section contains lists. It is intended for Holmes aficionados only. Others may prefer to skip it.)

In 1927, Conan Doyle drew up a list of his favourite Holmes stories in descending order. It went:

1. 'The Speckled Band' (*Adventures*)
2. 'The Red-Headed League' (*Adventures*)
3. 'The Dancing Men' (*Return*)
4. 'The Final Problem' (*Memoirs*)
5. 'A Scandal in Bohemia' (*Adventures*)
6. 'The Empty House' (*Return*)
7. 'The Five Orange Pips' (*Adventures*)
8. 'The Second Stain' (*Return*)
9. 'The Devil's Foot' (*His Last Bow*)
10. 'The Priory School' (*Return*)
11. 'The Musgrave Ritual' (*Memoirs*)
12. 'The Reigate Squires' (*Memoirs*)

'The Speckled Band' has all the best elements enumerated above. It is the 'locked-room mystery' Poe might have dreamed of, and although it stretches credibility, it does hold up; it is short, neat and almost all the action is seen at first hand. 'The Red-Headed League' puts an outrageous ruse against a common bank robbery and succeeds because the surreal element of the first is so distracting. 'The Dancing Men' has a proper code to be broken and a Norfolk/Chicago tie-up; but the central story lacks a twist. 'A Scandal in Bohemia' has one of the best titles and, in Irene Adler, a woman for whom Sherlock Holmes feels 'admiration', if nothing more;

it is also notable in that Holmes is outwitted by her; he loses. Yet the story lacks intricacy; the bird simply flies. 'The Empty House' is essentially a manoeuvre to bring Holmes back from the dead, after the end of 'The Final Problem', when he is assumed to have fallen from the Reichenbach Falls in a struggle with the arch-criminal Moriarty. It is more thriller than detective story, however, with Holmes and Watson in a stake-out at Baker Street with a waxwork dummy of Holmes behind a lit blind. 'The Final Problem' is also mechanical – a way of killing off Holmes, while Moriarty doesn't convince as a villain, let alone as the 'Napoleon of Crime'. 'The Five Orange Pips' has a memento mori motif (the pips) and a Ku Klux Klan background; it also uses a natural disaster (storm at sea) to mete out justice at the end – a common ploy when Conan Doyle wants to avoid a banal sense of revenge or legal retribution and to suggest that Holmes is on the side of a higher natural justice. The story itself, however, is far from his best and its inclusion merely confirms how much Conan Doyle preferred his early work – in the *Adventures* and the *Memoirs* – before he began to tire of Holmes.

'The Second Stain' is a different matter. It shows Holmes involved in high politics, but also has a proper sleuth clue in the eponymous stain and a genuine blow-me-down disclosure of who 'did it'. 'The Devil's Foot' takes Holmes to far-flung Cornwall, where some readers have found him ill at ease. I like it, though. It has excellent empire connections, a forgiving attitude to one 'villain' and another closed-room variation. 'The Priory School' runs on similar lines, though this time in an unspecified 'North of England' county. It has some excellent bicycle-tyre sleuthing and a shock perpetrator; the German teacher at the school in question is splendidly named Heidegger. 'The Musgrave Ritual' has another top title, some good trigonometry and an excellent 'living grave' denouement. It is perhaps the first crime story in which the 'butler did it' – and none the worse for that. 'The Reigate Squires', on the other hand (was ever there a better short-story titler than Conan Doyle?), is a routine tale, lacking distinctive features.

Later, Conan Doyle added a further seven favourites, one from the later *His Last Bow*, the others from the first two collections *en repêchage*. They, also in descending order, were:

1. 'Silver Blaze' (*Memoirs*)
2. 'The Adventure of the Bruce-Partington Plans' (*His Last Bow*)
3. 'The Crooked Man' (*Memoirs*)
4. 'The Man with the Twisted Lip' (*Adventures*)
5. 'The Greek Interpreter' (*Memoirs*)
6. 'The Resident Patient' (*Memoirs*)
7. 'The Naval Treaty' (*Memoirs*)

Three of these are outstanding. 'Silver Blaze' challenges 'The Speckled Band' as the greatest Holmes story of all, and it's odd that Conan Doyle overlooked it in his first selection. It tells of a Shergar-type mystery, though with a happier ending. It has a knock-me-down denouement, superb details (the mutton curry, the lame sheep), a convincing Dartmoor setting and one of the most famous lines in the canon about the dog that didn't bark in the night. 'The Crooked Man' has a terrific Empire/Home Counties collision, high passions of treachery and revenge, and a genuine crawl of horror. 'The Man With the Twisted Lip' is another closed-room mystery, with a big pay-off revelation that was in retrospect easily available to the reader; it seems to me one of the very best London stories, with an opium den scene thrown in for good measure.

For what it's worth, then, my top ten Holmes stories are – in descending order, as the author himself did it:

1. 'The Speckled Band'
2. 'Silver Blaze'
3. 'The Man With the Twisted Lip'
4. 'The Red-Headed League'
5. 'The Crooked Man'
6. 'The Musgrave Ritual'
7. 'The Priory School'
8. 'The Solitary Cyclist'
9. 'The Second Stain'
10. 'The Devil's Foot'

This would make a formidable collection. I have added only one ('The Solitary Cyclist' – young woman pursued by bearded man on bike, forced marriage, Farnham/High Veld link), but have changed Conan Doyle's order of preference a good deal. His favourite collection was clearly the second, the *Memoirs* (eight choices in total), which makes sense, as by then he would feel that he had found his rhythm but not yet grown tired of Holmes. Neither of us has been tempted to select from the last collection, *The Case-Book of Sherlock Holmes*, which seems to be the weakest.

'A LONELY GHOST'

WINSTON SMITH

There is no chance of Winston Smith or anyone else being a hero in the imaginary Airstrip One of George Orwell's *Nineteen Eighty-Four*, first published in 1949. This much is clear from the novel's opening, which gives details of a society in which, with the more or less willing connivance of its citizens, freedom – of thought or action – barely exists as a concept, let alone a possibility.

Unheroic Winston is thirty-nine, yet seems older. He has trouble climbing the stairs of Victory Mansions to his squalid lodging; he has a varicose ulcer on his ankle and a chronic cough. His surname suggests that he is an average man and his demeanour suggests compliance and defeat. It is important for George Orwell to establish early the totality of control; even the tiny pleasures of Winston's life – gin that tastes like nitric acid and rough cigarettes – are provided from a central commissary. Citizens of Airstrip One are crushed by the state but also dependent on it.

In an alcove beyond the gaze of the telescreen (a device that both broadcasts and intrusively watches), Winston Smith begins to write a diary. He doesn't seem to have much to say, though. Exhaustion saps his prose; he lays down the pen. He has noticed a 'bold-looking girl of about twenty-seven, with thick dark hair' and assumes that because she is a member of the Junior Anti-Sex League she is probably a spy for the party, looking out for 'thought crime' even in a man as drab as he is. Winston dislikes all women, 'especially the young and pretty ones', and particularly this one, with her 'swift, athletic movements'. He hates the 'atmosphere of hockey fields and cold baths and community hikes' they carry with them because they are a denial of the sex instinct.

Within the first twelve pages, therefore, Orwell has established that Winston is no hero, that heroism is impossible and that the girl with the scarlet sash of the Anti-Sex League is committed to celibacy. Where can the story possibly go from here? Well, in the unlikeliest directions, as it turns out, rebounding ultimately into the real world, where Winston Smith became an inspiration to Vaclav Havel and other dissident leaders in Eastern bloc Communist countries.

Orwell was not a novelist of the talent or skill of his contemporaries Graham Greene, Evelyn Waugh or Henry Green. His non-political novels such as *Keep the Aspidistra Flying* or *Coming Up for Air* are accomplished and enjoyable, but lack deep psychological insight, great themes, profound emotion or architectural ambition. He was a peerless essayist, however, and his work will endure (if future generations read) for the way that it captures essential truths about the way political systems worked in the twentieth century. Orwell's prose is a marvel of lucidity, democratically refined to make its ideas available to the greatest possible number of readers.

I first read Orwell at the age of fourteen, when his essay 'A Hanging' struck me with the force of revelation. It was written while he was serving in the colonial police force in Burma, and tells of a morning when he acted as escort to a local prisoner due to be hanged for civilian crimes.

> It is curious, but till that moment I had never realized what it means to destroy a healthy, conscious man. When I saw the prisoner step aside to avoid the puddle I saw the mystery, the unspeakable wrongness of cutting a life short when it is in full tide. This man was not dying, he was alive just as we are alive. All the organs of his body were working – bowels digesting food, skin renewing itself, nails growing, tissues forming – all toiling away in solemn foolery. His nails would still be growing when he stood on the drop, when he was falling through the air with a tenth of a second to live. His eyes saw the yellow gravel and the grey walls, and his brain still remembered, foresaw, reasoned – even about puddles. He and we were a party of men walking together, seeing, hearing, feeling, understanding the same world; and in two minutes, with a sudden snap, one of us would be gone – one mind less, one world less.

It was the first liberal challenge to the traditional sense of justice and retribution which had been at the core of what I'd learned till then, and it changed the way I looked at the world. I read the other essays in *Decline of the English Murder* and found them just as thrilling, even when they were dealing with things I knew little about. Almost every sentence seemed to strike home with the power of a simply revealed truth. Often in later life, when asked to give talks to students about 'creative writing', I have used the passage quoted above. I think there is perhaps only one occasion on which I have not used it, and that was when giving a class to a group of patients in Broadmoor Hospital in 2005, when I went instead with a poem by Thom Gunn called 'Considering the Snail'.

I first read *Nineteen Eighty-Four* while learning to speak French in Paris as a student. I saw it and several other tempting English paperbacks in a large *librairie* in the Boulevard Saint-Michel and thought how superior the French library system was to the English in having new books for readers to borrow. I wasn't sure what the limit was, but risked five at the checkout desk. I was presented with a bill so large that I couldn't eat lunch for ten days, but was too shy to quibble; my French language studies had not got as far as distinguishing between *librairie* (bookshop) and *bibliothèque* (lending library). Thank goodness for the free American Library in the rue Général Camou, which became my Monday destination for many weeks afterwards: Métro to Alma Marceau, then Pont de l'Alma across the Seine and brisk walk up Avenue Rapp, where a café sold a camembert sandwich – *sans beurre* – for a full ten centimes less than my local bar in place des Acacias. From the American Library I had my first experience of Henry James, Hemingway, Fitzgerald and Melville; and, as a reward for finishing *Moby-Dick*, *To Kill a Mockingbird*.

Reading *Nineteen Eighty-Four* again, and bearing in mind Orwell's acknowledged and partly self-imposed limitations as a novelist, I was impressed by how cleverly plotted it is. It is less of a tract and more of a novel than I remembered. Everything is set up to make you think that

Big Brother is Watching You: Edmond O'Brien as
Winston Smith in the 1956 film adaptation

Winston is drab, sick and powerless. And yet, the first thing he does – to
begin a diary – is probably punishable by death. Without knowing it, he
is brave. It is a balancing act of some skill to make the reader think that a
hero is not heroic; to gull you into thinking that no one, least of all a loser
like Winston, can fight the most oppressive monolith known to human
imagination, and then – almost before you understand it's happening – to
show him doing just that.

The nasty little Parsons boy from next door spots Winston at it before he has really begun: "'You're a traitor," yelled the boy. "You're a thought-criminal! You're a Eurasian spy! I'll shoot you, I'll vaporise you, I'll send you to the salt mines!"' Winston knows that the 'thought crime' of keeping a diary means he is already dead. But his recognition that his lifespan is now limited is what sets him free to continue. 'He was a lonely ghost uttering a truth that nobody would ever hear. But so long as he uttered it, in some obscure way the continuity was not broken. It was not by making yourself heard but by staying sane that you carried on the human heritage.' Orwell makes Winston's act of defiance seem small and hopeless; thus he makes him credible as an Everyman-hero. Yet at the same time, the whole tragedy of the twentieth century – the gulags, the concentration camps, the millions of anonymous corpses – seems contained in the simple thoughts that Winston expresses. They inspire us as readers to reach out to this imagined character and demonstrate to him that posterity did, after all, take the time and the trouble to care.

Winston, at thirty-nine, must have been born in 1945. His mother disappeared in one of the 'great purges', when he was about ten or eleven, therefore perhaps in 1956 (Orwell obviously could not have known that this would be the year of the Soviet invasion of Hungary, the watershed for Communism). Winston remembers from early childhood the day when 'an atomic bomb had fallen on Colchester', since when the continents of the world have been continuously at war. He thinks that Airstrip One was once called England and is fairly sure that London was always London. Orwell wisely does not give too many details of Winston's youth because there are some logical difficulties in accepting the degree of his forgetfulness. Winston meets an old 'prole' in a pub one day who can remember earlier days, but luckily for the logic of the book he is drunk and unreliable;

his memory was 'nothing but a rubbish-heap of details'. Winston presses him on whether he preferred the past, but the old man thinks the question merely refers to his personal health. It is hard to imagine that people aged between forty and sixty in 1984 would all have suffered amnesia comparable to Winston's; there would be colleagues in their fifties and sixties at the Ministry of Truth whom Winston could more profitably ask about the past, but perhaps it would be too risky for them to reminisce.

The elderly prole's response reminded me of a time I interviewed an old woman in a Moscow skyscraper as part of the research for a novel called *On Green Dolphin Street*. I asked her which of the many leaders she had lived under, from Lenin to Yeltsin, she had thought the best. She answered without hesitation: 'Stalin.' The interview was also part of a BBC *Omnibus* programme, and somewhere a film shows me choking on a piece of cake at this unexpected answer. The local BBC 'fixer' later told me not to be so surprised; many people, she said, agreed with the old lady. (She also reminded me of the story of an old man to whom the same question was put, his historical range of leader being from the tsar to Gorbachev. He also replied, 'Stalin,' adding, 'because when he was leader I had better erections.')

Orwell might well have argued that the unavailability of the past in Airstrip One is due to the ability of the totalitarian state to demoralise its citizens and capture their minds. The odd thing is that, writing in 1948, he could not have known this, since the extent of thought control in the Eastern bloc had not yet been documented. So *Nineteen Eighty-Four* is not just a cautionary fantasy based on deep political understanding; it is prophetic. Orwell also, incidentally, anticipates the functioning of what President Eisenhower later christened the 'military-industrial complex': an economy that needs perpetual war to service itself.

*

Winston's 'greatest pleasure in life was in his work', which is rewriting history to suit the party, with 'delicate pieces of forgery'. His colleague Syme is engaged on destroying Chaucer, Shakespeare, Milton and Byron by translating them into Newspeak, though one feels it might have been easier for the party simply to burn the books. Syme has spotted some problems in his work. The party will need new slogans to reflect the new, simplistic language. 'How could you have a slogan like "freedom is slavery" when the concept of freedom has been abolished?' he asks Winston. Instead of seeing the resilience of language as validation of his own diary project, Winston merely reflects that Syme is too clever by half and is therefore bound to be 'vaporised' by the state.

Language is one repository of freedom. The other one is love. We learn that Winston has visited a prostitute in a 'prole' area, and while the encounter is suitably grim it suggests that he has not given up: lust springs from energy and a desire for life to continue. The party sees the danger of such emotions and brainwashes all its women from a young age to reject natural urges. Winston's reason tells him there must be women who have survived this conditioning, 'but his heart did not believe it'. In some ways it is surprising that Winston's rebellion against Big Brother revolves so much around his love affair with Julia, the girl with the red sash. It seems a conventional, almost sentimental procedure in such an uncompromising dystopia. Yet Orwell is right in thinking – again, perhaps, ahead of his time – that individual passions and affinities are deeply subversive things. He at least had the witness of some Soviet dissidents and some concentration-camp survivors on which to reach the conclusion that while you have language and love, you are not fully enslaved.

If there is hope, Winston thinks, 'it lies in the proles'. His depiction of the lives of the 'proles' draws on H. G. Wells's *War of the Worlds* and on

Marx, though Orwell extended Marx's idea of the *Lumpenproletariat* from being a useless minority to making up the entire 'working' class. It is also predictive of current life in the West and the East in showing how millions of people can be kept relatively passive with relative ease in a post-religious world by mass entertainment. Films, football, beer and gambling are the party's prescription, but nothing quite matches the power of the Lottery, which, 'with its weekly pay-out of enormous prizes, was the one public event to which the proles paid serious attention. It was probable that there were some millions of proles for whom the Lottery was the principal if not the only reason for remaining alive. Where the Lottery was concerned, even people who could barely read and write seemed capable of intricate calculations and staggering feats of memory.' I remember that when I first read the book in 1971 I thought Orwell was laying it on a bit thick here.

For a moment it looks as though Winston is to become a sort of *marx-isant* activist, trying to liberate the proles, but happily Orwell narrows his focus back on to the struggle of one ordinary man against one extraordinary state. It is in the domestic details of life under totalitarianism that much of the grey charm of the book lies. Winston rents a room over a junk shop, a cosy little place that has awakened some 'ancestral memory' in him of a more pleasant life. His affair with Julia begins when she presses a piece of paper into his hand. On it are written the words 'I Love You'. Julia turns out to be an experienced lover. 'Hundreds of times – well, scores of times, anyway', she tells him. Winston likes her promiscuity because he sees it as subversive: 'The simple undifferentiated desire: that was the force that would tear the party to pieces,' he reflects, sounding, again ahead of his time, like a hippy marching on the Pentagon in 1967. 'Their embrace had been a battle, the climax a victory. It was a blow struck against the party. It was a political act.' Julia works as a rewriter of soft-porn stories for the

Pornosec division of the Fiction Department, recycling stock plots and situations. Winston tells Julia of his married life with his frigid wife Katharine who used to call their weekly sex act 'our duty to the party'. In passing, Winston reveals that Katharine was 'too stupid to detect the unorthodoxy of his opinions', and we see that the revolt of the diary and now the love affair with Julia are no sudden impulses. Drab little Winston Smith has been a long-time dissident: a 'sleeper', waiting for his moment.

The lovers meet in the room above the junk shop, and their meetings are charged with the feeling all lovers have: that time is against them. For Winston and Julia, who have transgressed against the state, this is no romantic pessimism, but a function of what they have done: 'There were times when the fact of impending death seemed as palpable as the bed they lay on, and they would cling together with a sort of despairing sensuality.' Orwell's interest is not primarily romantic, but the sense of time running out gives a touching intensity and sense of the universal to Winston and Julia's relationship.

When, after being arrested by the Thought Police, who have been spying on his love nest all along, Winston is being tortured in the Ministry of Love, he asks himself: 'If I could save Julia by doubling my own pain, would I do it? Yes, I would.' This, however, is fairly early in his ordeal; on the next page he is already conceding that 'In the face of pain there are no heroes.' As he is brainwashed into becoming a believing party member, Winston draws his defences back. Quite late in the process he is still able to maintain that what he represents is better in principle than what the party stands for. His torturer, O'Brien, asks him what this principle is, and Winston answers weakly, 'I don't know. The spirit of Man.' When O'Brien shows him what a wretched specimen of manhood he has become, Winston retreats to his final redoubt: he has not betrayed

Julia. In Room 101, however, even this last defence crumbles. With rats about to eat through his eyeballs, he screams: 'Do it to Julia! Do it to Julia! Not me! Julia!'

Winston Smith is a new kind of hero: one who loses. In his life, in his story, Winston is defeated, as he always knows he will be, by the superior powers against which no single man can prevail. The man who sold him the diary in the first place turns out to have been a member of the Thought Police, so even Winston's small rebellion was coaxed from him by the all-seeing authorities.

In the twentieth century, the hero tends to be a captive. He can no longer, like Tom Jones or Becky Sharp, make a free stand against society, or like Robinson Crusoe triumph through individual strength over the dangers of his physical and mental landscape. Winston's heroism exists in the fact that he dares to write down his story, dares to think and dares to love, knowing all the time that this will lead to torture and to death. Whether or not it leads to 'defeat' is another matter.

Orwell knew that the outcome of the struggle against totalitarianism would not be decided in the lifetime of the combatants. There were no 'winners' in the gulags or in Auschwitz. Whether the wretched end of Winston Smith and of his millions of real-life counterparts constitutes failure or success depends not on what they achieved, but on whether succeeding generations are prepared to make the imaginative leap of understanding; whether we can be bothered to read and learn; whether we can make that gesture of love and redemption.

When researching a novel called *Charlotte Gray*, I looked into the transportation of Jewish children in 1942–4 by the French gendarmerie to the Drancy holding camp outside Paris and thence in cattle trucks by rail to Auschwitz. The children – some French, some foreign – were volunteered by the French government to meet the 'quota' requested by the Nazis. The enthusiastic, in some cases competitive, French complicity was long officially denied after the war until, in the 1980s, a Rumanian-born lawyer called Serge Klarsfeld decided on a simple way of proving that 80,000 Jews had been deported. He named them. Of the estimated total of 80,000 deportees, he identified 75,721.

While going through the Paris archive of Klarsfeld's astonishing research, I came across this piece of writing:

Vous vous souviendrez. Le souvenir est un enseignement et un message d'amour ... le souvenir secoue la poussière du tombeau; le culte des regrets est un rachat du sépulcre: la vraie mort est l'oubli. A l'heure suprème, ce leur fut une consolation de s'endormir sur l'assurance d'avoir été mieux que de simples passants, puisqu'ils devaient trouver le bon asile de notre coeur qui se remémore.

A rough translation might go:

You shall remember them. Memory is an education and a message of love ... memory shakes the dust from their tomb; by our tribute of sorrow they are ransomed from the grave: the only true death is to be forgotten. At the final hour this was a consolation to them, to fall asleep safe in the knowledge that they were more than simple transients, knowing they had found lasting safety in the remembrance of our hearts.

'HE FELT BAD'

JIM DIXON

Jim Dixon, the hero of Kingsley Amis's 1954 novel *Lucky Jim*, made people laugh, and apparently laughter was scarce in Britain in the 1950s. In a letter to a friend, Ted Hughes referred to the decade as a 'tundra that we had to cross'. There was a shortage of food, jobs, money and fun; whatever the Festival of Britain tried to provide in 1951 as a 'tonic for the nation', there seems to have been little in the way of cultural joy in theatre, books or music (trad jazz and skiffle didn't quite do the trick), while architecture focussed on rebuilding the bombed-out docks and cities. Britain was a country that had stood alone against the Nazis in Europe and had summoned every atom of vigour and self-sacrifice to outperform even its own high expectations of itself. It had discovered heroes in twenty-one-year-olds with beer hangovers flying single-engine planes from grass airfields; it had gritted its teeth in the fearsome slit trenches of Anzio and the murderous air of the Normandy beaches; it had endured ordeal by fire in the waters of the North Atlantic, then joined the Americans and the Russians in the strength-sapping push to global victory. By the mid-1950s there was a looming, widespread sense of disappointment that a country which had done all this without complaining (much), and had earned the admiration of the world for its daring and resilience, seemed to have ended up with no spoils of war, but dead broke; that it should still be closing the pubs at ten o'clock, while its returning servicemen and women should have been offered nothing more than fog and rain and rationing, the 'Brains Trust' on fuzzy television and the same old bells of evensong. It is true that in 1957 Harold Macmillan declared that 'most of our people have never had it so good', but the prime minister's belief does not appear to have been widely shared.

Another thing that seems to have been irksome to grown-ups in the 1950s, particularly to unmarried people, was the lack of sex. A sizeable part of Jim Dixon's frustration springs from the fact that society at all levels seems to have conspired to prevent women from sleeping with him. During the first scene of the book, which sees him being irritated by Professor Welch, the head of department in the unnamed provincial university at which he works, Jim is really thinking with dread of his date that evening with Margaret Peel, the survivor of a recent suicide attempt.

It's not just that he won't sleep with Margaret, because she won't let him; it's more that unless he goes through the motions of asking Margaret out and not sleeping with her, he won't be in a position to get lucky with someone he really does like. In his first published scene between a man and a woman, Kingsley Amis opened up a seam of equivocal embarrassment that was to serve him so well that he later elevated it to a title, *Difficulties with Girls*. Everything about Margaret puts Jim in the wrong. She has tried to kill herself, which makes him feel guilty, although it's not his fault. She has another, 'real' boyfriend, a rotter called Catchpole, which makes Jim feel inadequate. She controls the question of sex, as women properly do; she can offer or deny, and there is nothing Jim, the man, can do about it. Jim wants Margaret to think that he fancies her, not because he does, but so that she will feel better about herself. He feels guilty that a bat-squeak of desire persists, yet also guilty that it isn't stronger. He feels guilty that she thinks he fancies her, guilty that he doesn't and guilty, really, that the feelings she has for him are not of a suicidal intensity. Not that he actually wants her to die, or that it would be his fault, or …

The point about the Margaret tangle is that Jim accepts that this sour chastity, sauced with guilt and tedium, is his fate. Young men like him – northern, grammar school, clever but not posh – cannot simply ask out a good-looking woman they like, have fun and have sex. In Jim's world, this doesn't happen, and this is as much a restriction on his happiness as his boring job in a second-rate institution and his chronic lack of funds or prospects. It is probably fair to assume that Jim Dixon has never actually slept with a woman. Even while he is with Margaret he studies the barmaid. 'He thought how much he liked her, and how much she'd like and have in common with him if only she knew him.' He leaves it at that; he accepts that it is somehow beyond his reach to befriend her.

Of all the literary-heroic qualities, the one that Kingsley Amis's main characters offered in spades was being the reader's point of identification. Men and women readers laughed at Jim Dixon in 1954 because his frustrating life, with only tiny childish triumphs (pulling silly faces, defacing magazines, nurturing fantasies of revenge) to compensate for the crushing unfairness and tedium of daily life, seemed to replicate their own. Almost all Kingsley Amis's main characters are whistle-blowers. In a modest, conversational way, they say, 'Is it just me, or is this bloke I'm meant to look up to self-evidently an idiot? Excuse me if I've got this wrong, but isn't that chap a complete fraud? Is a drink out of the question?' It's the modesty of the stance that is endearing, but which also reveals the weight of the settled world that these men are trying to shift a fraction on its axis. There is anger behind the laughter, but it's not the satirical heat of Joseph Heller's *Catch-22* or even of Malcolm Bradbury's later campus novel *The History Man*; it's more a sort of meticulously itemised and continuously compounded frustration; it is a polite, logical and English anger that needs time and nurture to reach critical mass.

In Jim's life, everyone is irritating in their own way: the fellow lodgers in his digs, the demanding student, Michie, Welch and all his family, all his faculty colleagues, even the landlady who puts the tea things down in such a way that it's impossible to speak to anyone except her as she does so. The entire world as seen by Jim Dixon is essentially a con trick. Jim, and, by flattering extension, we the readers, are the only points of sanity in this menagerie of folly and self-delusion. This, I think, was Kingsley Amis's strategy: to widen the scope of his heroes' disillusionment, item by item, so that it feasibly becomes a social satire as well as a private comedy. There seems to be hardly any generalisation about society or politics, either explicit or implicit; Amis built up the social picture by putting in the individuals, and their tics, one by one. This woman is annoying for the way she puts things on the table, this man for the way he adds unnecessary consonants to certain words in speech, this one for the way he's too mean to buy new razor blades. This is a society comprised of a thousand, individually scrutinised and digested irritations; the method is what you might call pointilliste, though I don't think Kingsley Amis would have. There are moments when it isn't merely the observation that is funny but the thought that an author could have taken the obsessive trouble to analyse and recreate such genuine but minute irritations from real life.

It's not long before Jim sees a woman he does like the look of: 'The fair hair, straight and cut short, with brown eyes and no lipstick … the large breasts and the narrow waist … the wine-coloured corduroy skirt and the unornamented white linen blouse.' His response is one of defeat. 'The notion that women like this were never on view except as the property of men like Bertrand [Welch's well-connected son] was so familiar to him that it has long since ceased to appear an injustice.' Not just defeat, in fact, but defeatism: 'Dixon had been too distressed at the sight of Bertrand's girl to want to be introduced to her.' This is pitiful, but sharp, and seems somehow truthful. Floundering at the Welches' ghastly musical evening, Jim escapes to the pub which, being out of town, closes not at ten but at ten-thirty. Jim has been pacing himself for the ten o'clock shutdown, and the extra half-hour proves critical. One of the great comic scenes of English fiction follows, culminating in the much-anthologised description of Jim's hangover, which ends: 'His mouth had been used as a latrine by some small creature of the night, and then as its mausoleum. During the night, too, he'd somehow been on a cross-country run and then been expertly beaten up by secret police. He felt bad.' My favourite line comes the night before, when Jim is making a drunken, though well-received, pass at Margaret, pushing his luck bit by bit, like a bomb disposal expert: 'As they lay on the bed, he made a movement not only quite unambiguous, but even, perhaps, rather insolently frank. Margaret's response to it, though violent, was hard to interpret.' Violent, yet hard to interpret … It seems to be an oxymoron, but it isn't; it tells you a great deal of Margaret's state of mind, as well, of course, as making you put down the book to laugh. Jim tops up his belly-ful of beer with port drunk straight from the bottle, the very bottle from which 'Welch had, the previous evening, poured Dixon the smallest drink he'd ever been seriously offered.' Even as the broad physical farce is unrolling, Amis does not neglect to chalk up one more small score to Welch's deficit. Being mean with drink was not a venal but a mortal sin in Kingsley Amis's eschatology.

When Jim meets Christine, Bertrand's pretty girlfriend, at breakfast the next day, something of the same technique is used to convey his strong feeling for her. Exaggerating his northern accent, he apologises for a misunderstanding the previous night and is gratified that she forgives him. She takes a lot of tomato ketchup, a good, unpretentious sign; likewise her square-tipped fingers, with the nails cut close. She has a rough, natural laugh in addition to the social noise she has made the night before, and when she laughs like this, a lock of her carefully brushed hair comes loose. Her front teeth are slightly irregular. 'For some reason this was more disturbing to his equanimity than regularity could possibly have been. He began to think he'd noticed quite enough things about her now, thank you.' The free indirect style takes us slithering from objective narration to silent monologue within the space of a few words. Later, as Christine is helping him disguise the fire damage Jim has inflicted on the Welches' spare room, he 'saw with fury that she was prettier than he thought'. The fury stems from his knowledge that he can never have her. The feelings she arouses in him are therefore 'indignation, grief, resentment, peevishness, spite and sterile anger, all the allotropes of pain'. He is cross with her for existing and, worse than that, letting him see her. 'Run-of-the-mill queens of love – Italian film actresses, millionaires' wives, girls on calendars – he could put up with … But this sort of thing he'd as soon not look at.'

Margaret, meanwhile, is revealed to be an emotional blackmailer of a pathological kind. '"You're so sweet to me,"' she tells Jim, '"and I'm getting much too fond of you." She said this in a tone that combined the vibrant with the flat, like a great actress demonstrating the economical conveyance of strong emotion.' The 'getting much too fond of you' is presumably a hint that she may allow Jim to 'have his way' with her if she, or he, is not careful – a prospect simultaneously alluring and shrivelling for Jim. The biting effectiveness of the characterisation of Margaret lies in the way that Amis suggests that her emotional self-indulgence, conceit, dishonesty and manipulation are characteristic of her sex. Much later, Jim meets the rotter Catchpole, the cause of Margaret's suicide attempt, and learns that not only were they not in fact lovers, but that the suicide attempt was faked. Catchpole was wary from the start: 'Quite soon I realized that she was one of these people – they're usually women – who feed on emotional tension.'

At this early stage in Amis's career, the idea of a flaw running through a whole sex is embryonic only, and is balanced by the portrayal of down-to-earth, honest, almost bloke-ish Christine, who will not tease Jim, but will sleep with him, no problem, if that's what it comes to. But I think there is no doubt that it's the suggestion of whole-sex characteristics that makes Margaret such a chilling character; and it was to be such fertile ground for Amis that the Christine figures began to fall away from his later books, in which all the women became developments of the characteristics first itemised in Margaret. 'Biting effectiveness' of individual characterisation is not the same thing as palatability, of course; and even Amis's warmest admirers have had to swallow hard at his later, generalised views of the female sex.

When chance allows Jim to ask Christine for a dance at the college summer ball, and she consents, he feels like 'a special agent, a picaroon, a Chicago war-lord, a hidalgo, an oil baron, a mohock'. He feels good. Something starts to change in Jim Dixon. It seems he might be able to take charge, to be active not passive. At the end of the party there is a magnificently sustained bit of trickery with a taxi. I have read *Lucky Jim* several times and I can't say I've ever worked out exactly how he does it, but Jim not only pinches a pre-ordered taxi from an elderly professor and his wife, he gets Christine into it and persuades the driver to break his company rules and travel beyond his limit. This is no longer Dixon the put-upon, but Dixon Agonistes. Christine tells him she is only nineteen years old (though he and we had thought her older); this, allied to a candid confession she makes about not being much good with men, emboldens Jim a little. Christine's relationship with Bertrand has nascent complications of an almost Margaret-like tendency, but Jim dismisses them with 'old-trouper confidence'. He is in unknown territory; he doesn't really know what he is saying to this 'unmanningly pretty girl', but he seems to be relying on a gamble: that if he keeps calm and says exactly what he thinks, then it's just possible that the two of them can form a rapport as two sane human beings might – not shaped or spoiled by the crushing machinery of idiocy, class-consciousness, conceit, prudery, bullshit, false nostalgia for the past, rationing and hypocrisy that make up the world that Jim has previously known. And he might eventually have sex.

Confidence begins to run in Jim's blood, as heady as the eight pints of bitter on the night of the Welches' musical soirée. He insists on getting change from a surly waiter; he stands up to the bullying Bertrand, telling him he knows about his dalliance with a married colleague of his. The men square up to one another. Jim knocks Bertrand down, stands over him and tells him, in characteristic Dixonian terms, what he thinks of him. 'It is', as David Lodge pointed out, 'the first occasion on which Jim's inner and outer speech exactly coincide.' 'The bloody old towser-faced boot-faced totem-pole on a crap reservation, Dixon thought. "The bloody old towser-faced boot-faced totem-pole on a crap reservation," he said.'

Jim's drunken lecture at an important event – another loved set piece – has him dismissed from his post at the university, but he is offered a better job, a sinecure as private secretary to a grandee in London. Catchpole's revelations free him from his thraldom of guilt to Margaret; Christine disentangles herself from Bertrand, and the lovers — as Jim and Christine will doubtless become — leave for the metropolis together. Jim's wager – that talking and behaving normally in a world of affectation might set him free – has triumphantly worked. The bogus life of the Welches will go on, but Jim's last act in the book is not to denounce it, as he wants to do, but merely to laugh at it. He is overcome with hilarity as he looks at Welch, *père et fils*. 'His steps faltered; his body sagged as if he'd been knifed.' For the first time, one of his comic-book gestures is for real. He has got lucky, Jim, very lucky. But it took a kind of heroism to back his hunch that behaving honestly might do the trick.

'READY FOR ANYTHING'

JOHN SELF

Martin Amis's extraordinary talents as a writer were clear from page one of his first novel, *The Rachel Papers*, published in 1973. Here was a stylist: a writer whose every sentence seemed pressurised by the tensions of its improbable juxtapositions. Where the father was happy to write 'Dixon paid the garage-man and the taxi moved off', as though challenging the reader to see how his meaning could have been more clearly conveyed, the son seemed reluctant to pass any sentence in which words were not pressed hard against one another to produce unsettling effects. In a characteristic Martin Amis passage, the high-flown is used to describe the vulgar and vice versa, and comedy springs from the disparity; but there is more to it than that. Almost every sentence contains a verbal surprise, a word or phrase forced into an unfamiliar context. Few novelists have been so recognisable from their prose; few have invested so much and so obviously in language as the principal pleasure of their books.

Thus John Self, the hero of *Money*, climbs out of his New York taxi. 'So now I stand here with my case, in smiting light and island rain. Behind me massed water looms, and the industrial corsetry of FDR Drive ... It must be pushing eight o'clock by now but the weepy breath of the day still shields its glow, a guttering glow, very wretched – rained on, leaked on.'

What makes you sit up is the number of different registers. 'Smiting' is biblical, 'island' is topographical, reminding us that we are on Manhattan; 'massed water looms' seems to be American pulp fiction; 'industrial corsetry' is a near-oxymoron; 'weepy' is feminine domestic; 'glow, a guttering glow' is mock-lyrical; 'very wretched' personifies the 'glow' but is otherwise punchy and direct; while the final phrase, 'rained on, leaked on', is both rhetorical with its repetition and conversational in the way it ends on a preposition. There is also the assonance, the rhythmic crescendo, the urgency of the present tense ... One could go on. The father might have written: 'When I arrived in New York it was raining but still just light.'

The question with such a style is whether it pays its way. It was clear in Martin Amis's early books that behind the street slang and the hipster lilt, quite a pedant was at work; he knew not only what his words meant, but was able to make harmonies from their conflicting connotations. You can only do this if you've done the spadework, looked up etymologies as well as reading widely (and Amis seemed to have learned a good deal from American novelists, most obviously Bellow and Nabokov; his prose sometimes had an almost mid-Atlantic flavour, which is one reason it works so well in *Money*, as the story jets between London and New York). With so many different registers there was a potential for cacophony, but the rhythm and effect seldom faltered; Martin Amis had that rare gift in a literary stylist, particularly in one as ambitiously rhetorical: he had perfect pitch. To those who could hear his rude, allusive music, these early novels were an intense delight. It was true that one read them principally for the thrill of the sentences, but they delivered more than just virtuosity to savour; they delivered a riot of laughter.

I don't know how well they were received at the time. Fiction reviewing was at a low ebb, and I have a vague memory of seeing some of Martin Amis's early books being slotted in at number three or four in a weekly 'round-up'. Such reviewers fretted about 'four-letter words'; the committees of literary prizes regularly ignored him; the books appeared on no bestseller lists. Yet to his admirers, these novels seemed to be in a different league from most things being attempted at the time, written at a higher level of verbal intensity; even his less successful books, such as *Dead Babies* or *Other People*, were, it was agreed, 'better than anyone else's good books'.

The Rachel Papers remains a classic of post-adolescent angst. Its main character, the preposterously candid Charles Highway, puzzles over the gulf between the heights of Literature and the squalor of the student life he experiences. His pathological self-awareness gives moments of exquisite comedy, as when he puts Rachel, the object of his lust, into a taxi and tells us: 'I waved goodbye with sinister, beckoning motions.' Many would-be writers had previously felt their way into print with a semi-autobiographical 'comic novel' about coming to London, getting drunk, falling in love and so on, but *The Rachel Papers* killed that sub-genre dead: it left it with nothing to say.

In his third novel, *Success*, Martin Amis ostensibly picked apart the high and low elements that had given such comic effect when put next to one another. One narrator, Gregory, is a posh dandy; the other, Terry, is a chavvy grafter. However, it soon becomes clear that while Gregory's life is art galleries, restaurants and orgies and Terry's is the office, the pub and no girlfriend, the style being used to describe them is actually the same.

It is Charles Highway's revved-up rhetoric of comic incongruity, of high style and eye-watering frankness. It is in fact Martin Amis's own distinctive voice, his great gift – and the problem he has always had to accommodate. In *Success*, he found a way of making the style appropriate to both Gregory and Terry, by allowing each to quote from and snipe at the other's narrative, leading us to suspect that the same person had in fact written both. It was a dangerous game, pulled off with panache, and *Success* is one of his most elegant and funniest novels.

In *Money*, the main character, John Self, is a gluttonous, vulgar, libidinous, alcoholic, materialistic, near-illiterate slob. What is heroic about him is, first, his excess and, second, the exhilarating way in which the excess is described, which not only makes the reader complicit in orgies of drink, drugs and pornographic sex but by its inexhaustible buoyancy seems to render the experiences almost innocent, almost childlike. Naturally this gives us what John himself calls 'a realism problem'. A man who is almost illiterate can't feasibly have access to the vocabulary, let alone the phrase-making ability, that characterise John Self's inner life and his observation of the world. This has been the continuing problem of Martin Amis's fiction: the style is the man, and the man is always Martin Amis. In *Money*, he found his most elegant and persuasive solution.

Self's face, he tells us, is 'wide and grey, full of adolescent archaeology and cheap food and junk money, the face of a fat snake, bearing all the signs of its sins'; his fat body is 'a clutch of plumbing, the winded boiler of a thrashed old tramp'. He's only thirty-five, though, and has done well as a maker of commercials for television with his own company, Carburton, Linex and Self. He is in New York to try to get a feature film under way, though is seldom in good enough shape to talk business. For breakfast he goes to a burger bar and has 'four Wallies, three Blastfurters, and an

American Way, plus a nine pack of beer'. After it he feels 'a bit full and sleepy, perhaps, but apart from that … ready for anything'. I doubt whether any novel has evoked the sleazy glamour of Mayor Ed Koch's New York as well as it is caught in the pages of *Money*, and it's more than just a snapshot of a moment, it has something of New York for all time. You could read *Money* simply as a travel book, if you liked, forget the fiction, and it would be the best one you could pack, even now – even without the hoboes mysteriously cleared from the Bowery and without the naked homeless people outside the high-end jewellers' shops on Fifth Avenue. It took a demented character and an overheated prose to rise to the challenge; by non-realistic means, a hyper-real picture of the city emerges.

John Self thinks he is representative of a new breed of ignorant, moneyed people who are rising in society, and by whom the educated class is frightened. His knowledge of Shakespeare consists of having been born in the upstairs room of a pub that bears the Bard's name and having visited Stratford, once, to make a commercial for a 'flash-friable pork-and-egg bap' called a 'Hamlette'. Persuaded by a friend to read *Animal Farm*, he thinks it's a children's story. 'What next?' he asks indignantly. '*Rupert the Bear*?' When he moves on to *Nineteen Eighty-Four*, he reflects, 'Airstrip One seems like my kind of town.'

Yet when *Money* came out, in 1984, Self didn't seem to represent a recognisable breed of person. The novel was written during the years of recession and public spending cuts when neither the cash-rich builders of the later boom nor the spivs of investment banking had yet made their mark. There is one reference to the 1982 Falklands War when Self eats a 'Malvinas Surprise', a 'triple mixed grill swaddled in steaks', but he doesn't really feel like a politically conceived character, more like one who is shaped by the exuberance of his author's own interests. In this way *Money* was less a report on the zeitgeist than a prophesy of the material binge that would characterise the century's end.

Reading in a tabloid about a girl dying because she is 'allergic to the twentieth century', Self reflects, 'I'm not allergic to the twentieth century. I am addicted to the twentieth century.' And this is another way in which this yob seems quite heroic: he is an optimist, he seems to give us licence to enjoy, not to spend our lives disapproving of, the corrupt state of the world we've made. 'YIELD say the traffic signs – but don't you listen! *Not* yielding, that's the thing. To strive, to seek, to butch it out – it's all a question of willpower.' This is endearing and uplifting, because we can already see that, despite his crafty reference to the closing lines of Tennyson's 'Ulysses', he is trapped by his own ignorance – and by something worse, his author. In London, he has met a character called Martin Amis, a writer, in a pub. Once in a New York brothel, he borrows the name Martin because he hates his own name. His smooth co-producer makes him sign legal documents twice, once under 'Co-signatory' and once under 'Self'; John thinks this is standard, and doesn't see that he is being set up to carry all the risk of the motion picture: he is his own business partner. Worse than that, he is revealed to be a figment of his author's imagination; and that is how this near-illiterate is able to describe so brilliantly the world he sees about him. John Self is the hero as prisoner par excellence: blinkered by his own ignorance, snared by a business scam being worked against him, enslaved by his carnal appetites and trapped by a postmodern authorial manoeuvre. The clue was in the name.

No wonder when he says, 'Look at my life. I know what you're thinking: But it's terrific! It's great. You're thinking: Some guys have all the luck!' we don't know whether to laugh or cry. As John Self begins to sense that he is trapped, there is a growing note of panic in his narrative. He is so jet-lagged that even his jet lag has jet lag; so hungover that he can't tell if he is drunk from last week or from lunchtime; even his insatiable libido begins to flag. 'The future could go this way, that way. The future's futures have never looked so rocky. Don't put money on it. Take my advice and stick to the present. It's the real stuff, the only stuff, it's all there is, the present, the panting present.' This is another factor in our sympathy for him: he lives as we would like to, if we dared. The fact that he has no choice – he couldn't plan for the future if he tried; he can't think strategically – hardly seems to matter: John Self is our representative at the feeding trough of the me-decade, at the bacchanal of the material appetites. As we sit reading in our small room with a cup of sugarless tea and our economy English light bulbs, we are thinking, Go on, John, have another fastfurter, have another triple shot, check out that strip joint, let's see what happens ... He obligingly buys 'a joint, a popper, a phial of cocaine and a plug of opium' from a dealer in Times Square and wolfs them all down together in a gogo-bar toilet. 'Anyway, I snuffled it all up, as I say – and felt a distinct rush, I think, as I came bullocking out of the can.' One is laughing too hard at the 'I think' and the 'bullocking' to have breath enough to call out, 'Way to go, John'; but it's the thought that counts.

   In a London scene, John Self is lectured by Martin Amis, who has been hired to rewrite the screenplay for the film Self is producing: 'In the epic or heroic frame, the author gives his protagonist everything he has, and more. The hero is a god or has godlike powers or virtues ...'. Toothache and hangover make it hard for John to follow this lecture on literary theory, but he remembers Amis saying, 'The further down the scale he is, the more liberties you can take with him. You can do what the hell you like to him, really. This creates an appetite for punishment. The author is not free of sadistic impulses.'

There is a sentimental way of reading *Money*, as though John Self is a 'real' character. Such a reader notices how often Self asks for signs of affection – kissing, tenderness – rather than, or in addition to, the pornographic sex that's all he can command; this reader may feel sorry for John Self, may hope that he can 'settle down' – perhaps with the dangerously named Martina Twain – and 'pull himself together', kick his bad habits and live happily ever after. I think this may be to miss the point. John Self is an avatar, a representative and a point of connection for the reader; but I think we are entitled to indulge the author's 'sadistic impulses' and enjoy the end to which he is reduced, sitting on the London pavement, waiting for his 'fat nurse' girlfriend, penniless, shabby, noticing that someone has tossed a ten-pence piece into his momentarily doffed cap. The character may have fallen on his backside, but there remains one hero standing in the book, and that is the life-changing vigour of language.

PART TWO

LOVERS

Love has a privileged place among the emotions. We don't try to regulate it, as we do most feelings. On the contrary, we have elevated it to the throne of reason. No one says 'I make my life decisions on the basis of sorrow, hatred or a feeling of slight resentment'; but even the most rational people make strategic decisions for themselves and their families based on love.

This sounds feasible until you try to reconcile it with the facts that the majority of marriages end in divorce (if we can use the word 'marriage' here in the sense of an attempted lifelong partnership between two people); all pre-marital love relationships come to an end, and most of the 'best' ones end unhappily. It is one thing to navigate by emotion not reason, but to steer by a feeling you know from experience to be unreliable and error-prone seems odd. I have sometimes wondered if literature is to blame.

Poetry had both expressed and idealised love between two people long before prose fiction became popular, but it was in the pages of the novel that readers most easily found the slow unfolding of a passion that they could identify with in all its heat, comedy and frustration. Novelists quickly saw that the form was well suited to the deep internalisations of emotion and to the agonies of misunderstandings between two lovers.

But in their successful exploitation of this aptness, did they perhaps misrepresent the ease or the happiness of love? Is the neurotic paradox outlined above – reasonable people repeatedly betting on a known loser – something that novelists helped to create?

Darcy and Heathcliff are sometimes held to represent different archetypes of male lover: one all reason and social form, needing complex negotiation to ally oneself with; the other a wild spirit requiring an abandoned, un-social female response. I expect magazines have even run questionnaires along the lines of 'Are you a Heathcliff or a Darcy type?'

As you would expect, this distinction is absurd. When he can condescend to feel, Mr Darcy experiences a strong sexual attraction for Elizabeth Bennet and the reader is free to infer that under Elizabeth's management, this feeling alters and deepens into something like 'love'. The important thing about love in *Pride and Prejudice* is that it works: after the half-comic tribulations, it enhances the lives of the protagonists, at least as far into the future as the book allows itself to look. We may – and will – look further, but for the time being, love brings happiness. In the case of Heathcliff, on the other hand, I doubt whether 'love' is really the word for the complex of emotions that he feels for Catherine Earnshaw. He has a need and a dependency that can't be satisfied in this world or the next. His passion has violent and destructive consequences: readers are awed by his rage, but no one envies it. Far from being a 'free spirit', Heathcliff is miserably anchored on the moor; he cannot in the end even tear himself from the stones of Wuthering Heights itself; his inner life has been deformed by experience of abandonment in childhood before the story starts. Darcy, a social being with friends and connections, is a freer man than Heathcliff and would have married someone else if he had not met Elizabeth. What he needs in a wife is vitality – to supply the force he lacks – but he could have found it elsewhere and in a woman he would have judged was more suitable to his family. Once Heathcliff has become attached to Catherine, he is haunted by the fear of a second abandonment, and this dread becomes a self-fulfilling prophecy. One could, I think, argue that Jane Austen has given a slightly false picture of the power of love between two people because it's hard to be convinced that the feeling will last between the characters as she has so artfully depicted them. Emily Brontë, on the other hand, has offered in *Wuthering Heights* no encouragement to anyone wishing to live their life by the lights of love.

Tess of the d'Urbervilles has in Tess a main character who trusts that the men she meets will be as pure in motive and as generous in their emotions as she is. This allows Thomas Hardy to illuminate, in an often pitiless way, several of the dangers of love. First, there is something that neither Darcy nor Heathcliff faced: the fallibility of the loved one. Angel Clare proves himself unworthy of Tess. Even his failings might not have been terminal if fate and the world had not also conspired against her. As if this were not enough, Hardy poignantly brings into play the greatest enemy of love, and that is time. The clock is always against lovers, their days of bliss are rationed, and this has seldom been more poignantly brought home than in the narrative of Tess and Angel's few stolen days together in the New Forest at the end of the book. There remains something desirable in the love Tess feels: she seems refined and elevated by it; her life is enriched by love. The reader may feel that while Tess's story ends as badly as it could, love itself has not been written off.

In *Lady Chatterley's Lover*, Lawrence put love and sex on the same page. Darcy feels lust but does not experience sex with Elizabeth in the course of the book; Heathcliff and Catherine never sleep together; Tess's baby is the result of an assault. The joy that Connie Chatterley finds with Oliver Mellors begins in physical connection, in lust. Sex opens a door for them both. Whether anyone can see them as examples or encouragement towards belief in love-as-life-guide is open to doubt. At the end of the book, they are apart and there is a sense that their mutual passion may be theirs alone and difficult for others to replicate. Their sylvan glade looks unreal.

In *The End of the Affair*, as the title implies, Graham Greene concentrates on the brief duration of love. Bendrix is a man who sees pain coming and would rather have it sooner than later. Like Tess, he encounters the fallibility of the individual, but in this case the flaw is not in the loved one but in himself. He and Sarah have profited from the easy availability of sex, but it does little to remove the obstacles to happiness. No one reading this novel could imagine that Graham Greene is advocating the finding of your ideal other half as the best way of ensuring fulfilment on earth.

Anna Wulf, the main character of Doris Lessing's *The Golden Notebook*, seems to have learned that lesson well enough. She looks for happiness not in one but in several lovers, and at first this looks like a plausible scheme. But as the book goes on, it becomes clear that Anna's brave new outlook can't conceal that at heart she is still sentimentally attached to the idea of the single perfect other. This comes as a shock to the reader, especially as Anna's conception of that other is more primitive and childlike than Tess's.

What hope now? Perhaps if 'love' is not enthroned as king, but allowed to be a sort of first among equals, might that be the pattern for a life that readers could fruitfully follow? This, ultimately, is the plan of Nick Guest in Alan Hollinghurst's novel *The Line of Beauty*. Nick is a lover who is not loved in return. His idea of love is, at the start of the book, naïve and unformed. His experiences change him, so that by the end he has come to see this elusive 'love' state as desirable still, but as being subsumed within a greater love: a love of the world, of art, of beauty – a love of being alive. The irony is that he may himself not be spared to enjoy this newly understood hierarchy of values.

These are only seven lovers from the thousands in literature. Clearly the charge that these seven authors have somehow falsified or minimised the dangers of love, its agonies and its tendency to fail or die, is quite unfounded. I would say these seven writers have, if anything, rather emphasised the pain, the brevity and hopelessness of the condition. Another seven might have yielded a different result; there are certainly thousands of romantic pot-boilers where love is triumphant. The novel at all levels of literary ambition is so well suited to charting the vicissitudes of the feeling that writers may have exaggerated its importance in a life. Either that, or the experience of the emotion itself has convinced them that human beings in their short stay on earth have no other access to transcendence.

"She is tolerable"

'She is tolerable, but not handsome enough to tempt me.'
– Mr Darcy appraises Elizabeth (1813 edition)

'BENEATH ME'

MR DARCY

I first read *Pride and Prejudice* at the age of fourteen. It was one of a handful of decisive books for me – decisive in the simple sense that they shaped my life. *David Copperfield, Pride and Prejudice, Sons and Lovers, The Catcher in the Rye* ... it was these books of the fifth-form canon, read in the space of that spring term, that made me think literature was the most important thing on earth. I borrowed them from a bookshelf in a classroom with wooden benches and took them up to my cubicle off the long passageway that was my home for three years. There, on the iron bedstead, while the life of the school went on around me, I felt myself unaccountably eager that Elizabeth Bennet should be united with Mr Darcy; Holden Caulfield seemed to express almost everything I had incoherently felt; and when at the end of *David Copperfield*, the hero turned rhetorically to the woman he loved, 'O Agnes, O my soul!', I found I was making strange snorting noises. These were caused by the fact that I was sobbing but trying to keep my eyes open so that I could read the sentences.

It was *Pride and Prejudice*, however, that broke me into the world of adult literature. I had heard of it, but found the title off-putting (*Northanger Abbey* and *Mansfield Park* were passable in an at-least-not-misleading way, but it was hard to think that anyone would willingly choose to read a novel entitled *Sense and Sensibility*); and the copy I read had illustrations of girls in dresses whose waists began just below the bust. It sat on my battered little table, concealed beneath the LP cover of *Aftermath* by the Rolling Stones, and I didn't like to think what the mutant wing forward in the next cubicle might make of it.

Ah, but the story. I hadn't expected Jane Austen to be such a rebel, so undermining of her elders and 'betters'. This was the first time I had seen respectable people such as Mr Collins and Lady Catherine de Bourgh not held up as an example but exposed for the shallow frauds I had always privately believed them to be. It also seemed to me a morally engaging book, in which the reader was constantly being asked to make fine ethical judgements about people's behaviour. Some of these were conventional – good manners, generosity and so on – but some of them were not; some of them had to be made on the hoof. Elizabeth, without much help from her family, had to improvise her own course and back her higher sense of right and wrong against the powerful but superficial judgements of society. Would she be up to it? It was exciting. In fact, it was more exciting than the thrillers I had begun to find not thrilling. If the smugglers got the bullion out through the heavily guarded port against all the odds before the bomb went off, then ... Well, then *what*, actually? Nothing much. But if Elizabeth could hold her nerve and back her own judgement against the world, then a lifetime of improbable happiness would open up for her. I didn't know at the time whether Jane Austen shared my priorities, but I felt that she did, and the minor setbacks and rewards handed out to the characters as the book went on did seem to show that her moral landscape was subtler and larger than that of the more conventional characters in the book. One of the thrills of reading is the suspense that comes from not knowing whether the writer has properly understood her own creation, whether she sees how dislikeable one character is and how worthwhile and interesting another might turn out to be. (Conversely, there is nothing more embarrassing than being surreptitiously begged to love an unattractive character – usually a sign that it is 'based on' the author.) I think it is part of Jane Austen's skill, perhaps unconsciously so, that she does not always make it clear that she has, as it were, got the point; she leaves that tension in the text.

For the most part, I could at fourteen follow the shifts of the moral argument without much difficulty, and could see, for instance, why and how we were gradually being asked to distance ourselves from the superficially attractive Mr Wickham, though I think that at that first reading I missed the clear criticism of Elizabeth's father. His benevolence is fine as far as it goes; but it does not go beyond the limits of his indolence, and a more vigorous man would have saved Lydia from disaster. At the end of the book, while Elizabeth's mother must stay at home, Mr Bennet is allowed to visit Elizabeth frequently at Pemberley, but the reward of seeing Elizabeth most often is reserved to Jane, the sister who has not put a foot wrong. Jane Austen was strict in prize-giving at the end of term.

As for Mr Darcy, I was not much bothered by his reserve and his rudeness. I think I sensed from the title and the way the author wrote of him that there was some inevitable momentum in his favour, and that it might be foolish to resist. The fact that he had been so misrepresented by Wickham seemed to seal it. Because a schoolboy is always at the mercy of a capricious adult authority, few things get beneath his skin so much as injustice; and my indignation at Wickham's lying and treachery made me so passionate in Darcy's cause that I was able, like Elizabeth, to allow that emotion to sweep away other, more well-founded, reservations about Mr Darcy.

Reading the novel again, in middle age, I formed a different view.

One thing I had forgotten was the primary colours and the rapid brush strokes with which Jane Austen gives us the characters at the start. On Darcy, for instance: 'for he was discovered to be proud, to be above his company, and above being pleased; and not all his large estate in Derbyshire could then save him from having a most forbidding, disagreeable countenance, being unworthy to be compared with his friend [Bingley].' This comes with a spin of irony, because it is the reported view of 'the ladies' at a ball, and we may believe their judgement to be hasty; however, once we get to hear Darcy unmediated, he confirms the local view. When urged to dance by Bingley, he replies: 'At such an assembly as this, it would be insupportable. Your sisters are engaged, and there is not another woman in the room whom it would not be a punishment for me to stand up with.' When Elizabeth is pointed out to him, he replies: 'She is tolerable, but not handsome enough to tempt *me*.' It is Jane Austen's own italics, in Mr Darcy's mouth, that condemn him; his judgement is not really about Elizabeth, it is about himself: he barely condescends to contemplate *her*. Elizabeth is all right as far as she goes – fine for some-one less fastidious, perhaps; but she is, to use a phrase of which Darcy is shown to be fond, 'beneath' him. And so unconcerned is he with other people's feelings that he even says this within Elizabeth's hearing.

When Jane Austen as omniscient narrator describes Darcy, her judge-ment is subtler than that of the 'ladies', but aligns with theirs. 'In understanding Darcy was the superior. Bingley was by no means deficient, but Darcy was clever. He was at the same time haughty, reserved and fastidious, and his manners, though well bred, were not inviting. In that respect his friend had greatly the advantage. Bingley was sure of being liked wherever he appeared, Darcy was continually giving offence.'

Here is a major problem. 'Well-bred' manners cannot be 'continually giving offence'. Jane Austen knew this and gives a simple demonstration of it when Darcy brings his cousin Colonel Fitzwilliam to Rosing's, home of their aunt, Lady Catherine de Bourgh. 'Colonel Fitzwilliam entered into conversation directly with the readiness and ease of a well-bred man, and talked very pleasantly; but his cousin [Darcy], after having addressed a slight observation on the house and garden to Mrs Collins, sat for some time without speaking to any body. At length, however, his civility was so far awakened as to enquire of Elizabeth after the health of her family.'

'Well-bred manners' are thus defined by Jane Austen as the ability to talk politely to people; Darcy lacks them. So the initial description of Darcy as having well-bred manners and continually giving offence is a contradiction in terms – unless by 'well bred' Jane Austen simply means 'posh' or 'grand' (in other words offhand, bordering on rude), in which case Darcy is tarred with the same brush as his aunt, Lady Catherine, a woman so conscious of her own 'station' in life that she becomes, para-doxically, an embodiment of vulgarity.

Later when Colonel Fitzwilliam is used to show up Darcy's boorish-ness, it can be argued on Darcy's behalf that he is by now tongue-tied by love or lust in the presence of Elizabeth, though this plea does not really stand up since the last we have been told of Darcy's feelings for Elizabeth is that, while warm, they are 'tolerable'. And even if they were not tolerable, a well-bred man would put others first. So it seems to me clear that in her first authorial passage on Darcy's character, in the comparison with Bingley, Jane Austen is showing us Darcy's critical limitations as a man. Quite what is causing them, she does not yet reveal – though I think we can already see some clue in his low spirits.

As for whether Darcy is 'clever', this is something we must take on trust from the author. He shows little sign of cleverness in the narrated action of the book. He misjudges the effect of his reticence about Wickham's true nature; he miscalculates the effects of his behaviour and of his awful choice of words in proposing to the woman he says he loves. If he is 'clever' it must be in thoughts and actions outside the scope of the narration – as indeed is, I think, the case: his interference in Jane and Bingley's romance is 'clever', albeit in an unforgivably self-serving way. To Jane Austen 'cleverness' may also have entailed a familiarity with books and ideas – a rather useless accomplishment in these circles, more likely to be a torment than a help to Darcy, as it is to Mr Bennet.

At this early stage, however, the outlines of the characters are still being given in bold, swift strokes. Sir William Lucas, for instance, is another who has made his money in trade and seems less afflicted by that knowledge than he 'should' be. Like the Misses Bingley, and perhaps Darcy in his own way, Sir William is vulgar; he has called his house 'Lucas Lodge' (the Regency equivalent, perhaps, of having a personalised number plate) and he likes his home because there he can 'think with pleasure of his own importance'. Jane Austen would return to this sort of person in Sir Walter Elliot, the father of the heroine in *Persuasion*. 'Sir' William's knighthood, like 'Lady' Catherine's title, is a comic indicator for Austen – and had he been *Sir* Fitzwilliam Darcy there could have been no way back from his buffoonish first appearance; it is on the rank of plain Mister – much repeated even by Elizabeth, who playfully declines to use any other form of address – that Darcy's hopes of rehabilitation depend.

Soon, Jane Austen gives us direct, if playful, access to Darcy's feelings. 'The beautiful expression of her dark eyes' commends Elizabeth to him; so does the 'perfect symmetry of her form' and 'the easy playfulness' of her manner. All this is 'mortifying' to him because he would expect to be drawn to someone whose 'manners were not those of the fashionable world'. She is 'beneath' him; she is slightly rough, and this is part of what he finds fascinating and exciting about her. If he were a less chilly man – more of a Wickham – he would woo her, seduce her and put her over his knee; and if Elizabeth were not suddenly becoming so aware of her own worth she might very well enjoy it. Darcy's foul mood is intensified by the dawning recognition that he will not be able to have sex with this woman, or draw on the vitality of her companionship, unless he pays a terribly large price – probably half of the Pemberley estate in perpetuity to the descendants of trade. No wonder he has such a 'disagreeable countenance'.

When at the next stifling social occasion he is forced by the blundering Sir William Lucas to invite Elizabeth to dance, she turns him down. Although he goes into a 'reverie', he is not wounded or sulky about the rebuff; indeed he tells Miss Bingley straight off about his admiration for Elizabeth. He is able both to tease Miss Bingley for immediately assuming he and Elizabeth are engaged and to shrug off her mocking compliment about his future mother-in-law. Suddenly there is a candour and a spirit in Darcy that we haven't seen before and which, if cultivated, could yet make him worthy of her.

But it does not last. We next see Darcy writing to his sister Georgiana with Miss Bingley looking flirtatiously over his shoulder and asking him to send Georgiana all sorts of good wishes. 'Will you give me leave to defer your raptures till I write again?' Darcy says. 'At present I have no room to do them justice.' This is almost frighteningly rude, but Miss Bingley is thick-skinned, and her brother does not intervene on her behalf. (Silly people are fair game in Jane Austen – up to a point (a point exceeded by Emma Woodhouse with Miss Bates on Box Hill) – to be teased without the author's disapproval.) More subtly worrying is the revelation, made by Bingley, that Darcy has a leaden prose style: 'He studies too much for words of four syllables.' Such a style suggests vanity and low spirits – Darcy's besetting sins. He tears into Bingley by suggesting that Bingley's contrasting lightness and rapidity are signs of a false humility, designed to reflect well on him. There follows a high-spirited but savage argument, into which Elizabeth is drawn. Bingley reveals: 'I declare I do not know a more aweful [*sic*] object than Darcy, on particular occasions, and in particular places; at his own house especially, and of a Sunday evening when he has nothing to do.'

This memorable image of the orphaned Darcy moping in his long corridors on Sunday evenings is a key to understanding him. It is here that Jane Austen begins to show her deeper conception of Darcy's nature, and his affliction. Bingley doesn't mind being attacked by Darcy, nor does he mind Darcy being rude to his sister, because Bingley doesn't mind anything very much: he may not be as 'clever' as Darcy, but he has an inexhaustible vivacity. And that is why Bingley is, improbably, Darcy's best friend: he has the supply of energy that Darcy lacks. If Bingley now marries Jane Bennet, Darcy will lose his access to the constantly available antidepressant effects of Bingley's company. Behind that saturnine countenance, therefore, two plans are starting to take shape. The first is to derail the Bingley-Jane marriage plans so that Darcy can keep his friend to himself.

And should that fail, there is a fallback scheme. Elizabeth Bennet could conceivably supply, as well as some déclassé sexual satisfaction, the human form of Prozac that Darcy is shrewd enough to recognise as his life's chronic need. Mr Darcy may not be the first depressive to feature in an English novel, but he is almost certainly the first to be a romantic lead.

After this revealing episode, Darcy resolves to show no further interest in Elizabeth. Miss Bingley's teasing about where he will hang the portraits of his new Bennet in-laws at Pemberley has brought the black dog from his kennel, and Darcy manages to pass the whole sullen day without speaking more than ten words to Elizabeth. He fears being drawn in further.

And what of Elizabeth? Wickham reveals that Lady Catherine's daughter has had from infancy an understanding that she will marry her cousin, Darcy. We watch closely for Elizabeth's reaction. She is simply amused at the thought of how poor Miss Bingley has flirted with him in vain. There is no pang, no lurch, no thought, like Emma's, that 'no one must marry Mr Darcy but herself'; so whatever unrealised desire may have mingled with her anger when she was first rebuffed by Darcy at Netherfield has been replaced by an enjoyable fascination for Mr Wickham and his red militia coat.

At the next ball, at Lucas Lodge, Charlotte Lucas reminds Elizabeth not to let her fancy for Wickham allow her to 'appear unpleasant in the eyes of a man of ten times his consequence'. But she need not have worried; it is Darcy who seems the more 'unpleasant', finding himself incapable of speech when he dances with Elizabeth. The words they eventually exchange are about Wickham. Elizabeth is frosty, believing Darcy to have behaved badly towards Wickham, and Darcy still believes it 'beneath' him to disabuse her. It ends with 'each side dissatisfied, though not to an equal degree, for in Darcy's breast there was a tolerable powerful feeling towards her, which soon procured her pardon, and directed all his anger against another.'

Jane Austen is now giving unironic accounts of Darcy's warm feelings towards Elizabeth, though the use of the word 'tolerable' is significant; he has his emotion under control: Elizabeth Bennet is to Mr Darcy still in essence a sexy back-up plan should Bingley marry Jane. Yet Darcy must know that Bingley is the marrying kind, complaisant, rich, conventional, and that if not Jane, then he will marry someone else, more 'suitable', and soon. Could Darcy wait a few years till he also finds someone of his own rank?[9] Or is his depressive condition so acute that in the absence of Bingley he must at once secure the dynamic services of middle-class Elizabeth? She has precipitated in him, I think, a complete stocktake of his own deficiencies both in the short and the long term. It is not surprising that he is silent and preoccupied: he has so much to find out about himself, so much to calculate and perhaps so little time in which to do so.

Elizabeth, meanwhile, cannot allow her own feelings to move forward at all until she has established the truth of the Darcy–Wickham history; and so there is an impasse at this point, with neither party understanding the other or aware of their own feelings. Darcy is moving a little ahead in the game, however. When the unctuous Mr Collins dares to address him, Darcy's response goes from 'astonishment' to 'unrestrained wonder' to 'contempt'. Collins, like Miss Bingley, is licensed to be mocked with impunity by virtue of his own insincerity. When it comes to the more ticklish business of not looking exasperated by Mary Bennet's excessive and

---

[9] He is the grandson of an earl – the title having descended to his uncle (whose younger son is Colonel Fitzwilliam). Fitzwilliam was his mother's surname; she was Lady Anne Fitzwilliam, the present earl's sister, before her marriage to Darcy's father.

incompetent playing, Darcy keeps a face 'impenetrably grave' – a face worthy of Emma's Mr Knightley at his most humourless, which is saying something. It is left to Mary's father to end their agony with one of Jane Austen's most often quoted lines: 'That will do extremely well, child. You have delighted us long enough.'

For a time, the focus of the story leaves Darcy and Elizabeth. The narrative remains 'light and bright and sparkling', as Jane Austen was later, critically, to judge it – for instance in the authorial comment on the negotiation between Charlotte Lucas and Mr Collins: 'But here she did injustice to the fire and independence of his character', which is as straightforwardly playful as Jane Austen can be; though the episode quickly darkens as Charlotte's plight is revealed: 'Mr Collins to be sure was neither sensible nor agreeable; his society was irksome and his attachment to her must be imaginary. But still he would be her husband.' It is cautionary to think that while Elizabeth is prettier and livelier than Charlotte, she is poorer and in some senses even less 'marriageable'. These are the facts of spinster life. By rejecting Mr Collins herself, Elizabeth has doubled the stakes and backed her own innate qualities against those that 'society', and her mother, values; and Collins's demonstration that he can pull a 'better' catch in Charlotte is designed to reprove Elizabeth. This adds to the tension for the reader: Elizabeth had better be right.

Colonel Fitzwilliam, playing the Bingley role of foil to Darcy, tells Elizabeth why Darcy is so offhand. 'It is because he will not give himself the trouble' to be polite. This low-spirited man lacks the energy to be agreeable; Bingley and Fitzwilliam know him of old, so this behaviour predates Elizabeth and cannot be put down to lovesickness. Darcy continues to visit the Collinses' parsonage, where Elizabeth is staying, but can find nothing to say. He moves his chair closer to Elizabeth, then back again, as though measuring out, as Terry Eagleton noted, the social and geographical distances he would need to cross if they were to be united.

And then Colonel Fitzwilliam reveals to Elizabeth the terrible news that Darcy has intervened to break off Bingley's attachment to Jane. While Elizabeth is furious with indignation, Darcy makes a characteristically ill-timed and misjudged declaration of love for her. Despite 'all his endeavours', he says, he has not been able to overcome his feelings. Elizabeth rises to the occasion, wondering why if it was against his will, his reason and his character, he bothered to tell her that he liked her. When she taxes him with alienating Bingley from Jane he changes colour, 'but the emotion was short'; he rallies and declares himself proud of his interference. He goes on: 'Could you expect me to rejoice in the inferiority of your connections? To congratulate myself on the hope of relations, whose condition in life is so decidedly beneath my own?'

And that really ought to be the end of it. Darcy's proposal is more offensive than Mr Collins's, and shows less self-awareness. What he has done and said are beyond forgiveness. It is not much to Elizabeth's credit that Jane Austen allows her to reflect that 'it was gratifying to have inspired unconsciously so strong an affection'.

Darcy then does what he should have done before, which is to put straight the matter of his history with Wickham. The manner in which he does so, however, threatens to make matters worse. The Bennets' poor breeding was less of a problem, apparently, for Bingley than for Darcy (Bingley being presumably 'beneath' him). 'But there were other causes of repugnance'. What a word to use of the family you hope to marry into! And as if his own family was so splendid: his sister is an underage bolter and his aunt the most vulgar woman in Kent. But Darcy does not see this. For him, further obstacles lie in the fact that Mrs Bennet's family is in trade ('objectionable') and the racy behaviour of Kitty and Lydia Bennet (though neither has yet, like his own sister, eloped). Darcy further reveals that he not only pointed out to Bingley how vulgar the Bennet family was, but convinced him that guileless Jane didn't care for him at all. He persuaded Bingley not to return to Hertfordshire and then 'condescended to adopt the measures of art' by omitting to tell him Jane was in London, and 'Perhaps this concealment, this disguise was beneath me. – It is done, however, and it was done for the best. – On this subject I have nothing more to say, no other apology to offer.' It is rather as though it was not his fault that the thing that was 'beneath' him became his own action; he makes it sound like something he has stepped in – regrettable, but scarcely his fault.

This is a man without shame, whose shamelessness is made worse by the fact that he has *intermittent* access to good judgement. When he is without it, however, he is a manipulative, hypocritical, self-centred depressive, aware of some of his faults but unapologetic for them – bound by arrogance to ignore them because they are his, and therefore, by his definition, not really faults at all. While admiring the completeness with which Jane Austen presents this psychopathology, the reader by now is very fearful for Elizabeth's happiness. If she is desperate to escape the embarrassment of her home, to fly into matrimony (as it seems she is), what's wrong, you ask, with Colonel Fitzwilliam – a sort of Darcy with manners, and without chronic psychological disability? Well, Fitzwilliam has 'made it clear that he had no intentions at all, and agreeable as he was, [Elizabeth] did not mean to be unhappy about him'. She is certainly in a frisky mood, though; all men are now a possibility in her eyes. She is 'not yet one and twenty', but she wants to escape from her family, and this makes her vulnerable. It is this jeopardy that gives the novel its vital frisson.

At about the halfway mark, Jane Austen has had enough of bold strokes and primary colours. The plot, or rather, the technique, thickens. *Pride and Prejudice* stops being a bravura comedy and becomes a more intricately shaded moral negotiation – less like Oscar Wilde and more like Henry James. Darcy has been wronged in the matter of Wickham. While he was foolish and weak not to be more open about Wickham's character, there is no doubt that he behaved properly – and generously. Whatever else his failings, Darcy is not mean with his fortune.

Elizabeth's defining quality is that she prides herself on her good judgement; she backs it against the mores of the fashionable world. While she is largely taken to represent the second quality of the book's title, she has plenty of the first as well. Naturally, therefore, she is mortified to find herself so wrong-footed. She is ashamed and humiliated. The essential transformation of her attitude to Darcy is based on a factual correction; but its emotional driver is the embarrassment and self-criticism she feels. How can she regain her self-esteem? She's not as beautiful as Jane, as studious as Mary and doesn't have as much fun as Lydia and Kitty. Her good judgement is what defines her; it's her unique selling proposition. As a generous-spirited person, she must make it up to him. In the impulsiveness of her shame and of her generosity, Elizabeth Bennet allows the revision of her attitude to Darcy about the Wickham episode – which was based on her haste or 'prejudice' – to sweep away all the other reservations she has about his character and behaviour, which are not based on false judgement or 'prejudice' but on fact, truth and the reliable witness of his old friends. Out of shame for being wrong about Wickham, she forgives Darcy for trying to ruin the life of Jane, the person she loves most in the world. Her wounded pride produces such a spasm of remorse, and so keen is she to regain her own, and to a lesser extent Darcy's, good opinion of herself that she is now prepared to overlook his most unforgivable short-comings ('Could you expect me to rejoice in the inferiority of your connections?'). The misjudgement about Wickham is over-corrected by a greater misjudgement about Darcy. Such is the danger of pride in a gener-ous and impulsive nature.

But nothing now can save Elizabeth, or Jane, except extraordinary good fortune.

Back at home, Elizabeth finds an uproar as Kitty and Lydia prepare to go to Brighton. Darcy has so put her off her family that she 'felt anew the justice of [his] objections'. She is even inclined to think him right for having put Bingley off marrying Jane! Mr Bennet is robust: 'Poor little Lizzy! But do not be cast down. Such squeamish youths as cannot bear to be connected with a little absurdity, are not worth a regret.'

At the beginning of the third and final part of the novel, Elizabeth arrives at Pemberley, Darcy's house, while she is on a sightseeing tour with her relations in trade, Mr and Mrs Gardiner. She is struck by its natural beauty. Darcy is a man of the Peak District – rugged country, far from arable Hertfordshire; 'and at that moment she felt, that to be mistress of Pemberley might be something!' She also notes that the furniture is 'neither gaudy nor uselessly fine; with less splendour and more real elegance' than Lady Catherine's.

Elizabeth then has a bizarre encounter with an old retainer, Mrs Reynolds, who says of her master that she has 'never had a cross word from him in my life' and that 'he was always the sweetest-tempered, most generous-hearted, boy in the world'. This opinion goes against the testimony of Bingley, Fitzwilliam and, later, of Darcy himself. It is hardly surprising that 'Elizabeth almost stared at her. – "Can this be Mr Darcy!" thought she.'

No, not as we know him. But whether the old retainer is soft in the head or whether Jane Austen merely wished to be playful, this encounter remains unexplained. It has, though, a powerful effect on Elizabeth, who views Mrs Reynolds as the best possible witness. 'What praise more valuable than the praise of an intelligent servant?' she wonders, though without asking whether 'intelligent' is the apt word. Mrs Reynolds serves a purpose in the plot; perhaps there was no time to tie up the loose end. This is a shame, because I think Jane Austen means the testimony to be important. In her world, as today, being rude to people in serving positions – waiters, bank clerks and so on – is an infallible indicator of the 'superior' being despicable; you need look no further. And she surely means the converse to apply.

The grounds of Pemberley are wild and imposing in a controlled way, and at the height of her romantic delight in them Elizabeth is surprised by the appearance of Mr Darcy himself. She is mortified to be seen as a daytripper at the house of a man who recently proposed to her, but suddenly – inexplicably – it is all right. Darcy, far from being his usual surly and discomfiting self, is all charm. This is the second appearance of the 'other' Darcy in his alternative, lively persona. Nothing is too much trouble – even being polite to people in trade. Luckily Uncle Gardiner comes up trumps and Elizabeth is exhilarated that Darcy should see that not all her relations are embarrassing. But the puzzle remains. 'Why is he so altered? … it cannot be for *my* sake that his manners are thus softened.' Perhaps Darcy himself barely knows, because the explanation of such inconsistent moods is more neural than circumstantial.

Elizabeth's response is still not to fall in love with Darcy, but to be grateful to him. She is relieved that he was once in love with her and that, far from holding a grudge against her for the brusque way she rejected his clumsy proposal, he has treated her with unexpected courtesy and kindness. She has left hatred behind; she has a positive opinion of his moral worth and now a warm feeling of gratitude. Jane Austen has previously hinted as clearly as propriety allowed her at a strong sexual attraction and it is therefore interesting that at this stage she still withholds the word 'love'.

The news breaks of Wickham's elopement with Lydia. Darcy is sympathetic to Elizabeth and chastises himself for not having done more to prevent it. Mr Gardiner and Darcy contrive to buy off Wickham, fix a wedding and limit the damage, though not before Darcy has once again managed to upset Elizabeth by not revealing that he was present at the ceremony. He has had pratfalls enough for us to know that he will for ever be accident-prone; but the difference now is that the better side of his nature seems to be in control and he is putting his hand in his own pocket to repair the damage.

His explanation of what he does, though, shows the same egocentricity, the same curious attention-seeking. He blames himself for Wickham's bad character because he 'had thought it beneath him to lay [Wickham's] private actions open to the world.' He allowed Wickham to run off with his own fifteen-year-old sister, Georgiana, to woo unimpeded the woman he has himself proposed to and then to run off with *her* fifteen-year-old sister, Lydia, because to say anything would have been 'beneath' him ... These are the actions and inactions of a very peculiar and troubled man.

Elizabeth's uncle Gardiner recounts that Darcy was 'obstinate' in insisting that he must do everything himself, because the elopement was all his fault. Darcy is undoubtedly generous with his money, helpful to the Bennet family and kind in his attitude to Elizabeth – a good thing if he loves her. But his behaviour here has something desperate and false, something manic about it. Love, perhaps? But no: because when, soon afterwards, he comes back to Longbourn with Bingley it is the old chilly Darcy again, not the glad-handing host of Pemberley. He says 'as little as civility would allow', leaving Elizabeth 'astonished and vexed'.

Now Elizabeth needs a *deus ex machina* – and help is at hand. Her change of heart towards Darcy, we have seen, is propelled at first by embarrassment at her own misjudgement and then by gratitude at Darcy's unprecedented good manners to her at Pemberley. But the momentum of her revision has now stalled under the weight of Darcy's gloom – to be restored by a most unlikely source: Lady Catherine de Bourgh, who sweeps in to Longbourn to persuade Elizabeth to renounce any plans of marrying Darcy. Elizabeth reacts with commendable high spirits by at once renewing her interest in just such an outcome. It is Lady Catherine who compels Elizabeth to voice her thoughts, to make them real and so believe in them herself. 'In marrying your nephew,' she splendidly begins, 'I should not consider myself as quitting that sphere. He is a gentleman; I am a gentleman's daughter; so far we are equal.'

News reaches Darcy that Elizabeth has not given Lady Catherine any assurances. From somewhere beneath the layers of gloom, Darcy hauls up the energy to try again. His new vein of self-reproach is more agreeable than the constipated vanity of his first proposal; Elizabeth is inclined to go with the momentum of her emotions, but the huge, perhaps unbridge-able, difference of temperament between the two is stark. Each has much to feel ashamed of, but Elizabeth, knowing that her mistakes were honest, has already forgiven herself and moved on. She says brightly, 'You must learn some of my philosophy. Think only of the past as its remembrance gives you pleasure.'

Darcy's reply makes clear who he is – a man suffering from chronic depression, dwelling on the past, but unable to take responsibility for his own actions: 'Painful recollections will intrude, which cannot, which ought not be repelled,' he says; and it is the most revealing thing he says in the novel. He goes on to correct the servant, Mrs Reynolds's, account of his character and to confirm the darker views of Bingley and Fitzwilliam; but alas, for all he has learned from Elizabeth, he still cannot take responsibility for himself. He blames his dead parents for 'spoiling' him; he will not see that his character and actions have been for some years his own to shape. He is unhappy about himself, critical even, but is locked in a spiral with thoughts that 'cannot, ought not to be repelled'. He has, furthermore, no interests; he doesn't *do* anything. He will lend his fishing rods to Mr Gardiner but doesn't contemplate joining in the sport. In modern therapeutic terms, he needs to understand his own emotions more deeply, to get to know himself, to take exercise to release endorphins, to abandon the protective persona ('beneath me') he has adopted and to forgive himself for what he is and has been. There is much to forgive, much 'work' to be done, and it is the sadness of the book that we suspect that he will never be able to do it. When Elizabeth asks him why he was so silent on his last visit, when all seemed set fair between them, he says he was 'embarrassed'. Even Elizabeth, all of whose defences are now down as she heads for the altar, cannot let this go: 'But tell me, what did you come to Netherfield for?' she asks in exasperated fondness. 'Was it merely to ride to Longbourn and be embarrassed?'

It will be hard for her to accept that in her husband the lack of vital energy that underlies depression will always dominate the intermittent bursts of activity, the little upswings that punctuate his melancholy. All that Darcy can do now is marry Elizabeth, his lifelong Prozac in an Empire-line dress: dear, busy, middle-class Lizzy with her wit and common sense, who will be good at sex, kind to his sister and will laugh at his aunt. It is more, really, than he deserves for his single outburst of politeness and his periodic financial largesse.

And Elizabeth? The first time she uses the word 'love' of Darcy is after they are engaged. And when did her love begin? 'I must date it from my first seeing his beautiful grounds at Pemberley.' She is teasing Jane with this reply, but, significantly, is never required to give a better one. She may be in love with Darcy or she may not be, but she rides the momentum that leads towards marriage. And why not? For Elizabeth Darcy there will be sex with a man she finds attractive, money, children, a large house and an escape from her embarrassing mother; there may yet be conversation if Darcy is in the mood; she may even come to see the 'clever' side of him, now that his days of bungling and misjudgement are over. Perhaps she really does 'love' him. Over the last two centuries, Darcy has exercised an undoubted power over women readers. It may be difficult for some of us to understand, but it would be foolish to deny that Elizabeth was not the last woman to be strongly drawn to this rude and gloomy man.

One feels that Darcy has the better of the deal, however – until the final twist in the complex negotiation. The key to Elizabeth's happiness is not Pemberley with its sounding cataracts and specimen trees, not Mr Darcy with all his millions; the clinching moment, the detail that lets the reader close the book content, comes when, partly to be rid of his mother-in-law, Bingley quits Hertfordshire and buys an estate a mere thirty miles from Pemberley. Now Elizabeth is united with her heart's twin. At least once a week she can have Jane's naïve chit-chat – 'You *didn't* Lizzy!' – over coffee, or tea, or dinner – and then why not stay the night? It's a life, after all, and an arrangement as good as any person can realistically hope for; so the close of *Pride and Prejudice* becomes against the odds one of the most satisfactorily happy endings in English literature – but only because in the second half of the book Jane Austen's artistry has let us see all the compromises, shadows and deceits. The most important of these little lies is the fact that Elizabeth will never tell Jane that Darcy tried to scupper her marriage to Bingley, 'for although Jane had the most generous and forgiving heart in the world, [Elizabeth] knew it was a circumstance that must prejudice her against him'.

Jane's arrival in Derbyshire brings one other bonus for Darcy: Bingley, his back-up antidepressant. As the years go on and the children of both marriages grow up, the men will gravitate more to one another in shooting, fishing (if Darcy can rouse himself actually to bait a line and join in), card games and trips to town, while the sisters will spend not just nights but weeks together; it will tend to revert to the boy/boy, girl/girl pairing with which it began.

One should not dwell too much on the thought of Mr Darcy's mood at sixty years old on a wet Sunday evening: 'aweful' is not the half of it. I prefer to think that Elizabeth, who has magnificently backed her own sense of right and wrong against the conventions of society, will always have enough energy to spare from galvanising Darcy to be happy with her children and with the person she loves most – with Jane.

'MORE MYSELF THAN I AM'

HEATHCLIFF

I first read *Wuthering Heights* at the age of sixteen, though I had seen the Laurence Olivier/Merle Oberon film on a black-and-white television one fuggy Sunday afternoon. I remember finding the plot oddly complicated for a novel that focussed so much on two people. There was the framing device of the traveller come to rent the house, the housekeeper, the fact that there was a boy called Linton, but that Edgar Linton was also referred to by his surname alone. Was Catherine or her daughter Cathy the 'real' heroine? And it was hard to go on liking Heathcliff when he became so filled with bitterness. A young reader not long out of Agatha Christie needed surer points of identification. One thing did thrill me, though, and that of course was the elemental power: there was an urgency, a sense of a story somewhat beyond the author's control, and the confusion seemed a testament to the overwhelming force of the emotions that Emily Brontë had invoked. They had reduced to matchwood the structure of the novel built to house them.

Heathcliff is a character who seems to have two lives, one in popular mythology and one in the pages of *Wuthering Heights*. In the former, he is romantic, wild and uncompromising. It was perhaps not these qualities that the then Prime Minister Gordon Brown meant to invoke when he compared himself to Heathcliff; what Mr Brown was after, I think, was a disdain for show or social nicety he thought he shared with Heathcliff. In Mr Brown's mythology, perhaps, both men were 'the real thing' – passionate for truth, and above pettiness. To most people it would be hard to think of two characters more dissimilar than Heathcliff, the moorland gipsy, and Mr Brown, the pallid creature of a life in committee rooms framing 'composite' motions; but strange things happen when fictional characters take on an imagined life beyond their pages …

I had not read *Wuthering Heights* since 1969 until forty years later I opened an old second-hand Penguin on a flight back from New York. A previous reader had done a family tree in blue ballpoint in the inside jacket. Unfortunately, he had been defeated by the complexity of the plot and had assigned Thrushcross Grange to the wrong owner and made Hindley marry Catherine. He was not alone. Part of the weird intensity of the novel derives from the tight and complex links between a small number of people, and most editions do now carry a printed family tree.

Charlotte Brontë's cautious introduction admitted many faults in the book 'hewn in a wild workshop, with simple tools out of homely materials'. It is 'moorish, and wild, and knotty as a root of heath'. Emily had little knowledge of the world, or of other people; Charlotte conceded that the novel must appear a 'rude and strange production' to people unfamiliar with the West Riding, its moors and its inhabitants. She was apologetic for the roughness and occasional profanity of the language.

Most of all, though, Charlotte apologised for Heathcliff. 'Whether it is right or advisable to create beings like Heathcliff, I do not know: I scarcely think it is.' She was quick to claim that Emily conceived Heathcliff as evil from the start, 'never once swerving in his arrow-straight course to perdition'. A parson's daughter, she defended her sister's sense of conventional morality. 'Heathcliff betrays one solitary human feeling, and that is *not* his love for Catherine.' No, it is in his 'rudely confessed regard for Hareton', the son of his enemy, Hindley.

Well, whatever Charlotte Brontë anxiously claimed in her sister's defence against Victorian critics, Heathcliff does not tower over the other romantic characters of the nineteenth-century English novel because he is occasionally tolerant of his nephew-by-adoption. He does so, for all Charlotte's italic denial, because of his feeling for Catherine.

Emily Brontë gains a great deal from having her lovers as childhood friends first. It ratifies their affection; it roots it in innocence and removes the slightly comic sense that can attach to the random meetings of adult lovers – 'We met by chance at a party given by an old friend who …' After a brief false start in which Catherine views the dark-skinned newcomer with distaste, they quickly establish a wild intimacy: it is Catherine and Heathcliff *contra mundum*, and we watch with enthusiasm and only a little sense of dread. It is affecting because such intense friendships are normally between children of the same sex; this one is cross-gender and cross-race. It taps deeply into the romantic idea of affinities – of another world in which the little white-skinned Yorkshire girl and the brown-skinned boy from God knows where could once have been happy, were once indeed a single entity before the inconvenient facts of being human

– being incorporated, living in a house, a place and a time – have made things impossible for them.

It is the other-worldliness of their feeling that is so powerful and upsetting. Our very first encounter with Catherine is not as a human girl but as a ghost at the window: 'Let me in – let me in!' Significantly, the ghost has a 'child's face', because it is the young Catherine who cries out to return and whom Heathcliff longs to recover. Heathcliff's response to the spectre gives us a sense of the enduring torment of his feelings for Catherine before he has even been introduced into the story in his chronological place. This means that, for the reader, the child Heathcliff is already father to the man – a being whose fate is pre-determined and whose childhood raptures are therefore doubly poignant.

He is first delivered to Catherine more or less from a sack, like a mongrel dog. He talks 'gibberish' and is referred to as 'it'; Nelly Dean, the house-keeper, is instructed to 'wash it, and give it clean things and let it sleep with the children'; left to her own judgement, it is implied, she might have put it in a kennel. He is bullied by Catherine's brother Hindley but withstands the blows 'without winking or shedding a tear' – a worrying sign in a victim.

Catherine is impulsive, talkative, high-spirited and humorous, but not deeply cunning or selfish. Her weakness is in her feeling for the strange, self-contained boy. 'The greatest punishment we could invent for her was to separate her from him,' Nelly Dean recalls. When Catherine's father dies, Nelly finds Heathcliff and Catherine in the children's room, long past midnight: 'The little souls were comforting each other with better thoughts than I could have hit on: no parson in the world ever pictured heaven so beautifully as they did, in their innocent talk: and while I sobbed and listened, I could not help wishing we were all there safe together.' Even the simple Nelly has sensed that their union will have to wait for another world. The moors are, at first, a substitute for that better place, and the two children like to run off and spend the day there, laughing at the punishment they receive on their return. For a book so associated with its landscape, there is surprisingly little description of the moor while Catherine is alive; perhaps Emily Brontë sensed that if the moorland were to retain its universal force as an alternative reality it had better not have too much specificity of detail.

The idyll is short-lived. They come to Thrushcross Grange, where the civilised but bloodless Lintons live. The animosity between them and Heathcliff is immediate. Heathcliff would not want to live there 'even in return for flinging Joseph [the canting servant at home] off the highest gable and painting the house-front with Hindley's blood'. Young Isabella Linton thinks Heathcliff looks like the gypsy who stole her tame pheasant; her father thinks him 'a little Lascar, or an American or Spanish castaway'. Heathcliff has tried to rescue Catherine's ankle from the jaws of their savage dog by thrusting a stone down the animal's throat.

Catherine is not so sure. The Lintons have a nice house, and pretty dresses, and music. We share Heathcliff's agony to see her start to be seduced, to see the secret ideal of their passion betrayed for a tinkling recital or a fancy-dress ball. It is a hard-edged representation of many such severances in real life when what hurts so much is the thought that the other party to love may all along not have meant what they said about the primal importance of the shared private world.

When Catherine returns after five weeks, Heathcliff is appalled and cannot bring himself to speak to her. He confesses to Nelly that he wished he had a light skin like Edgar and was as rich as him, and Nelly, rather splendidly, tells him he is handsome and urges him to believe himself an Indian prince who can laugh at a 'little farmer' like Edgar. But Catherine is changed; she has become haughty and arrogant, even though she retains her affection for Heathcliff. She lives, in fact, a double life between the two houses, polite and mannerly at Thrushcross, but less affected at home. Heathcliff, in his anger, also changes. He gives up his studies and takes self-destructive pleasure in 'exciting the aversion rather than the esteem of his new acquaintance'.

The decisive scene comes when Catherine confides in Nelly that she has dreamed of being in heaven, but disliked it. She was thrown out of heaven by the angels and came back to earth on Wuthering Heights, where she woke sobbing with joy. So she is not allowed even the vague comfort of lovers who believe they will be reconciled in another place, after death. I think this is ultimately what is so troubling about *Wuthering Heights*: it confronts the issues of death and time head-on, and its answer is extremely bleak. There is no heaven beyond this earth, and if ever you did reach such a place, you would beg to be returned. It is in the world that lovers must square their impossible circle.

Everything Catherine says to Nelly is overheard by Heathcliff, who is hiding out of sight. He hears her say that she has 'no more business to marry Edgar Linton than I have to be in heaven'. In fact, she knows what heaven does to her: it makes her long for Wuthering Heights. But since Heathcliff has been humiliated by her brother Hindley, Catherine rashly declares: 'It would degrade me to marry Heathcliff now; so he shall never know how I love him: and that, not because he's handsome, Nelly, but because he's more myself than I am. Whatever our souls are made of, his and mine are the same; and Linton's is as different as a moonbeam from lightning, as frost from fire.'

Whatever the flaws of this novel, in design and execution, it will always be read with awe, I think, because of the unaffected way that Catherine

Earnshaw says these terrible things. 'He is more myself than I am.' The whole pity of human love is in those words.

And there is more. 'If all else perished, and *he* remained *I* should still continue to be … My love for Linton is like the foliage in the woods: time will change it, I'm well aware, as winter changes the trees. My love for Heathcliff resembles the eternal rocks beneath: a source of little visible delight, but necessary. Nelly, I *am* Heathcliff. He's always, always in my mind: not as a pleasure … but as my own being.'

This is what unconditional love feels like – a sensation of 'little visible delight', to be sure; in fact, this love, as Emily Brontë depicts it, is more than awe-inspiring, it is to be feared. We could wish to share Mr Darcy's feeling for lively Elizabeth, but no one would want to feel what Catherine and Heathcliff feel for one another. It is also interesting, I think, that while many female readers declare that they are 'in love' with Darcy and almost all male readers are attracted by Elizabeth, to feel any such personal response to Catherine or Heathcliff would seem impertinent. They are self-contained and almost sexless; they belong to one another and to no one else. There is, since childhood, no satisfaction in that belonging – only a brief, wild ecstasy and then a pain that death itself will not remove. Heaven will eject them both, and they are doomed to be together and apart, for ever, on the moor.

By a sadistic plot twist worthy of Thomas Hardy (who was seven years old at the time of the book's publication), the hidden Heathcliff leaves in despair after overhearing Catherine tell Nelly she would be 'degraded' by marrying him – but before she has expressed her passionate love for him in the words quoted above. Mortally wounded, he disappears from Yorkshire.

Meanwhile, for Catherine there is marriage to Edgar Linton. When Heath-cliff returns from his mysterious exile he shows 'no marks of former degradation', according to Nelly. 'His upright carriage suggested the idea of his having been in the army,' she says, though admits that 'a half-civilised ferocity lurked yet in the depressed brows and eyes full of black fire'.

Heathcliff is not really changed. Mr Darcy is a contingent man, defined by his low spirits, but also by wealth and social standing, by friendship, lust, love, by management of wealth and by interference in the affairs of others; to some debatable extent he is even capable of change and modification under the influence of Elizabeth. If he had not met Elizabeth, he would have married someone else – a girl less 'beneath' him, perhaps, whom he would meet in London. But Heathcliff is not a compound or a mixture to be altered by reaction; he is an element. He is passion incarnate. He is not capable of being broken down or changed in any way. He exists only as a fire of love for Catherine, and his relationships with other human beings exist only at an animal level. What does he do while he is in exile? It doesn't matter, and Emily Brontë may not even know. The slight softening of his exterior and his new military bearing are superficial things, and they do not last. The only doubt about him is the extent to which his nature has been formed by cruelty and neglect suffered before the story begins and subsequent rough treatment at Wuthering Heights. In Nelly Dean's narra-tive there does seem a suggestion – and we are free to see it as sentimental or not – that Heathcliff had it in him once to have been a 'better' man.

When Isabella Linton, Catherine's new sister-in-law, decides she loves Heathcliff, Catherine tries to warn her off as one might warn a toddler not to play with a pit bull terrier. This second marriage does take place, though, and it is not long before Isabella is asking, 'Is Mr Heathcliff a man? If so, is he mad? And if not, is he a devil?'

At this stage of the book, you feel that the fascination exercised by Heathcliff's intransigence is beginning to wane. Emily Brontë may have borrowed too much from the Gothic and not enough from the realistic; a little more Miss Austen and a little less Mrs Radcliffe might have helped. When Heathcliff seems driven to violence, like Hamlet or Othello, by the terrible constriction of his fate, we are in awe of him and of the purity of his passion, but from the time of his marriage to Isabella onwards he seems often to be motivated by something baser – by spite or petulance, or by a mental disturbance of small interest outside its own aetiology.

Before then, however, Heathcliff is to partake in one of the most terrible scenes in nineteenth-century fiction, the death of Catherine. Nothing is extenuated by Emily Brontë; all is set down in bold, unflinching terms: 'You have killed me – and thriven on it, I think,' is the dying Catherine's opening shot when he appears at her bedside.

In the exchanges that follow, love is shown to lie close to hatred. They bewail the fate that has made them incapable of life – or death – without the other. It is no use trying to find relief in the Gothic tenor of the scene; it is truly harrowing, and very difficult to read. This is not how normal people live or feel; it is not, thank God, a version of the reader's life; but in its mortal hopelessness it strikes at a truth we would rather not contemplate.

'I have not broken your heart', Heathcliff furiously responds, ' – *you* have broken it; and in breaking it you have broken mine. So much the worse for me, that I am strong. Do I want to live? What kind of living will it be when you – oh, God! Would *you* like to live with your soul in the grave?'

Catherine begs for his forgiveness, and at the very last moment he is able to find some nobility of heart. 'I forgive what you have done to me. I love *my* murderer – but *yours*! How can I?'

There is nothing more to say. 'They were silent – their faces hid against each other,' Nelly tells us, 'and washed by each other's tears.' That night Catherine gives birth to a 'puny, seven months' child' – young Cathy. Two hours later, Catherine dies. The reader has to blink a moment to remember if we even knew that she was pregnant. One doesn't like to think of Catherine having had sex with Edgar, and it feels odd that Isabella is impregnated by Heathcliff. The love of Catherine and Heathcliff is not physically consummated, though his kisses for her on her deathbed clearly have a sexual content. The separation of love and sex in *Wuthering Heights* is very troubling; doubtless there have been many theses on 'embodiment' and 'disembodiment' in this novel. It is the exclusion of sex as a natural comfort and consolation that makes the metaphysical agonies of the lovers all the more difficult to bear.

The book is barely halfway through its course, but with the death of Catherine the vitality goes out of it. Heathcliff has nothing grand left in him, only a descent into bitterness and thence the borderlands of insanity. Before then, he utters his terrible curse: 'You said I killed you – haunt me then! The murdered *do* haunt their murderers, I believe. I know that ghosts *have* wandered the earth. Be with me always, take any form – drive me mad! Only *do* not leave me in this abyss, where I cannot find you! Oh, God! It is unutterable! I *cannot* live without my life! I *cannot* live without my soul!'

It is very hard to reach any sensible conclusion about the artistic merits of *Wuthering Heights*, and I'm glad I'm not a teacher or a critic who needs to find a 'line' on it that withstands the cross-examination of others. When I spoke to the writer and psychoanalyst Adam Phillips, he had had a similar experience. We had both read it as an extracurricular book in our teens without having been taught it; then, on returning in middle age, found that it was not at all the 'love' story we remembered. Adam Phillips thinks Heathcliff lives in fear that the first great rejection of his life, by his parents, will be repeated. Perhaps there is something self-fulfilling in this mortal dread. Adam thinks that the prime emotions involved in the relationship between Heathcliff and Catherine are need and want, but believes there is also 'love'. I am not quite sure. Both of us were hesitant about coming up with any all-embracing interpretation.

F.R.Leavis, I remember, called *Wuthering Heights* a 'sport' – a horticultural term referring to a shoot that's been grafted on to the stalk of a different plant, and takes. The result is exotic, but also, like all genetic experiments, slightly troubling. The term does, I think, fairly reflect both the critic's difficulty in trying to place the book and the sense in which it can't really be accommodated in the mainstream of English fiction. *Jane Eyre* can doubtless be shown to have its roots in romance and in the Gothic, but can also be placed with a reasonable degree of comfort in a tradition that runs from Defoe and Richardson through Jane Austen into Dickens. *Wuthering Heights*, though? It is Shakespearean at moments, but garish and clumsy at others.

I hope it's not a readerly cowardice to confess oneself, however admiring, defeated by a book. If *Wuthering Heights* continues to be read, it will be chiefly because of the character of Heathcliff. Catherine has most of the best lines, but Heathcliff has the curse that rings in our heads as long and as terribly as any howl of Lear or Macbeth.

'TO SEE YOU AGAIN'

TESS DURBEYFIELD

At some early stage in my thinking, aged about seventeen perhaps, I developed some fixed ideas about what a novel 'ought' to be. I tried to work out from the books I most admired what it was, if anything, they had in common. It seemed to rest on a series of paradoxes – and to the student mind a paradox is a splendid thing.

If someone in a pub, I reckoned, told you an amazing anecdote, you feel you want to pass the story on; the best tribute the saloon-bar raconteur could hope for is, 'You should put that in a book.' As a child, I read books largely for this blow-me-down quality – the more amazing the better; so Alistair MacLean's *Night Without End* or *Fear is the Key* were the best things I knew. When it came to Sherlock Holmes, there was an additional pleasure to be found in the characters themselves and in some of the settings – those wistaria-covered suburban houses, for instance, and the details – hansom cabs, fog and so on; but I still judged them primarily by how extreme or 'thrilling' they were. Thus I liked 'The Speckled Band' best of the short stories, even though it was clearly improbable.

Then, after I had read *Pride and Prejudice* and *Sons and Lovers*, everything changed. The Bennets and the Morels weren't intended to be weird; they were meant to be ordinary. Yet by focussing tightly on the inner life of the main characters, their authors had not only made them live, they had made their lives seem of extraordinary importance. Paradox One formed in my teenage mind: the inner life, while lacking guns and car chases, is more exciting than the outer life.

And there was something more than that, I thought. I didn't see Paul Morel as simply a more exciting version of James Bond – as a secret agent of the internal world. He did something Bond couldn't do: he resonated with me. At the age of fifteen I had as little in common with a Nottingham miner's son and his first love affairs as I had with a Cold War spy and his Walther PPK. The difference was that Ian Fleming rubbed my nose in the difference, while D. H. Lawrence somehow suggested that part of me was to be found in Paul and vice versa. Paradox Two: by delineating the individual with great skill, by faithfully relaying each beat of his heart, the author could suggest that he was *more* than an individual: he could open out something in his character, however distinctive, that you, however improbably, could share. Through the particular, the universal could be revealed. This surely was the trick of the novelist's art.

Somehow it didn't matter if the characters were deliberately understated men-in-the-street, asking to be seen as typical, or whether, like Dickens's, they were highly coloured. The only test was whether under the pressure of the novelist's scrutiny they revealed some deeper shape. Clarissa seemed to demonstrate such qualities, Tom Jones certainly did. Both were middling sort of people who found themselves in unusual circumstances. What was interesting was not that Clarissa was a victim or that Tom was a rake, but what their conduct told you about life outside the confines of their own stories; it chimed with the feelings, the very nature, of those of us who had neither been raped nor fought a duel.

This now, in retrospect, seems obvious. Yet somehow, I also developed another 'rule', Paradox Three: that while the novelist is free to write about bizarre people and extreme events, he must not then, for didactic or moralistic reasons, pretend that they are a typical sample, randomly selected. In *Vanity Fair*, for instance, the name and a great deal of editorial content in the course of the novel suggested that Thackeray did wish to prove to his readers that 'all is vanity'. For this authorial point to be made, I felt, the novelist had to convince the reader that his characters were representative. To take an example from the newspaper: you couldn't persuade people that celibacy is the key to happiness by telling the true story of unfaithful Mr Wayne Bobbitt, the man whose wife chopped off his penis. The example is simply too extreme to have any application outside its own bizarre circumstances. To put it more strongly, Thackeray's greater theme of the vanity of the social world can only be convincing if he could say: 'I could throw out Becky, Amelia, Dobbin and the rest of them, pick half a dozen other characters – at random – from the same milieu and although the novel might not be as entertaining, its moral and thematic drift would be the same.'

In this, Thackeray just about succeeds, I think, but it was a test I felt from the beginning, when I read *Far From the Madding Crowd*, *The Mayor of Casterbridge* and especially *Jude the Obscure*, that Thomas Hardy never did pass. He had a moral and philosophical agenda, but he didn't have the scientific or historical detachment to prove his points. Hardy was not the novelistic equivalent of Cecil Sharp, who travelled England to record the last of rural folk songs before they died out; he was not a man who listened to his beloved county, to its hills and villages, and then wrote novels that represented the tendencies of life and fate among the people. He seemed to me, rather, someone who had heard a strong pub anecdote, then, by his undoubted skill as a novelist, rooted it in credible people, assigned its most outlandish aspects to realistically conceived characters and then at the end turned to his audience and said, 'Doesn't that show how wretched life is?'

Would the moral impetus have been the same if he had chosen not Tess, but a different milkmaid? Not Michael Henchard, but another grain merchant? I thought not. His retort, I suppose, would have been, 'But it's Tess's and Henchard's stories that I chose to tell.' To which I might have said, 'That's fine, but by preselecting an example helpful to your conclusion, you have sacrificed your claim to universal resonance.'

This paradox was rather hypothetical, and hard to express precisely, but it was enough to stop me enjoying Hardy's novels as much as I should have done when I first read them, considering how much I warmed to the characters themselves and the way he wrote about the countryside they inhabited.

The first thing I noticed on reopening *Tess of the d'Urbervilles* after thirty-five years is how lasciviously fond her author is of Tess, with her 'mobile peony mouth and large innocent eyes'. From the start, we are asked to believe that this country girl knows something of the ways of beasts but almost nothing of men; that she is a 'vessel of pure emotion untinctured by experience'. She is, like the Virgin Mary, of immaculate conception; even passers-by are 'fascinated by her freshness' and would 'wonder if they would ever see her again: but to almost everybody she was a fine and picturesque country girl, and no more'.

Hardy is working hard here, I think, to suggest that, while Tess is exceptional, she is chosen more or less at random. All fresh young country girls glimpsed in passing have a life story: here, he suggests, is just one. It is vital, I think, for us to buy into this implication if Hardy is not to be thought guilty of constructing his novel backwards to illustrate his wider scheme.

The first important incident, and it is in some ways the most important in the book, is when nothing happens. When Tess is out with a group of other girls dancing in a field, a passing student, Angel Clare, does not ask her to dance. He pauses only for a moment, dances with the girl nearest to hand (she doesn't even have a name), then continues with his journey. He has noticed Tess, however, and she has noticed him. Had they become acquainted at this moment, all might have gone well between them. Time is the enemy of love, Hardy knows; they run on axes that seldom agree. It is no use merely meeting the loved one and being loved in return; the timing must be right for both. And by the time Angel and Tess meet again, it is too late.

Tess's father, an idle drunkard, believes his family to be of noble stock, and Tess's mother sends her to 'claim kin' with a local gentleman called Alec Stoke-Durberville in the hope of getting work or money or both. Alec is a sort of pantomime villain, though 'despite the touches of barbarism in his contours, there was a singular force in the gentleman's face, and in his bold, rolling eye'. He lights a cigar and eyes the fresh young thing through veils of blue smoke. Tess has the 'disadvantage', Hardy tells us, of looking 'more of a woman than she really was'. She is told that she will grow into her voluptuousness; but for the time being, allied to her girlish freshness, it makes a powerful combination for the fascinated Alec.

It is not long before Alec is making a move. He makes Tess hold the reins of the pony and trap, so that with her hands occupied she cannot push him away when he gives her 'the kiss of mastery'. He seems honestly perplexed that she resists: 'You are mighty sensitive for a cottage girl!' The build-up to some explosive outcome is subtly done. In his sympathy for Tess, Hardy does not underestimate what she unwittingly does to inflame Alec. Of course, it is not her fault she is so comely, with her peony mouth and womanish figure; but she has come alone, unbidden, to ask a favour, and such independence requires a degree of protective self-awareness. A hypothetical jury in the reader's head is ready to condemn the slavering Alec, but may be open to some plea in mitigation.

Tess goes to work in the d'Urberville house, where Alec treats her playfully, calling her 'cousin'. Tess begins to trust him a little. She loses her initial shyness, though acquires a 'shyness of a new and tenderer kind', by which Hardy presumably means the modesty that precedes 'submission'. This is quite clear: she is prepared to accept Alec's good-will, but no more. One evening, Tess is embroiled in a fight with some village hoydens (two of whom are former 'conquests' of Alec's) when Alec comes cantering to her rescue and scoops her up on to his horse. She is at his mercy, though he does not immediately exploit this fact. He asks her if his attentions are always unwelcome and she says they are – though not as emphatically as she might. Alec reveals that he has bought a new horse for her father, and Tess thanks him 'with a painful sense of the awkwardness of having to thank him just then'. Alec rides on at random to prolong the pleasure of having Tess's arms round him. After a while, he can feasibly claim to be lost, and leaves Tess with the horse to go on foot to see where they are. When he returns, he finds her asleep.

As a result of what follows, Tess becomes pregnant. Hardy does not say whether Alec rapes Tess or whether Tess consents. The terms he uses make it clear that it is a coarse and unfortunate coupling, though he suggests that some of Tess's allegedly noble ancestors may have 'dealt the same measure even more ruthlessly to peasant girls of their time'. So Alec was ruthless, but not as ruthless as he might have been. We will have to wait to find out whether this was technically a rape or not.

A few weeks later, Tess tearfully tells Alec that if she had ever loved him, she would not 'hate myself for my weakness as I do now! … My eyes were dazed by you for a little, and that was all.' She then says, 'I didn't understand your meaning till it was too late.'

After an angry exchange on the lines of what women say and what they mean, Alec admits: 'I did wrong – I admit it.' He says he is prepared to offer her better work indoors as compensation.

The extent of Tess's consent is still not clear, though her use of the words 'weakness' and 'dazed' suggests compliance at some point, and the words 'I didn't understand your meaning' suggest he did at least ask her consent, albeit opaquely, to something. On the other hand, he says, 'I did wrong'. The only sequence of events that tallies with all these words is that Alec 'took advantage' of Tess; that he urged her to go further than she really wanted, though at the crucial moment, her eyes 'dazed', she allowed him to proceed.

Tess's mother is not much worried by the fact that her daughter has lost her virginity, but can't understand why she didn't catch Alec in marriage. Tess knows that she could not marry a man she does not love, however convenient it might be; in the same way that Elizabeth Bennet has the taste to recognise that Darcy's furniture is 'better' or less showy than Lady Catherine's, so Tess has the natural taste and standards of someone more educated than herself. Ninety-nine milkmaids out of a hundred would bag the rich husband, but Tess, like Elizabeth, is one of 'nature's ladies'; she has received some education; or as she later puts it, 'I am only a peasant by position, not by nature!' What matters to her is that she didn't 'wholly care' for Alec before the incident and does not 'care for him at all' after it.

At this point Hardy, who has been elusive, becomes plainer: 'She had dreaded him, winced before him, succumbed to adroit advantages he took of her helplessness; then, temporarily blinded by his ardent manners, had been stirred to confused surrender awhile.' Surrender is not the same thing as consent, and nor is 'awhile' (i.e. for a moment) the same thing as really wanting to make love, but the balance of evidence at this point would not be enough to secure a rape conviction. It is enough to make us hate Alec and sympathise with Tess, but the fact is that Hardy's handling of the incident is subtle, incomplete and deliberately designed to prompt more questions than it answers. He had the vocabulary and the authorial courage to make it clear that Alec did rape Tess had he so wished; but he doesn't. He sees much more dramatic mileage in confusion, in doubt, in half-agreement, in 'momentary weakness' than in outright barbarism; and his judgement in this is vindicated, because it makes Tess less of a passive victim and more of a tragic figure. A child killed by a speeding car is ineffably sad, but it is not 'tragic'; the waste of Hamlet's life caused by the freakish coincidence of external circumstance and internal predisposition is what makes tragedy.

Soon Hardy begins to mobilise another player in Tess's drama: the natural world. Reflecting on her 'spasmodic weakness', Tess becomes profoundly unhappy, leaves her parents' home only at night and knows

'Tess flung herself down upon the rustling undergrowth … in palpitating misery broken by momentary shoots of joy.' – Tess contemplates her future with Angel under the burden of her secret past (1891 edition)

that at twilight 'the plight of being alive becomes attenuated to its least possible dimensions'.

In a beautiful passage at the end of Chapter 13, Hardy describes her night-time walks in which she feels the landscape express her inward feelings of grief. This 'pathetic fallacy' is perhaps comforting to her; but later, she becomes alienated even from the much-loved Wessex woods and fields, imagining that she is a 'figure of Guilt intruding into the haunts of Innocence'.

Hardy tells us that 'she had been made to break an accepted social law, but no law known to the environment in which she fancied herself such an anomaly'. It is this sense of having violated nature that is the hardest thing for Tess to bear, and Hardy milks it, if that can be the word, for almost all it's worth. The baby is a 'natural', i.e. illegitimate, child, but the bearing of it and the suckling of it in the fields where she works makes Tess feel oddly 'unnatural', 'living as a stranger and an alien here, though it was no strange land she was in'. Hardy pauses to muddy the waters a little more over the child's conception. A woman worker in the field had heard that there was more than 'persuasion' in the matter and that it might 'have gone ill with a certain party [Alec] if folks had come along', but Hardy also reminds us of a 'slight incautiousness of character' in Tess.

On one thing he is clear: it is not the condition of being an unmarried mother that makes Tess miserable, but her 'conventional aspect' – her spontaneous feeling of social shame. Just as her desire to marry a man she 'loves' is a luxury or a self-indulgence unaffordable to most of her village friends, so her sense of having transgressed socially seems to belong to a different social stratum, and is not shared by her co-workers in the field. In any event, just when the uncritical friendship of the village girls is beginning to reconcile Tess to her situation, the child becomes ill and dies. And with the death, Tess changes 'from simple girl to complex woman'.

She renounces all thoughts of aristocratic association on her father's side, and determines to be what her mother was: 'All my prettiness comes from her and she was only a dairymaid.' Her arrival in a different part of the county is greeted by a prolonged and repeated calling sound. 'It was not the expression of the valley's consciousness that beautiful Tess had arrived, but the ordinary announcement of milking time.' The cows are ready for her; indeed their udders are so full that they are oozing drops of milk on to the ground. Poor Tess: so much part of the land that the hills cry out in welcome, yet alienated from it by her strangely beautiful eyes and, paradoxically, by her unnecessary sense of guilt at having been party, with whatever degree of willingness, to the most natural act of all. This play on the paradoxes of what is or what is not natural runs like a subtle current through the book.

At the dairy, Tess is reunited with Angel Clare, who is learning husbandry in preparation for a life in the colonies. If Tess is a child of nature, Angel is the slave of thought, and the affinity each feels for the other is grounded in a fascination with the unknown. Angel is dealing with problems of career, belief and of a snobbish and religious father, Tess with the death of a baby not lovingly conceived and her consequent sense of dislocation from the universe. It is easy to be impatient with Angel on the grounds that Tess's difficulties are severe, while his are the indulgence of privilege; but he is a good man in his narrow way, and he appreciates the better part of her. He gives her fancy nicknames from myth; to which she replies, 'Call me Tess', and so he does. The love that grows between them is simple and mutual. For Tess, it is a whole move-ment of the heart, a little despairing, for all she knows of fate and life, touched also with compassion for her fellow milkmaids, who cannot have him; for Angel, it begins in a fascination for her face, her mouth, perfect except for the tiny flaws that give it humanity. They are in some ways a mismatch, but not an impossible one. With Elizabeth and Darcy, the fris-son lies in watching how good a deal she can strike, if Darcy it must be. With Heathcliff and Catherine, the reader is simply appalled. But with Tess and her dark eyes, all innocence on the surface, all sensual sorrow underneath, and Angel with his education and his patina of worldliness, yet innocent, barely lustful at a lower level, there is a mutual purity of regard and the possibility of future happiness that seems all the more desirable for being so unlikely. The reader cannot but help, with whatever misgivings, to begin to hope.

In a rush, Angel proposes, but Tess says she cannot marry him. She will not tell him why. He responds with a patience and generosity that rebuke the absent character of Alec. The reader feels that if Tess were to tell him the truth, he is at bottom such a decent man and so inflamed by love that he would tell her that he doesn't mind the fact that a villain took advantage of her. Frustratingly, Tess refuses to disclose her reasons for refusing him. 'You seem almost like a coquette,' he protests, and we almost think so too.

Tess overcomes her misgivings and agrees to the marriage; we see her passion for Angel when she clasps him to her and kisses him. She thinks him beautiful and saintly and clever; and in this she is mistaken. Clare is not a bad man, but he is 'more spiritual than animal', 'rather bright than hot'; his feelings are 'ethereal' and 'fastidious'. He loves her dearly, but not with the 'impassioned thoroughness' of her love for him. What Hardy delicately suggests is that Angel (as his name implies) lacks sexual ardour and the forgiving generosity that goes with it; he does love Tess, but he is not a fool for her; he does not have the driving sexual passion that will overlook small faults. If only he could borrow a little of Alec's devilry and use it to cast a warm animal glow through all his thoughts, to make himself a little 'hot' as well as 'bright'…

While the marriage approaches, there is a period of moving reconciliation with nature ('Thus, during this October month of wonderful afternoons') in which Tess once more feels part of the natural world, and Angel walks with her, feeling it also through her sensibility, which in this respect is superior to his own. It is a brief idyll. Tess is still troubled by thoughts that she is unworthy, and Angel's fine riposte that worthiness has nothing to do with social class but only with being 'true, and honest …

and of good report' unwittingly makes things worse for her. She is not much concerned about her social status, but 'good report' is exactly what she feels she has lost. The wedding brings her no relief, only a sense of 'culpable reticence' and guilt that Angel has not married the real Tess, but one she 'might have been'. As they drive off, they hear a cock crow three times, in a reference to Peter's denial of Christ; and for a moment you feel Hardy mumming and gurning in the foreground of what had been a delicately painted picture. Emboldened by Angel's confession that he had once 'plunged into eight-and-forty hours of dissipation with a stranger', Tess tells him of her own past with Alec.

Angel's response is everything she feared. 'The woman I have been loving is not you', he declares, but 'another woman in your shape.' He seems determined to misjudge her, even with all the evidence before him that she is essentially, in the words of the novel's subtitle, 'a pure woman'. Angel can forgive Tess, but he can no longer love her. From this moment, the novel approaches tragedy in the sense that there is some irreducible molecular trait of character in each protagonist that is caught in an inevitable reaction with circumstance. 'Within the remote depths of [Angel's] constitution, so gentle and affectionate as he was in general, there lay hidden a hard logical deposit, like a vein of metal in soft loam, which turned the edge of everything that attempted to traverse it.'

When I first read the book, I found Angel's response so unsympathetic as to be almost incredible. If he really loved Tess, I thought, he would love her for what she was, with all her past. Now, I am not so sure. If you were to find out that the person you loved was not what they seemed, how would you feel? The effect of infidelity is similar; it is not so much the perfunctory action that is damaging as the knowledge that the adulterer had been withholding some important part of him or herself from what had been shared in trust. Or suppose you found out that your husband of thirty years had not been working for an oil company but for MI6. You would 'understand' the reason why he had not told you, but would it not cast a sickly backward light over your marriage, to think that you had given everything but had never really known him?

The circumstances of Tess and Angel could hardly be more individual. On the one hand is a milkmaid with a dead illegitimate child, the by-blow of a nasty near-rape, and an odd sense of being a lady with a degree of education and aspiration a little above her actual position in life, yet somehow estranged from her home in nature; and on the other is a gentle, radical, affectionate man, an atheist in revolt against his father, a colonist-in-waiting, a fey adventurer with a stubborn streak. Yet in their tragedy is something universal. Do we not all fall in love with 'versions' of a person? Love is 'blind' to those aspects it does not wish to see, and in its early stages can even involve a semi-conscious closing of the eyes, or aversion of the head. If we saw all potential objects of love in the round – clear, with all their faults as well as all their virtues ... Well, it could never be done, because we bring our own eyes and minds to the job of looking. But if, hypothetically, it *could* be done, if we could see truly through 360 degrees, we would presumably all fall in love with the same person. So Tess and Angel's agony, though distinctive, maddening, almost unbearable to read about, does represent some universal human truth and this is what makes it so troubling, so affecting.

Hardy can still loom like a clumsy chorus. 'God's *not* in his heaven: all's *wrong* with the world', he makes Angel reflect as he and Tess separate, rescuing the sudden bathos only with the rhythm of the sentence that follows, 'When Tess had passed over the crest of the hill he turned to go his own way, and hardly knew that he loved her still.' But he regains his mastery with the inevitable momentum of events. After Tess has taken her lurid revenge on Alec, Hardy grants her a short taste of heaven with the man she loves. On the run from the law, they find a deserted house in the New Forest where they hide away and I think – though Hardy is evasive on this point – find physical expression of their love. What they are fleeing from, like so many lovers, is Time. Angel 'peeped out also. It was quite true; within was affection, union, error forgiven: outside was the inexorable.' How long can love–happiness last? A day? A year?

Like Catherine Earnshaw, Tess Durbeyfield looks to another world and time for salvation:

> 'Tell me now, Angel, do you think we shall meet again after we are dead? I want to know.'
> He kissed her to avoid a reply at such a time.
> 'O, Angel – I fear that means no!' said she, with a suppressed sob. 'And I wanted to see you again – so much, so much! What – not even you and I, Angel, who love each other so well?'

Angel is silent, because his whole character has been fired by the heat of his atheism. The three key moments in this novel all occur when nothing happens: the first, when Angel does not ask Tess to dance; the second when she has told him her secret and asks if he can love her and he makes no reply; and the third when once again he shows what he believes by remaining silent.

Reading this novel again, I did not think that Hardy had failed my imaginary test of the third paradox. Although at times he is almost clownish ('the cock crew again') in his attempts to point up what is going on, I didn't feel that he was trying to burden the individual circumstances of Tess with more than they can bear. Nor did I feel that her life, while strange, was necessarily unrepresentative. Hardy successfully persuades us that she is chosen because her story is the most interesting, but that other girls' lives would not show altogether different shapes. In this, he makes her fellow dairymaids at Talbothays work hard for him. They are not just a bucolic chorus; all are in love with Angel and one of them kills herself for it.

Perhaps no line Thomas Hardy wrote in prose is more moving than that awful cry of Tess's, 'And I wanted to see you again – so much, so much!' One feels a knife through the heart on reading it.

And the thought it contains was to be the dominant theme of Hardy's poetry, which would shortly become his life's work.

'ESSENTIALLY SHAMELESS'

CONSTANCE CHATTERLEY

Constance Chatterley, the heroine of D. H. Lawrence's 1928 novel *Lady Chatterley's Lover*, is a cheery girl from a bohemian background, who, like most people, bounces through life without much thought, but then finds herself surprised by the very stark outlines of the choices that confront her as a mature woman.

As a teenager, she is packed off with her sister to Germany, where she loses her virginity to a talkative student. But she is not much interested in sex. The important thing for Connie is the 'freedom' of the woman's life and a desire to leave behind the sordidness of the modern world. She thinks it is a shame men are more earthbound and insist on 'the sex thing'. Time and experience will change her mind.

In Lawrence's mind 'sordidness' exists principally in the mechanised society of factories and mines. They have scarred the landscape of the older, pagan England of Robin Hood and his merry men and have reduced the vital force of the men and women to a dribble. In 1917, Connie marries Sir Clifford Chatterley, a mine owner with a brown stone mansion called Wragby Hall, a 'warren of a place without much distinction', but with large grounds. They have a month's honeymoon, before he returns to Flanders and is shipped home 'almost in bits' – paralysed from the waist down, unable to walk or to make love to his new wife and thus produce an heir. The war is the greatest expression of the dehumanising effects of an industrialised society, and the characters in this novel are trying to find ways of living in the terrible aftermath, to find 'new little habitats, to have new little hopes'. It is a post-apocalyptic landscape in which men and women are thrown back on to the fundamentals of what they are.

There is some early comedy in the book about the pretensions of the arty set that the Chatterleys move in. Brittle short stories and fashionable plays are not the answer to the problems of a shattered civilisation, as the vapid conversation of the Wragby coterie illustrates all too well. Connie does her best to encourage the literary ambitions of her husband, who becomes 'successful' in a trite way as a writer of 'society' short stories, and to run the gloomy house. Encouraged by her father, she takes a lover, a slick playwright called Michaelis, though the arrangement is not satisfactory for her because he does not engage emotionally with her when they make love. He comes to his own 'crisis' too quickly, and although endowed with an extraordinary ability to remain *in situ* until Connie in turn has finished, he is dismissed by her as being 'selfish'. He is in any case not a man for a long-term connection; he is a butterfly who 'couldn't keep anything up' – an unfortunate phrase in the circumstances, given his bedroom trick, though Lawrence is too solemn about sex to hear the double entendre.

There is something naïve about Connie. While she is arty and unfaithful and 'liberated' for her time, she is also inclined to be gauche; and what is beguiling about her is an unexpected modesty. She has few social airs and is open to experience. She shares neither the Tevershall miners' wives' mercenary calculations of their worth, nor the dried-up *noblesse oblige* of her husband's class. What she has is the potential for extreme and disinhibited sensuality.

There are doubtless many such people of either sex, though fewer who find their primer or fuse. Oliver Mellors is the gamekeeper on the Chatterley estate, a man who knows much more about life, death and nature than Connie does. He has a scheme for living and a set of priorities. The hut, with his old army blanket where he raises pheasant chicks to be shot by visiting aristocrats, and his modest cottage, with its white oilskin, bread in a basket and blue mug of beer, are literally the 'new habitats' of the post-apocalyptic world. But Mellors is the survivor of the massacre who retains the knowledge of a better life; he is the village elder who provides the vital link with the past. He disdains the idea of money and social advancement, both of which he is fitted to obtain, in favour of living a simpler life, more radically attached to the land and to the lingering, still trustworthy, animal aspects of the human. Socially, he is an intriguing mixture, and hard to pin down. He is, like Tess, bilingual in dialect and standard English; a former officer, he ends up helping his landlord's daughter in her training to be a teacher.

The war of 1914–18, with its mechanised slaughter of ten million men, appeared to have eliminated for all time the idea that *Homo sapiens* was in any sense a chosen or superior species. The rats, the birds and the rabbits that played and sang among the charnel houses of Verdun and Passchendaele did so with no symbolic or reassuring purpose as far as the soldiers were concerned; on the contrary, their small animal lives showed an utter disregard for the proximate shame of humanity.

Although he does himself not put it in so many words, Mellors represents a thin flame of hope that after all they have done to themselves and to the world, human beings can again find dignity enough to exist alongside other creatures – not as their betters, but as equals, with lungs and blood and longings. It's a modest hope, and modesty is the key to Mellors's character. As we have seen, it finds an answering note in Connie's humble openness to experience.

The heart of this novel is a proposition that was radical at the time and is still not a comfortable one today. Sex and love were present from the beginnings of literature – the Bible, Homer, Horace, Catullus – and also from the early days of the novel in such characters as Moll Flanders, Clarissa and Tom Jones. In British fiction, however, there tended to be a distinction between, for instance, Lady Bellaston, whom Tom Jones was allowed to sleep with, and Sophia Western, whom he 'loves' and will marry. The fact that we all know he does not 'sleep' with Lady Bellaston at all, but is fully awake when he makes love to her, was part of the issue as far as Lawrence was concerned. By the use of euphemism ('sleeps with', 'makes love to' in the absence of an inoffensive word in English for the prime human act) and by the separation of 'just sex' from 'true love', writers had colluded with their readers in making a false and damaging distinction.

A drunk man may visit a prostitute and perform an act which lasts a few moments, without even knowing the name of the woman or seeing her face, and that would presumably be 'just sex'. Or there is Tess's awful love-cry that she had hoped to be reunited with Angel after death, 'so much, so much'. These would seem to be at opposite ends of a spectrum. The implicit contention of *Lady Chatterley's Lover*, however, is that not only do these two examples, being so extreme, tell us little, but also that the very idea of a 'spectrum' is false. What the book suggests is that the relationship between love and sex is more complicated; that sex is not the delinquent brother of 'true love', regrettably tolerated within a pure relationship; but that if men and women understand one another with a deep and modest trust, and that if the physical and neural connections between them are unusually strong (two admittedly large 'if's), then sex at its most passionate and shameless can actually open the door to a deeper and more life-affirming love. It is sex, says Lawrence, that, properly understood, is the purer entity – the driver and enabler. If he were compelled to revisit the old dichotomy, he might rename its poles 'pure sex' and 'just love'.

It is not, to be honest, a view that has found much favour. Young women today must deal with the economic needs of work and the noisy claims of sexualised fashion in a society with high rates of venereal disease. It's not surprising that, however superficially louche their behaviour may sometimes be, they have tended to cling to the old polarity. Who can blame them? In a post-authoritarian, fully deregulated world, any certainty may be better than none. 'True love' as opposed to 'just sex' seems a decent thing to cling on to – certainly until something better comes along.

But Connie is a child in a new, post-traumatic world. She is an explorer. Sir Clifford gives her guarded permission when he says, 'If lack of sex is going to disintegrate you, then go out and have a love affair.' A few moments later, the new gamekeeper, Oliver Mellors, appears as though by command. Connie is frightened by the sudden appearance, first of his dog, then of Mellors himself; he has a 'red face and red moustache', is dressed in old-fashioned gaiters and velveteen; he is like a small woodland creature and shows himself to be 'quite frail really' when he has to push Sir Clifford's wheelchair uphill. Like many of Lawrence's men characters, he is lean and far from bonny, but with a hard inner flame.

From this moment, the narrative has a new sense of something quickening, of something sure to happen, especially when Sir Clifford hires a gossipy local woman, Mrs Bolton, to look after him, thus liberating Connie from any further physical connection with him: 'She breathed free, a new phase was going to begin in her life.' Connie comes across Mellors by chance in the woods, where he is making a cage for his pheasant chicks, and almost at once, Lawrence narrates from Mellors's point of view – a clear sign that he is a privileged character. The first thing we learn is that 'a little thin tongue of fire flickered in his loins' when he senses Connie watching him; and the second is that he 'hated her presence there' – perhaps because he has a foreboding of what it will lead to. At this point, Mellors enjoys the feeling of self-sufficiency in his pared-down life and has no wish to share it with a woman. But it is not long before Connie returns, and their first physical contact comes when he comforts her as she weeps. She is crying 'in all the anguish of her generation's forlornness', and it is significant that Mellors's first caress is one of consolation – for all that was lost between 1914 and 1918. They make love, and it fills them with peace, but also with sadness. Mellors is wistful about starting again with feelings he thought he had left behind: 'She had connected him up again, when he had wanted to be alone.'

The physical sensations of sex grow more intense. Lawrence does not scruple to describe how Connie's orgasm feels to her – 'one perfect concentric fluid of feeling' – but tries to connect it to unseen natural forces: 'The voice out of the uttermost night, the life! The man heard it beneath him with a kind of awe, as his life sprang into her.'

Passages like this one are really the crux of this novel's being and reputation. Many readers have found them portentous. Feminists have found them impertinent. Some have criticised them as being lewd (and they become more frank as the story goes on); others have mocked them for being, on the contrary, too high-falutin'. Some have complained that Mellors is 'phallocratic' or 'phallocentric', that his love-making is all thrust and little foreplay, and that it is 'wrong' to portray a woman as enjoying that male-instigated kind of love-making – that all these descriptions represent male fantasies of dominating passive women.

To me, the important thing is that these are descriptions of two particular people, both clearly delineated by the author. I don't think Lawrence is saying that all sex is like this; what he is saying is that for these two people it was. Mellors is a former lieutenant in India who has returned to the ranks, as it were – decommissioned himself in the army and in life. He is separated from a hard, rapacious wife with whom he has had previous experience of sensuality, of how it can liberate, inflame and destroy. Now he wishes only to be left alone with the wild animals of the wood. Connie is a woman of her generation, many of whom were deprived of husbands by the war. Yet in her modest, arty way, she is adventurous, and she is not prepared to let the flame of her life dwindle into extinction because of what the war has done to her husband, her country and all their ideas of what it means to be human. To me, it is psychologically credible that these two people in a world that both of them see as post-apocalyptic would try to create 'new habitats', new meanings in the simplest naked connection that human beings can make.

To look, then, at the criticisms one by one. There is certainly an air of portentousness, an attempt to evoke a biblical force in the way Lawrence refers to Mellors as 'the man', as though he were all men, or Adam. This, of course, is exactly Lawrence's point. Humanity is back to its roots, and must start again. But perhaps he is trying to have it both ways here:

forcing Mellors to be individual and universal at the same time. This is a little hard to take. And is the description lewd or is it absurdly elevated? It tries to be high and low; it wants to say that in this carnal act is our joy and our true self; but because we are human, not bestial, it may be two things at once. It may, to use the author's terminology, be simple 'fucking', but it may also be transcendent. And really, if the act can never transcend its physical limitations of friction and release then humankind is exactly what it appeared on the fields of the Somme: not merely on a level with the rats and birds, but lower than them, because more cruel.

The question of how a reader responds to the artistic representation of sex will always be difficult and subjective. Personally, I am unembarrassed by sexual description in books (though obviously many such passages are unsuccessful and some are absurd), but I find it uncomfortable to watch sexual acts on screen, particularly in a public cinema; with some people it is the other way round. These are privacy reflexes which vary from person to person, and I think one merely has to respect other people's sensitivities. The idea, however, that sex can never be written about in an elevated way is the property of a certain kind of sniggering person, encouraged by some privileged education in this country. Unlike the differing privacy concerns, it is not, I think, a viewpoint that commands much respect.

Much has been written about the difference between the erotic and the pornographic in literature, the former being praised, the latter despised. This is another false polarity, I think – like 'just sex' and 'true love'. The most impressive aspect of Lawrence's writing about sex in *Lady Chatterley's Lover* is that it is neither erotic nor pornographic – for the simple reason that it is not concerned with the sexual response of the reader. Lawrence cares only about his characters: this is what Mellors did, he tells us, and this is what Connie felt. The collateral tumescence or otherwise of the reader is not his concern, and that, presumably, is why he is sometimes called 'puritanical' or 'po-faced'. The aim of the erotic is the same as the aim of the pornographic: to arouse. The former is simply an upmarket version of the latter, and Lawrence is not obviously interested in either.

Finally, the criticism that Mellors is 'phallocratic' is not really a literary criticism at all. It is personal gossip. We don't actually know how much time Mellors spends in foreplay, though his first act of tenderness is to kiss Connie's navel, which Lawrence may have meant the reader to think of as a prelude to oral sex. The first point, however, is that some women do enjoy what Mellors does with Connie (and Doris Lessing has plenty to say on the preferability of the vaginal to the clitoral orgasm in due course); it may be unpalatable to a certain feminist turn of mind, but repeated rhythmic penetration is what some women like best (see, for instance, Catherine Millet's *The Sexual Life of Catherine M.*), and there is little that political theory can do to alter neuronal preferences. The more important point, however, is not an anecdotal but a properly literary one. This is how it happened, says Lawrence, this is what Mellors did, this is what Connie liked and this is where it took them. The only proper literary question is whether he is convincing in his portrayal of what he claims they did and what he claims they felt.

For all that Lawrence is pushing the reader to think more about the power of sexual love, he does not lose sight of the everyday concerns. Connie, of course, wonders what it would be like to have Mellors's baby and is properly enraptured by the thought. He, meanwhile, having lost his solitary life, forfeits also his peace of mind, and so becomes lonely and agonised when separated from his new connection; and in a haunting scene at the end of Chapter 10 he is drawn from his bed at night to go near to the big house where his lover lies asleep. He stands with his gun by his side in the dark driveway, wondering if he could sneak into the 'warren' of rooms and find her. Mrs Bolton, meanwhile, is waiting for the dawn, because it is only at sunrise that shell-damaged Sir Clifford can relax into sleep. As she pulls back the curtains to see if the day is coming, she reveals the figure of Mellors, staring forlornly at the house, like an animal in the dawn light, craving its mate. She has only to see him to know the truth. 'Goodness! The knowledge went through Mrs Bolton like a shot. He was Lady Chatterley's lover. He! He!' This unnerving switch of viewpoint does not stop what has gone before from being one of the most beautiful passages that Lawrence ever wrote, though, interestingly, he undercuts it further with a little humour at the end. The sudden changes of register work well here, though it must be said, much less well elsewhere in the book, where some of the writing seems not so much daring as slapdash.

There is no getting away from the fact that this book does have its absurdities. Some of Mellors's theories about lesbians and black women are risible; some of the would-be elevated descriptions fail to take off. When Lawrence is at his best, the simplicity of his writing can have a literally breathtaking quality; you inhale at the daring of the short cut he has taken to the heart of a matter, which often seems to concern the lives and deaths of miners. A few words in *Sons and Lovers* can give you all a man's life. In *Lady Chatterley's Lover*, some of the short cuts are perfunctory or unintentionally comic.

When it comes to sex, however, Lawrence always concentrates. After Connie and Mellors have danced in a rainstorm, he strokes her haunches, letting his hands linger on the 'secret places' while he talks to her about her excretory functions. Connie laughs – as the reader may, too. Then Mellors weaves a bouquet of wild flowers in her pubic hair, the tender and the comic in harmony as she prepares to leave shortly for Venice, where, with her husband's encouragement, she is to try to become pregnant in order to provide an heir for Wragby.

Before she goes, Mellors takes the last step of intimacy by entering Connie by the 'secret place' he had previously touched with his finger. The prose is sufficiently opaque that it had to be explained to the jury at the obscenity trial in 1960 that this was indeed sodomy.

> Though a little frightened, she let him have his way, and the reckless, shameless sensuality shook her to her foundations, stripped her to the very last, and made a different woman of her. It was not really love. It was not voluptuousness … Burning out the shames, the deepest oldest shames in the most secret places. It cost her an effort to let him have his way … She would have thought a woman would have died of shame. Instead of which, shame died. Shame, which is fear … She felt now she had come to the real bedrock of her nature, and was essentially shameless.

It is a difficult episode. Not every reader will be persuaded by the assertion that 'she had secretly wanted it'. The passage of time has not helped Lawrence's choice of words – 'this phallic hunting out', for instance. Again, it seems to me a question not of what women as a generality 'really want', but of whether this act of intimacy on the eve of the separation of two individual lovers whose emotions have been driven to a rarefied state by the candour of their sexual activity is feasible or not. Is this what Mellors would have done, and if so, is Connie's transcendence of shame into new purity a convincing outcome? The way that the male author presumes to explain the woman's deepest sensations has seemed provoking to some readers on the grounds that a man could not 'know' such things. To others, who believe the creative imagination is sovereign, such moments are simple demonstrations of how an author is entitled to know every cell of the characters he has created. My view is that – to turn it around – a woman novelist is entitled to present her male character's every neural sensation – but she had better be convincing. It is a risk.

The story ends unhappily, as love stories do. Connie is pregnant with Mellors's child, but Mellors's estranged wife demands to be taken back. She moves into his cottage and finds evidence of the affair; word reaches Sir Clifford, who dismisses Mellors. It is a mess. Mellors tries to reconcile himself to a life of chastity in a new job in a new place. Connie cannot marry him, because Sir Clifford will not divorce her, and the book ends with the lovers apart, hoping for reunion.

Lawrence has become unfashionable. Even some of the scholars who spoke up in his defence at the obscenity trial later referred unenthusiastically to the novel, while the introduction to the Wordsworth Classics edition reports: 'There is very little recent work on the novel because it has fallen so severely out of favour.'

Fashion is often a good guide, in an inverted way. It would be facile to say everything fashionable is worthless and that everything deemed politically incorrect, dated, absurd and so on is always, on the contrary, valuable. Literary fashion is right about as often as it is wrong, but probably not *more* often. And the 'fashionability' or otherwise of a book is no better – or worse – a guide than the length of its title or the colour of its jacket. You have to read with an open mind. *Lady Chatterley's Lover* is a flawed book with many moments of absurdity, but it is, I think, a brave one that makes its central point with conviction. Constance Chatterley is a believable human being who wants to find happiness and intimacy in a world all but destroyed. That she should come so close to finding what she craves, yet by means so utterly unforeseen by her at the outset, seems to me credible, comic and moving.

'I'D RATHER BE DEAD'

MAURICE BENDRIX

What 'Fate' is to Hardy, Roman Catholicism is to Graham Greene – a loud gatecrasher at a muted family gathering. Whatever else they have to deal with as artists, both writers have first to try to make this intruder seem not just welcome, but somehow natural in their otherwise realistic, often humdrum settings. The extent to which they can manage it will to a large extent define the success of each novel.

Maurice Bendrix, the main character and narrator of *The End of the Affair*, is a writer of modest distinction and an embittered nature. He makes it clear from the first page that, despite its title, this will be a book not about love but about hate. Greene gives him a helping hand with one of the most depressing epigraphs ever attached to a novel, a quotation from the French Catholic essayist, Léon Bloy: 'Man has places in his heart which do not yet exist, and into them enters suffering in order that they may have existence.'

Bendrix goes for a drink in a pub on Clapham Common with Henry Miles, a friend he 'hates'. 'The Pontefract Arms was still decorated for Christmas with paper streamers and paper bells, the relics of commercial gaiety, mauve and orange, and the young landlady leant her large breasts against the bar with a look of contempt for her customers.' Everything about the sentence tells us what to expect. It is January, but the landlord has been too lazy to take down his cheap decorations, which celebrate not religious joy, but commercial gaiety, in one gaudy colour – orange – and one invented by a chemist, mauve. The landlady is young, but has large breasts, as though she has 'let herself go' or wears an ineffective bra; there is something sluttish in the way she leans them 'against the bar' (perhaps Greene means 'on the counter'); but despite her own vulgarity, she looks down on her customers. Here is laziness, squalor, lack of spirituality, simultaneous sexual pull and revulsion, snobbery and alienation – all proficiently expressed. As readers, we feel drawn in by the exactness of the detail and tempted to align with the misanthropy; but, even while relishing the Greeneland gloom, we are already worried by the narrowness of the world view and by the lack of ambition in the conception of theme and character that the sentence seems to promise.

Henry confides to Bendrix that he thinks his wife, Sarah, has been having an affair and wonders whether he should consult a private detective to have her followed. In the end, it is Bendrix who goes to the agency, and has an interview with a man called Savage, who tells him, 'There is nothing discreditable about jealousy, Mr Bendrix. I always salute it as the mark of true love.' This is a palpable hit, though one that disdain for the speaker forbids Bendrix from acknowledging at the time; privately, though, he is candid about his part of himself: 'I am a jealous man... I was jealous even of the past'. In any event, Savage details his man Parkis to follow Sarah, and when this Parkis reports back to Bendrix, it turns out that Sarah has indeed been meeting a man not her husband, and in a furtive, emotional manner. Unfortunately, the man in question is Bendrix.

This is clever storytelling. Initially, we were intrigued to find out what had made Bendrix so embittered, but sensed there was to be no adequate or interesting explanation: he is the way he is less because of imagined and understood history than because his author wishes to use him as a conduit for some cosmic pessimism. With the plot development, however, we can put aside our dislike of Bendrix and our disappointment at his author's conception of him, for a good reason: he knows the story. We are now back at the Beginning of the Affair, where, after watching a poor adaptation of one of his books in the cinema, Bendrix takes Sarah to dinner. He has invited Henry, too, but Henry is too busy with Civil Service work, which is just as well, because as they leave the restaurant, Bendrix tells Sarah, 'I'm in love.' They go to a hotel in Paddington. Bendrix takes some pleasure in this – but not much, because at once he is jealous at the thought of Henry kissing Sarah when she gets home. However, he takes some comfort in the fact that their love-making will have a chance to improve, because he feels sure the affair will go on.

And so it does, but it brings little joy; indeed, Bendrix's first reflection on his new condition is: 'The sense of unhappiness is so much easier to convey than that of happiness.' We know almost nothing at this stage of what it means to Sarah, because Bendrix takes little interest in the feelings of others. They make love on the sitting-room floor with Henry ill in bed upstairs, and 'when the moment came, I had to put my hand over her mouth to deaden that strange sad angry cry of abandonment'. The sounds are those of Sarah, but the adjectives are those of Bendrix, and we don't know if they are accurate. Compare Constance Chatterley: 'It was like bells rippling up and up to a culmination. She lay unconscious of the wild little cries she uttered at the last.' Perhaps the two women make the same sound and the difference is that only one man has the capacity to enjoy it; Mellors 'heard it beneath him with a kind of awe, as his life sprang into her'; Bendrix almost suffocates her.

What we do know about Sarah is that, unlike Bendrix, she does not suffer guilt, and that, for her, 'remorse dies with the act'. In this, Bendrix says, she is almost like a Catholic, able to expunge sins by confession – though, like him, she is an atheist at this point in the story. The important difference between them is that she seems capable of disinterested love. She wouldn't mind if he had another lover: 'I want you to be happy. I hate your being unhappy' – in which case she has made a curious selection by choosing a man clearly incapable of such emotion. For him, by contrast, 'I'd rather be dead or see you dead ... than with another man ... Anyone who loves is jealous.'

Perhaps the emotion they feel should not really be called by the same name, that of 'love'. In Bendrix there is want and fear; in Sarah there is self-fulfilment and benevolence. What Bendrix feels is close to what a small, stressed child might feel towards its absent mother; in Sarah, there is more of the attitude of a parent to a grown-up child. Despite its large number of words, English struggles to pin down emotions. We are better with colours, where to talk about a deep moss green or a delicate coral pink will give a fair idea of the difference. If the only word we had was 'tinted', the picture would be less clear. Yet 'love' has to serve a number of elemental feelings, of their compounds and mixtures, that cover a range at least as wide as that in the colour spectrum. And that is before the element of sex is even admitted.

Bendrix picks up a girl in Piccadilly and takes her for a drink in a pub, where he finds he can feel no desire for her. 'My passion for Sarah had killed simple lust for ever. Never again would I be able to enjoy a woman without love.' He comes to loathe Sarah's insouciance, the way she can happily pass hours without him, while a 'devil' in his brain keeps prompting him to jealousy; and this devil is 'not Sarah's enemy so much as the enemy of love'.

At about this point, Graham Greene seems to lose patience with Bendrix's powers of narration, and has Parkis go and steal the diary that Sarah has conveniently, if improbably, kept throughout the course of the affair. Greene only used first-person narration twice (*The Quiet American* is the other instance) and professed to find it very difficult; he said he was emboldened to try it here by re-reading *Great Expectations*. At any rate, Bendrix finds fond references to himself in Sarah's diary, though he can take no consolation from them, reflecting only that: 'It's a strange thing to discover and believe that you are loved, when you know there is nothing for anybody but a parent or a God to love.' Such a thought might prompt someone to value more highly the lover who has held them in this high regard; for most people it would be not so much a 'strange' as a 'wonderful' discovery; and if Greene had had a more complex conception of his main character, this moment could have been made to illuminate it.

However, Greene does not like to stray from a narrow line of paradox. As he has told us on the first page, this love story 'is a record of hate'. In almost all his major characters, Greene will go for the quick frisson of neat contradiction rather than the long satisfaction of unresolved complexity. One thinks of Pinkie, the boy gangster in *Brighton Rock*, or Fowler, the old Indochina hack in *The Quiet American*. They are initially interesting because where you'd expect A, Greene gives you B. But it is always B. It is always the opposite of what you expect, so that in the end you don't expect A any more, you expect B. And B is what you get – neatly, narrowly and proficiently done, but done without variation.

Bendrix boasts of his routines as a writer: 500 words a day, come hell or high water, never more, never less, happy to break off in mid-scene if the daily 'quota' is done, to be read over last thing at night before sleep, no matter what time it is. It is exactly this submission to a self-imposed restriction that is so limiting in Graham Greene's books. What are presented as 'professionalism' and self-discipline are in fact voluntarily imposed creative limitations. And one does not have to be a Freudian to believe that the motive behind such habits is fear: fear of over-reaching what he knows he can pull off with mechanical certainty, fear of playing a game with a different hand; fear, above all, of failure. Greene hit on a pungent mixture for his cocktail: religious doubt, gloom, acidic comedy and a simplistic conception of character, delivered in a disciplined prose. But he is a barman who serves only one drink.

Many readers have been happy to hang out in Greene's saloon, ordering the same drink, and I've enjoyed an evening or two there myself, particularly with the more comic, less religious books, or 'entertainments', such as *Our Man in Havana*. Greene's talent was large and intercontinental; his insistence on finding new settings for his fiction was a reproof to lesser novelists. When the Catholicism can be made to seem integral to the characters and their situation, as it is most successfully in *The Power and the Glory*, something stirring and memorable does emerge. But at other times there is a tendency to revert to formula; and sentences as suggestive as 'It's a strange thing to discover and believe that you are loved, when you know there is nothing for anybody but a parent or a God to love' make one aware of what was sometimes sacrificed to fear in the name of professionalism.

The loss is particularly frustrating in *The End of the Affair* because at its best it verges on something grand. What both Bendrix and Sarah are good at expressing is how time is the enemy of love. Greene himself said that Bendrix is a man who knows that pain will always come with love and thinks he might as well get his pain over with sooner rather than later. As for Sarah, 'She had no doubts. The moment only mattered. Eternity is said not to be an extension of time but an absence of time and sometimes it seemed to me that her abandonment touched that strange mathematical point of endlessness, a point with no width, occupying no space.' In this rare moment of empathy, Bendrix does identify the pain of love – the desperate need of lovers to inhabit that moment of timelessness, while knowing that it is against all the laws of nature. Like most lovers, Bendrix and Sarah are planets whose orbits thrillingly overlap, but only as part of a longer, gravitational destiny that will pull them into other paths as surely as it has brought them together.

From Sarah's diary, Bendrix learns that she planned to leave Henry to be with Bendrix and wrote a note to tell him so. But at that moment Henry returned to the house, having found out about the affair, and Sarah could not leave him 'because I've seen what his misery looks like'. Later, Henry confesses to Bendrix: 'I'm not the marrying kind. It was a great injury I did to Sarah when I married her. I know that now.'

Men incapable of passion and intimacy should not marry women who crave and need such things: they will only make their wives miserable, and that discontent will rebound on the husband. Henry's insight is a sharp one, though nothing in Greene's presentation of the dry civil servant has prepared us for this spark of emotional intelligence. The marriage of Henry and Sarah appears to have been sexless for so long that some readers have even suggested it is 'unconsummated'; if this is the case, it is hard to imagine what it is in a Sarah without sex that first appealed to Henry.

Sarah's diary, meanwhile, reveals little of any consequence. She is much affected by whether Bendrix has been 'sweet' or not to her, and troubled by thoughts of religion, but Greene does nothing to explain the mystery of why such an apparently unaffected, life-loving and attractive woman should either have married a bore like Henry or fallen in love with a man as sterile as Bendrix. It is as though he has not fully imagined Sarah.[10]

And still there is the gatecrasher, Catholicism, to be accommodated. In another neat plot turn, we discover that Sarah has indeed been 'seeing' a man since the end of her affair with Bendrix – a rationalist demagogue called Smythe, a soapbox pamphleteer devoted to the idea that God does not exist. Sarah has needed to see him because she has made a vow to God. While she and Bendrix were making love, a German bomb fell on

---

[10] There may be a 'based on' problem here. Sound evidence suggests that Sarah is modelled on a real-life lover of Greene's, an American called Catherine Crompton, who married an English life peer to become Lady Walston (or as Wikipedia in its wikiway has it: 'Graham Greene's own affair with Lady Catherine Walston played into the basis for *The End of the Affair*'). It is possible that, knowing the woman so well, Greene forgot to make her available to the reader in her fictional form – Sarah's character has hardly any characteristics – though this seems an odd oversight for such an experienced writer.

A few years ago, there was a new book whose *raison d'être* was to argue that Sarah was *not wholly* drawn from life. That a publisher should think it worth printing a book entirely devoted to the idea that one of Britain's most famous novelists had partly invented a character tells you all you need to know of the current popular assumptions about how novelists work.

Even this was surpassed by something I heard at the same time from a grand financier I met at a party, who told me he had every intention of going to see the Ralph Fiennes/Julianne Moore film of *The End of the Affair* 'Because, you see, my daughter's godmother is the *current* Lady Walston.'

the house. Believing him killed by the blast, she made a deal with God that if he lived, she would give him up for ever. In the ensuing two years, Sarah has been visiting Smythe to try to persuade her that she can break her vow with impunity. God, meanwhile, has been reeling her in like a hooked fish, reawakening some childhood Catholic conscience. It turns out that the love triangle does not really involve Henry after all, but has an uncertain divinity at its apex.

Greene excuses himself from the challenge of offering a resolution to Sarah's awkward plight by killing her off. He then attempts to embed the Catholic theme into the novel by another late plot twist, in which we discover that a large purple birthmark on the face of Smythe has been 'miraculously' cured: the rationalist has been unmanned. The book ends with Bendrix hating not only himself, Sarah and Henry, but also the God whose tentacles he now feels reaching out to him: 'I hate You, God, I hate You as though You existed', where the capital letters suggest that disbelief is ceasing to be an option for Bendrix. And in the very last sentence of the book, as he walks towards the pub for his evening drink with Henry, he thinks: 'O God, You've done enough, You've robbed me of enough, I'm too tired and old to learn to love, leave me alone for ever.'

Much of this verges on the ridiculous. The action appears *voulu* – stuck on by the Catholic author, not generated organically, so that sufferings of the characters seem to have been piled on by their creator rather than springing from their interior worlds, which are in any case inadequately rendered. And yet … Despite the book's shortcomings, there seems something hard and truthful at its core. One may not like Bendrix, or even find him believable, but he does show how a narrow view of 'love' is certain to lead to despair. What he feels for Sarah is sexual want and longing, which then become an addiction from which he can't free himself. There is little tenderness between them; one cannot imagine him giving her pet names, asking about her childhood, making efforts to understand her as a fellow human; and when she comes, he puts his hand over her mouth. But his desperation is compelling. Why should he not call his mixture of dark yearnings by the name of 'love'? After all, he admits that he is too old and tired to 'learn' how to love properly. And if he sometimes resembles a petulant child, does that not fairly reflect the fact that, in the face of large emotions, we are all childlike? Which of us can say that our strongest feelings are pure and dignified? Which of us can revert to the false dichotomy of 'pure love' and 'just sex' and report with certainty that we experience only the best parts of each? Above all in Bendrix we feel the wretched shortness of life and the way that time and chance conspire against our hope of finding happiness through one another. All culture is for it; almost all history is against it.

'MEN WHO WOULD HURT ME'

ANNA WULF

In the late 1960s and throughout the 1970s the British novel, with some noble exceptions, became bogged down. It seemed that novelists had stopped doing the thing they were principally paid to do – make things up. Instead, they seemed reduced to writing accounts of their own lives, with sometimes scant attempt even to disguise which of their friends and neighbours they had 'put in'. The nadir was reached with the so-called 'Hampstead novel' – a slim thing that often had a philandering male television executive and a disgruntled wife as its main characters. These books had no interest in prose itself, no vision beyond the end of the street, no insight into people – largely because they hadn't created them but had 'borrowed' them from life – and no conception of how to make theme and structure work. It was dire stuff. No wonder the newspaper 'group reviews' in which they were bluffly summarised, half a dozen a time, were interspersed by occasional magazine pieces entitled 'Is the novel dead?' It certainly looked ill – perhaps terminally so.

As a reviewer and then as the editor of a small literary magazine, I read a lot of these books. For the magazine, I would sometimes ask people to recommend their favourite novels in features entitled 'Modern Classics' or some such thing. Few contemporary novels were chosen more often than *The Golden Notebook* by Doris Lessing. It appeared to have been a bible to the literary women of the generation before mine and was spoken of as the definitive feminist novel. Lessing herself was clearly a writer of great talent, and I therefore took it on trust that *The Golden Notebook* was all that its devotees claimed.

Imagine my surprise, as they say, on actually opening it. At first sight, this was not just a Hampstead novel, this was the mother and aunt of all Hampstead novels. I felt like someone who had spent ten years listening to Oasis before hearing his first Beatles record. All those sanctimonious women, all those one-dimensional male horrors, all these people who did jobs in 'the media' while consulting shrinks in NW3: this was where they had all come from, this was the Ur-text.

It was, to put it mildly, not what I had been expecting. We begin in 1957 with Anna and her friend Molly, two women in their thirties who pull the wings off a pathetic fly of a man called Richard, Molly's discarded husband. Richard is the basis of a type much loved by later feminist novelists: the bully who is also a milksop, the 'man-baby'. They tell him he is a 'pompous little snob', that he is 'anti-semitic'; and as if that were not enough, he has been to Oxford and Eton and works in 'the City'. It's hard to know who is more unpleasant, Richard, or the women who sneer at him. Anna, like many characters in the Hampstead novel, does not have a job; she lives, with her daughter and a lodger in Earls Court, off the royalties from a novel she has written. There are, however, two potential points of interest in this otherwise unpromising set-up: first, Anna is a half-believing Communist and, second, she may be heading towards some mental disintegration. 'Everything's cracking up' is the first thing she says in the book.

The state of Anna's inner life is given in different-coloured note-books, which we read between sections of the novel that tell us about her outer life with Molly and their friends and lovers. The use of multiple narratives stemming from one character seemed remarkable at the time, and is still unusual today. The first notebook has a long recollection of dissolute times in Africa with a group of Communists. Although one is a 'master of dialectic' who 'despised people who allowed their lives to be disturbed by personal emotion', what they really like doing is drinking and having sex. The characters, while solemn in discussion, are frivolous in the way they live; it is possible to sense why Anna might start to feel divided in herself. And although the men in particular seem ridiculous, we are at least out of Hampstead.

We also see what a terrible chooser of men Anna is. Just as we feel that if Hardy is to convince us that Fate is against the rural poor he must convince us that to some extent any random sample of a life will prove his point, so a feminist novel must convince us that its male characters are not hand-picked for their deficiencies. The men in *The Golden Notebook* are indeed repulsive, but they are chosen by Anna herself – sometimes not only despite their shallow egotism but because of it. What this soon made me wonder was whether this was really intended to be read as a 'feminist' novel at all. What is clear is that Anna herself feels repelled by this period in her life, during the Second World War – 'I'd rather die than live through any of that again' – and alienated from the self she describes in Africa.

Another notebook gives an account of Anna's cautious dealings with the Communist Party. It seems terribly dated and hard to take seriously ('Writers' group meeting last night. Five of us – to discuss Stalin on Linguistics'), but perhaps we should try. The period is before 1956 and the invasion of Hungary, when it was still possible to disregard reliable reports of repression, purges and mass murder in the Soviet Union and to view that country as the victor over fascism and to see in its flawed society at least an attempt at social justice. Not easy – but just about possible. Anna and her friends know the game is up, really, but as one of them puts it: 'The reason why we don't leave the Party is we can't bear to say good-bye to our ideals for a better world.' Bombed and rationed London of the early 1950s certainly seems to have held out little else for the idealistic.

Doris Lessing then gives us some of Anna's own writing, in the shape of an autobiographical fiction about a character called Ella and her love affair with a man called Paul. He is vain, married and deceitful, she is childish and petulant. She elevates whims into entitlements. She feels the need to use men physically in the hope that it will make her feel more of a 'completed' woman. Meanwhile, her self-indulgence, her willingness to take offence and her vulnerability combine to make her seem quite dangerously unbalanced. Anna seems occasionally to sense this when she breaks into Ella's story to point out its shortcomings. Many of the characters in *The Golden Notebook* seem to be writing a novel – a form they regard not as a potential work of art but as a natural medium for their self-regard.

The hollowness of promiscuity is starkly laid out. Of her boss, Ella reflects: 'He had not one spark of that instinctive warmth for a woman, liking for a woman, which was what she felt in Paul. And that was why she would sleep with him.' She would sleep with him *because* he dislikes women? Ella/Anna is a very confused person, but this decision seems more than muddled; it seems masochistic. 'I was looking for men who would hurt me. I needed it', Anna confesses later.

Curiously enough, it is Paul who first voices the idea of a war between the sexes: 'The real revolution is women against men.' This idea becomes something the characters vaguely latch on to as a substitute for the Communist revolutions that have failed them; but it never seems something that has been thought out by the author or her characters. Anna does voice the idea at one point: 'The resentment, the anger, is impersonal. It is the disease of women in our time ... The woman's emotion: resentment against injustice, an impersonal poison.' But although Anna thinks she is a fighter, she is too damaged, too selfish, too pathologically dependent on being 'loved' by a man, and, above all, too muddled to be the role model for a new politics.

Time has not been kind to *The Golden Notebook*, and it has, perhaps inevitably, lost some of its apparent audacity. Its admirers often spoke of how it was the 'first' novel to talk of this or that aspect of female experience – menstruation, for example; and it is hardly Doris Lessing's fault that almost every novel by a woman for the next 20 years seemed to feel obliged to describe its heroine's first period. Lessing tried to put things in perspective with an introduction, written in 1971. 'This novel was not a trumpet for Women's Liberation', she wrote; and the aims of that movement would, she thought, be shown in time to be 'very small and quaint'. Clearly, she felt aggrieved at the way her book has been misrepresented, perhaps by its feminist admirers: 'Some books are not read in the right way because they have skipped a stage of opinion, assume a crystallization of information which has not yet taken place.' She also seems frustrated by readers' inability to understand the structure, which, itself compartmentalised, implies that such a process is unhealthy in a life, and that Anna's future depends on her ability to unify all the aspects of her existence.

These points seem perfectly justified. Less so, is a sort of brash impatience. Lessing laments the absence of an English nineteenth-century equivalent of Tolstoy or Stendhal to describe the 'intellectual and moral climate' of its nation. Dismissing Hardy and George Eliot, she proposes her own book as the twentieth-century equivalent. Her impatient 'At this point it is necessary to make the obligatory disclaimers' is not enough to lessen one's embarrassment at the gulf between *Anna Karenina* and *The Golden Notebook* (even if *The Grass Is Singing* can look anyone in the eye). Nor does blaming the 'parochialism of our culture' quite explain why people have not responded as she wished; a novel of this scope – or length, even – ought to carry within it a means of being properly interpreted.

One can't help feeling that the book has simply been historically unfortunate. Anna is a neurotic who has been misinterpreted as a feminist. The Communist milieu, chosen because at the time it seemed the most historically serious crucible of ideas, has come to look dishonest. The sexual promiscuity of the characters no longer appears 'liberated', but reckless and damaging. The social setting of North London, psychotherapy and adultery was devalued by a legion of less talented writers who came after.

It is all very unfortunate, because as the novel goes on, those who have stayed with it will see that Doris Lessing has a different conception of Anna as a woman in crisis. However, it is not as a feminist role model or as an Everywoman defining herself in a male-dominated world; it is as a psychiatric case. Once you cease to read *The Golden Notebook* as a political novel and consider it as a psychological one, it becomes less strained and more interesting. In her Blue Notebook, Anna recounts her visits to a psychoanalyst called Mrs Marks, known to her as 'Mother Sugar'. In full Freudian mode, she sets about analysing her dreams, and what is unusual is how resistant she is to the analyst's interpretation. These sessions may seem dated (and the psychoanalytic profession is among the quickest to stress how rapidly it has evolved, and keeps on evolving); but these passages, however enervating they can be for the reader, do support the idea that Lessing is trying to find new ways of creating character.

Doris Lessing herself acknowledged that it is from the case history angle that more and more people tended to see her book. The letters she received used to be, she says, principally about the 'sex war, about man's inhumanity to woman and woman's inhumanity to man'. Second most numerous were letters about politics 'probably from an old Red like myself'. And 'the third letter, once rare but now catching up on the others, is written by a man or a woman who can see nothing in it but the theme of mental illness'.

However, while Anna Wulf makes more sense in this context than as a proto-feminist, there is a limit to this interpretation as well because Doris Lessing's interest in psychiatry is too slight for her to furnish a plausible diagnostic picture. 'Anna and Saul Green [her final lover] "break down"', she later wrote. 'They are crazy, lunatic, mad – what you will.' Alas, 'what you will' is not good enough. People don't '"break down" into each other, into other people, break through the false pattern they have made of their pasts' and so on; it just doesn't happen. In a book that is quite scrupulously realistic about political events, containing many pages of newspaper clippings, it doesn't seem enough to shrug off the central problem of your main character with the words 'what you will'.

Anna and her alter ego Ella continue on their promiscuous road, but show no interest in their 'lovers' as people, only as machines for gratifying – or more often not gratifying – their ravening sense of entitlement. You have to dig very deep into your heart to find any sympathy for a woman so pathologically self-centred, so utterly deluded about life and love that she sees half the human race as depersonalised. On the other hand, the men that Anna chooses deserve little more. The most frustrating thing about the final sections of the book is that as Anna's 'madness' grows more intense, it becomes less clear whether these men are chosen for their very awfulness, as masochism becomes the principal symptom of Anna's neurotic quest, or whether she and Lessing really think these men represent their sex.

I believe the former. Even if Lessing's idea of 'breakdown' is a literary one with no basis in medicine, it remains the underlying principle of this novel with its fragmented structure, and I think we are obliged to read the last sections as being filtered through a badly disturbed mind. This interpretation doesn't make Anna any more likeable, or believable, but it helps explain the shape of the book, which asks us to believe that in the end Anna, by allowing Saul Green to help her write in the golden notebook of the title, not only cures her writer's 'block' but dispels the sense of false nostalgia for a younger self that has caused it; by penetrating her most private self – her writer's notebook – Green enables Anna to combine the fragments of her life from the different-coloured books into a reconstituted entity. Why it should be Saul Green rather than any of the other smug adulterers is not explained; but in Anna's masochistic neurosis, it may have been a question of quantity not quality. In other words, she needed to reach a certain number of men, to plumb a certain depth of humiliation, in order to 'break through' into a better existence; and Green, like all the other men, is just a tool.

And that is as close to a coherent explanation of Anna as I can come. There is some support from the text. 'I was a woman terribly vulnerable, critical, using femaleness as a sort of standard or yardstick to measure and discard men ... I was an Anna who invited defeat from men without being conscious of it'; or: 'It was easy to respond to the coldness, because it could not hurt me, like tenderness'; or, again: 'I was looking for men who would hurt me. I needed it.'

The most chilling thing about Anna is that even at her most demented she can relapse into conventional language. 'I am hopelessly in love with this man', she writes about Saul. But we know that Anna is not capable of love in the sense that Tess or Constance Chatterley or Sarah Miles might be – or in the sense that she is here using the word. She clings to the idea, though, not like a crazed veteran of some imagined war, but like a schoolgirl: 'I'd forgotten what it was like to be in love like this so that a step on the stair makes one's heart beat.' And here in the depth of her self-delusion one can, I think, find something vital in this character.

There are times when poor, muddled Anna appears to have been created by an anti-feminist campaigner – Kingsley Amis, perhaps, in mischief-making mood. However, a reader is as much caught in time as a writer, and everything that currently conspires against this novel will, presumably, change; so that future readers will bring different precon-ceptions from new cultural climates. If so, my guess is that the interest will not be in the area of feminism or the 'sex war' or of psychiatry, and certainly not of Communism. I think it may be read as a book about promiscuity. Anna Wulf may survive as an example of how not to conduct a sexual life. If Constance Chatterley shows how sex can open the door to love, Anna Wulf shows just how exceptional, and how fortunate, Connie was. In this light, Doris Lessing may then get more credit than she does now for having dived into the mid-century and, with whatever confused results, having emerged with a blood-spattered report from some of its battle lines.

'SHOCKINGLY UNCONDITIONAL'

NICK GUEST

The gay novels that began to come out, as it were, in the 1980s were of a different breed from their predecessors. Early twentieth-century examples, such as *The Well of Loneliness*, Radclyffe Hall's lesbian novel of 1928, or E. M. Forster's *Maurice* (begun in 1913) were soulful in tone but restrained in content. James Baldwin's *Giovanni's Room* was hot enough to be given by the politician Jeremy Thorpe to a boyfriend to put him in the mood for sex, but an atmosphere of sadness and frustration permeated most mainstream gay fictions. Forster was so anxious about the reception of *Maurice* that he refused to let it be published until after his death in 1971; Mary Renault did publish novels about intimate female friendships but more often found it easier to write about fifth-century BC male Greek warriors, whose bisexuality was an historical and 'acceptable' fact. Late in life she disavowed the gay rights movement.

The gay politics of the 1970s and the advent of the AIDS epidemic in the early 1980s made reticence seem pointless. For the first time, newspapers investigated the lives of gay men, chiefly in the United States, and any lingering idea of the vaudeville 'pansy' died with them; the gist of what emerged was that gay men were fitter, stronger and more virile than their heterosexual cousins, possessed of prodigious appetite and speed of recovery. Many of the anecdotal statistics (twelve – or was it sixteen – 'encounters' a night) almost defied belief, but were recorded with the solemnity of revisionist history.

Most of the new 'out' novels seemed more concerned to document the gay experience than to use the resources of the fictional form. Edmund White's *This Boy's Story* and *The Beautiful Room is Empty*, for instance, catalogued a life of continuous sexual encounters, though the people involved seemed little more than body parts with men's names attached. There seemed to be no attempt to develop character, theme or pattern, and White's contention that his main character was naturally blank because he needed the effects of 'gay lib' to define him did nothing to help the reader struggling to engage with a personality-free protagonist. Alan Hollinghurst's first novel, *The Swimming Pool Library*, published in 1988, seemed partly motivated by a similar documentary urge, though it showed some stylish comic touches and suggested that here was an author who might make something of the life-and-death issues that lay uncomfortably close behind the restless human urges, and that in the right hands the artistic possibilities of the novel might contain and shape the reportage, rather than be lost to it.

In Nick Guest, Hollinghurst found the character who could navigate the fine line between social comedy and terminal darkness, between the straight and gay worlds, between innocence and experience. Nick appears to have been shaped to a considerable extent by what the author needed his main character to be and do, but also, in his admittedly slight way, seems credible and fully realised. 'Characterisation' is not in fact the main strength of *The Line of Beauty*, a novel written on musical lines and more concerned with theme and orchestration than with depicting mental landscapes. There is little analysis of motive and almost no psychological explanation of why people are the way they are. The details that help fix and define the characters are few in number and often of a comic or physical kind, but they are precise and suggestive.

Nick is a shallow young man. His main interest is in atmosphere, surfaces and 'beauty' – especially as revealed to him through art and sex. When we first meet him, he is a virgin, come to lodge in a swanky house in West London with an old friend who, like him, has just left Oxford. He answers a small ad in a paper. As a result, he meets Leo, a keen bicyclist of West Indian parentage. After two drinks in a pub, Nick takes Leo into the bushes of a nearby communal garden and sodomises him. Not for Nick any virginal misfire or performance anxiety: he is a natural at sex, with a strong libido and socially at ease with his preferences – so much so that we do wonder slightly why he has waited till the first chapter of the novel to get started.

Wide-eyed Nick goes to parties in grand houses and snorts cocaine. He is a bit of a fibber and compromiser, but never in a serious way – only to remove some momentary friction from the charmed life that he and his friends are leading – 'Sometimes his memory of books he pretended to have read became almost as vivid as that of books he had read.' He is in love with the aching beauty of it all – the handsome boys, the lines of white powder, the classical music, grand architecture and the prose of Henry James. There is no real harm in him; there is only a semi-naïve enthusiasm for the world and its intense passing sensations. The house in which he lodges belongs to a bombastic Conservative MP called Gerald Fedden, who is also a devotee of pleasure, though in a more traditional way: through power and money, with sex a close third. He is, like Nick, relatively harmless – not without charm – and is amiably tolerant of Nick's presence in his house. In return for a free ride, Nick is always on hand as a social lubricant, defusing arguments, filling vacant seats at dinner and above all taking the tiresome daughter Catherine off her parents' hands.

Catherine is diagnosed 'bipolar', but also has the symptoms of spoiled rich-bitch syndrome. She drinks and smokes too much, has an awful photographer boyfriend (though she tells Nick, with characteristic candour and choice of words, that he is a 'blinding fuck') and then an even worse estate agent, who Nick, to his chagrin, silently lusts after. 'Cat' is selfish, impulsive, ill-read (she misses something by a 'hare's breath'), but, despite it all, rather charming. She sees through the pretensions of her family and their friends. She is the only character who is not calculating; she is perceptive and bracingly blunt. Her friendship with Nick is touching because they share many of the same hedonistic pleasures; but Cat's intolerance of the phoney throws an uneasy light on Nick's own obsession with fleeting 'beauty'. Surfaces may be beguiling, Cat's experience seems to say, but sometimes surfaces are just what they seem: superficial. Nick's story turns on this paradox, and at the end, he is caught by a mortal doubt.

First, though, there is Nick as a lover. When at the start of the book Cat tells Nick he is a snob, he replies, "'I'm not really,'" ... as if a small admission was the best kind of denial, "I just love beautiful things."' With its neat ironic turn, this is a typical Hollinghurst sentence – but an important one. It tells us almost all we need to know about Nick: 'beautiful things' are what he loves most. A few pages later: 'Nick's taste was for aesthetically radiant images of gay activity, gathering in a golden future for him, like swimmers on a sunlit bank.' Again, there is a mocking tone. Nick is inexperienced, the author tells us, but where's the harm in that? The first part of the book is called 'The Love-Chord' and when Nick goes on his first date to meet Leo, he thinks that 'his ambition was to be loved by a handsome black man in his late twenties with a racing bike'. However gently he does it, Hollinghurst seldom misses a chance to tease his boyish main character. When Nick hears that Leo is wearing his sister's shirt, 'that made him love him even more' and again, the word 'love' is being used playfully. On his second meeting with Leo, we are told that he 'wanted pure compliments, just as he wanted unconditional love', but there is room to doubt if he really wants anything of the sort.

The interesting thing about Nick is that he is both deceiving and deceived. He is sly and creatively dishonest, but partly because he does not quite understand the world, or his sudden arrival in its blissful mainstream. When someone apologises for having shocked him, '"Not at all," said Nick, to whom life was a series of shocks, more or less well mastered.' This is acute as well as funny, I think, because without his wide-eyed quality, Nick might seem predatory. He finds it difficult to differentiate between the new experiences he is having, while trying to place a relative *value* on them is far beyond his capabilities. The 'love-chord' itself turns out to be something Nick hears in his head when he is with Leo, but is unable to place. In a moment of panic he wonders whether in fact it was written by the despised Richard Strauss to illustrate 'some vulgar atrocity'. Soon he is 'in love [with Leo] to the point of idolatry', but the context in which this is revealed – on seeing Leo in his work clothes for the first time – is comic enough to cast doubt on the reality of the emotion invoked. The truth is that 'love' is to Nick an aesthetic experience, and a largely imagined one at that, on a par with listening to a Bach cantata on his 'sunlit bank'.

After Leo decides to cool the affair and to go his own way, Nick finds himself with Wani, a rich and glamorous Lebanese friend from Oxford he has previously thought out of his league. The 'love' word is again used from the beginning, though still attended by glimmers of irony: 'He wanted only love, and today perhaps a kind of obedience, from Wani.' In order not to alienate his rich and powerful father, Wani can't be open about his homosexuality; even in private he is cool towards Nick, as though he considers him a bit déclassé. Nick more than gets his own back when they are snorting coke upstairs at the Feddens' and hear Cat and her estate agent making love loudly next door. Turned on by the noise, they have sex themselves, but Nick fantasises that he is with Ronnie, a man they had once picked up at a swimming pool, so 'as Wani pulled out and Nick squeezed his eyes tight shut, it could almost have been Ronnie in front of him, instead of the man he loved'. We later learn that Nick has stopped telling Wani that he loves him 'because of the discomforting silence that followed when he did'. Whatever Nick feels for Leo and for Wani, it is not 'love' as Tess or Constance Chatterley understood it.

The book covers four years, from 1983 to 1987, the triumphant years of Thatcherism, from the afterglow of the Falklands campaign to the huge election victory, though it doesn't seek to make political capital of its own. Cat makes some studenty anti-Thatcher remarks and her boyfriend Jasper is an estate agent, a worn symbol of the new vulgarity. Gerald Fedden turns out to be a financial cheat as well as an adulterer, but Hollinghurst treats him almost as indulgently as he does Nick. In fact, Gerald and Nick are, in some deceitful ways, kindred spirits. The most abrasive character is a Tory MP called Barry Groom, the man who 'can't say hello'. Even here, Hollinghurst's interests are less political than comic: 'There was something so irksome about Barry Groom that he had a fascination: you longed for him to annoy you again.' If this novel was really the 'satire on Thatcherism' some reviewers found, it would be a pretty thin one, with its estate agents and MPs' insider dealing. The fact is that Nick couldn't care less about politics, and considers spoiling his ballot paper in the election. He, and his author, have grander things in mind.

In the final section of the book, Nick has a visit from Leo's sister Rosemary, who tells him Leo has died of AIDS and that she is tracing all his boyfriends. Nick reassures her that he is fine. 'I was lucky. And then I was ... careful.' As with most things Nick says, this is not entirely true. Hollinghurst handles the scene very lightly, however, like a composer merely hinting at the return of a major theme as the piece nears its end.

Scandals erupt, and Nick is evicted from his enchanted lodging. In two contrasting scenes, he fights to save his reputation. Cat's mother accuses him of neglecting Cat, but in doing so reveals that she herself doesn't know the name of the medication her daughter is on. Round one to Nick. But then Elena, the dignified housekeeper Nick believes he has always charmed, tells him that ever since he arrived she considered him 'sciocco'. Nick hopes she might mean 'a bit crazy'. But no: she means she always thought he was 'no good'. 'What praise more valuable than the praise of an intelligent servant?' Elizabeth Bennet wondered; and what criticism more damning?

When the end comes, it is with the sweep and crescendo of the full orchestra; you recognise the theme that has been hinted at, varied, and is now expounded in its melodic fullness. After saying goodbye to the dying Wani, Nick is going to have a further HIV test. 'It came over him that the test result would be positive.' He imagines how he will receive the news in the doctor's waiting room. 'He was young, without much training in stoicism.'

Throughout the book, Alan Hollinghurst presents Nick's strong sexual instincts as being congruent with his artistic preferences. The 'line of beauty' itself represents a Hogarthian aesthetic ideal visible to Nick in art, architecture, music and the shape of the male body. As a consequence of his aesthetic self-assurance, Nick has largely conquered his sense of surprise, to become blithe and integrated as a personality. The fact that Leo, his first love, and Wani, his second, both die of AIDS has done oddly little to disturb his serenity. The doubt that rises like an awful tide over the closing pages is this: were all the areas of appreciation and delight quite as similar as they seemed? Were they all equally valid? A man might die for love of another and not regret it; he might sell his soul for a Beethoven quartet. But if Nick's HIV test proves positive, as he fears, will he feel that he might be facing death for the wrong thing – a glimpse of thigh, not real 'love'; for a single issue of a 'style' magazine that he and Wani have finally put together rather than a Henry James masterpiece?

'It was a sort of terror, made up of emotions from every stage of his short life, weaning, homesickness, envy and self-pity; but he felt that the self-pity belonged to a larger pity. It was a love of the world that was shockingly unconditional.' So there is a twist within the twist. Perhaps, after all, it doesn't matter if the objects of his love were of different intrinsic value. Since nothing lasts, it is perhaps as good to die for something slight as for something profound; Oscar Wilde would probably have thought so. And that, in the final sentence, is revealed as the true nature of Nick's love: 'It wasn't just this street corner but the fact of a street corner at all that seemed, in the light of the moment, so beautiful.'

PART THREE

SNOBS

Snobbery is more than stuck-up people looking down their noses at someone they think is 'beneath' them; it's an anxiety that touches on the individual's sense of identity in relation to the society in which he or she lives. The novel has realistically direct access to the inner life; it can also convey economically the working of large social groups. More than any other literary form, it has examined the conflicts between these two worlds, inner and outer, and it's therefore not surprising that snobs in the widest sense of the word have been such a productive character type in the novel.

What makes snobbery fascinating to read about is, first, the simple comedy of self-delusion. What superficial trait or trick makes a person imagine he is 'better' than his neighbour? It's the pettiness of the defining distinction and the absurd tangles into which snobbery leads its sufferers that are enjoyable to witness. But there's a more serious side to it as well. To be concerned about where you stand is not necessarily a character flaw. It's difficult, for instance, to imagine that a fully integrated and un-snobbish member of any society could have reached that happy state without at least having considered his position in relation to others. Could you even be thoughtful or generous if you had never thought about how you compare to other people? Can you honestly be immune to snobbery if you have never had a dose of it?

Snobbery is the diseased twin of a healthy impulse. There are many ways of defining the nature of the sickness. You could say that it's normal to chart your position horizontally among family and friends and society, but that a snob wants also to place himself vertically in an imagined hierarchy. Or, in a recent book called *Status Anxiety*, Alain de Botton defined modern snobbery as a kind of 'synecdoche' – the grammatical term in which the part is taken for the whole. Work is an example. So when the first thing someone tells you is that they are a lawyer, a nurse, a shopworker or a violinist the snob may immediately place them on a rung in his imagined structure without finding out any more about their personal qualities or experiences. In his mind, there would be no distinctions within the nurse category; so Florence Nightingale and an unhygienic, thieving auxiliary would to him be indistinguishable. It needn't even be something as defining as a job; it could be people with hair over their ears, or goatee beards or Midlands accents (so Shakespeare, for one, would lose out on all three counts).

I prefer to think of snobbery as a kind of astigmatism or focussing defect. We tend to dismiss snobs as by definition stupid, but this is not necessarily true, as the following fictional characters may show. Snobs may in fact have insight and knowledge; they may be unusually curious and have plenty of information about other people; but an inability to focus on what matters – to see the shape of the spinney not the texture of the bark on a single tree in front of you – means they are prone to catastrophic errors of judgement. And while such errors may be comic in their first presentation, leading to a humiliation of the snob, they can also be wounding in their effect; they can ruin lives.

*

Good novelists know and exploit all the paradoxes of the condition. Few people, I imagine, would disagree that Charles Dickens and Jane Austen are the two greatest British novelists of the nineteenth century; and I think it's interesting that *Great Expectations* and *Emma*, which many would take to be their most flawless books, both have a snob at their heart. The way that Pip and Emma misunderstand themselves and other people allows their authors not only to map a journey of each one's moral education – comic, embarrassing and moving by turns – but to give a nuanced picture of the society they inhabit. The bright but intermittently false vision of the main characters allows the authors to give added texture to the social picture. The law-abiding and respectable world of the Kent marshes and the coexistent world of crime and degradation are made to seem more real and more overlapping by Pip's uncertain grasp of the distinction. The subtleties of Highbury society in *Emma*, part hierarchical and part ethical, are clearer to us for the fact that the main character ricochets among their representatives like the 'he' in a game of blind man's buff.

It is the same with the characters whose lives they affect. Joe Gargery lives on in our minds not through his personal qualities (great though they are), but through the way that he is alternately illuminated, obscured, valued and betrayed by the unreliable focus of Pip's understanding. Emma's prolonged refusal to see clearly what is in front of her brings Mr Knightley almost to his knees in frustration – a state of humbled anguish that enables him to complete his own sentimental education.

As you can see, this is a long way from *Noblesse Oblige*, Nancy Mitford's and Evelyn Waugh's admittedly playful but ultimately silly essay on whether you should say 'napkin' or 'serviette'. Snobbery in the hands of a good novelist can be more interesting than that – also more various. Mr Pooter in *The Diary of a Nobody* is a classic snob, in that his vision is defective. So anxious is he to cling on to the position of respectability to which he somehow ascended, so hypersensitive is he to imagined slights and to threats, that he is blind to a simple and overwhelming fact: that he is happy. Such a flaw is potentially the terrain of tragedy, but luckily for us George Grossmith wrote for *Punch* and wanted a happy ending, so Pooter's vision is allowed to self-correct, and the scales almost literally fall from his eyes.

Jean Brodie, on the other hand, is not allowed to reach any sort of self-knowledge; indeed she never even finds out the identity of which girl 'betrayed' her. Her snobbery is cultural, but it is symptomatic of a deep dishonesty in her character. Her lack of vision, unlike Emma's or Pooter's, is consciously indulged, and that is the justification – at least in the religious scheme that lowers over the book like Edinburgh drizzle – for her harsh treatment at the hands of the author.

In James Bond we see the beginnings of a snobbery of brand and manufacture that has proved resilient now for more than fifty years – for all that other writers have pitilessly sent it up. Snobbery is, like all viruses, adept at mutation. It has proved itself a great survivor, going underground for decades at a time, then re-emerging in some new, infectious form. There are, as we shall see, extenuating circumstances for Bond's connoisseur snobbery, but none for the writers who plodded along with their designer luggage in Fleming's footsteps. And finally there is Chanu Ahmed, an intellectual snob who, by a nice irony, is exactly the kind of person most intellectual snobs look down on. Monica Ali's achievement is to use Chanu's astigmatic reading of his place in the world as a way into examining not only the experience of immigration, but abiding questions of identity, love and self-delusion. Chanu's London life is one that Dickens would have recognised.

Of the four character types looked at here, the snob is the one that passes into books least mediated or altered from life and has paid the greatest dividends to his author–investors. The snob and the mainstream novel could almost have been made for one another.

'NONSENSICAL GIRL'

EMMA WOODHOUSE

The trouble with Emma is that she has had things rather too much her own way; the trouble with *Emma* is that it's a novel of such scintillating brilliance, and so quick on its feet, that anything a reader can say about it seems doomed to bathos. If you were to hear the Amadeus Quartet playing Mozart on a summer evening in the Hall of Mirrors at Versailles with your lover on your arm and a glass of Bollinger 1990 fizzing on your tongue, it would probably be vain to try to put the sensations into words.

Emma Woodhouse is a character fortunate enough to inhabit a fictional world that has perhaps never been surpassed as a mechanism for revealing the self-deceits, hopes and passions of its human inhabitants. Perhaps its closest corollary would be in drama – *A Midsummer Night's Dream*. The plot of *Emma*, which goes round in concentric circles, appears, despite its moments of confrontation, almost frictionless; it is as though Jane Austen had discovered the secret of perpetual fictional motion, and the reader might join the story at almost any point, or return at some time in the future to find it still dizzily revolving.

Much of the kinetic energy is supplied by Emma herself, instigator and observer of almost all the action. Emma is naughty, but we don't seem to mind. She has lost her mother so long ago that she can barely remember her, and we grant her some indulgence for this loss, especially when we see how tolerant she is towards her selfish father. A good daughter, then, and someone interested in the well-being of others: it's Emma, as she's keen to point out, who has set up the happy match between her old governess Miss Taylor and the kind widower Mr Weston. Emma is 'handsome', we learn, in the third word of the book, and Jane Austen gives the reader an idea of the effect that her beauty has on others by allowing us to overhear Mr Knightley and Mrs Weston discussing it. 'Considering how very handsome she is, she appears to be little occupied with it', the austere Mr Knightley concedes. So Emma is lacking in vanity as well as being, according to Mrs Weston, 'loveliness itself'. When she takes up the case of pretty Harriet Smith, the illegitimate child of someone or other who lives as a parlour-boarder at a school in the village, she shows no sense of competition with Harriet. So far there is nothing in Emma to dislike, though a few authorial hints and some grave words from Mr Knightley suggest that trouble lies ahead.

The problem declares itself when Emma talks about Harriet's liaison with a tenant farmer called Robert Martin. 'The yeomanry are precisely the order of people with whom I feel I can have nothing to do', says Emma, and we flinch at this snobbishness. Yet there is some logic to it. Emma sees herself, accurately, as a woman of leisure who should devote herself to helping others, either the poor or her friends. The yeomen farmers can look after themselves and would be patronised by her interference;

and if she is snobbish towards Robert Martin, her intention of 'improving' Harriet by marriage shows a rather fine disdain for hierarchy.

Mr Knightley tells her that she is quite wrong about the relative social standings of the two people and that a yeoman farmer easily outranks a penniless illegitimate. He also pleads Martin's good sense against Harriet's silliness, but is happy to conduct the main part of the battle on the grounds of social status alone. They agree to differ, though the argument leaves Emma feeling the more shaken of the two: 'She did not always feel so absolutely satisfied with herself, so entirely convinced that her opinions were right ... as Mr Knightley.' This is one of many silky touches with which Jane Austen lets us see that it is not only Emma whose character needs work.

Perhaps it's not snobbery that's so much Emma's problem as immaturity. She is 'not quite one and twenty' and is reluctant to accept the constraints of womanhood. She wants one last go in the playroom of childhood and is using her status and charm for self-indulgent purposes. There is also the question of the books Emma hasn't read. She has made many nicely organised lists, but hasn't actually opened or digested the books themselves; she lacks self-discipline. Emma stops her ears to the voices of the adults, but it seems hard to begrudge a motherless girl with the burden of a sickly father this one last chance of fun. Like the rest of us, she will be grown up for quite long enough.

The problem lies, as problems do, in the feelings of others: in the harm her games might do. Robert Martin is cast down when the woman he loves rejects him. Emma, meanwhile, encourages Harriet Smith to set her cap at the new vicar, Mr Elton. In an almost farcical sequence of events, Mr Elton misunderstands and thinks it is Emma herself who is interested in him. Even after she has painfully disabused him, Emma is reluctant to take stock of herself properly. Mr Elton is a shallow man, so his discomfort is not be taken as seriously as Robert Martin's; he does not love Emma and she feels that she 'need not trouble herself to pity him'; but she ought by now to suspect that there is something wrong with her understanding of other people.

In a passage that shows how much remains for Emma to understand, she reflects on Mr Elton's hubris in even thinking he might win her hand, when the Woodhouses are clearly the second most important family in Highbury 'whose fortune ... was such as to make them scarcely second-ary to Donwell Abbey [Mr Knightley's house] itself', while the wretched Mr Elton has no connections at all, except in 'trade'. This snobbish little aria is followed by a genuine contrition about how wrong she has been to raise Harriet's hopes; so we see the superficial and the admirable aspects of Emma side by side. Contrition and regret, which usually play a second-ary part in the emotional landscape of a novel, after the primaries of love, lust, anger and so on, are among the strongest passions in *Emma*, and this is one of the reasons why it is emotionally so interesting.

At this stage, the different parts of Emma's judgement are not inte-grated. She is not altogether wrong about Mr Elton: he would be a hopeless husband for her. But she is right for the wrong reasons. It's not because he is vulgar that Mr Elton is a bad match for Emma; it's because he's vain (later also cruel) and because she doesn't like him. Emma's snobbery is a synecdoche: she takes the part for the whole, so that vulgarity and bad connections are all she can see of Mr Elton. Her understanding of herself is similarly afflicted: she considers herself 'above' Elton without understand-ing that the obligation of her own status is that she must either marry a social equal or throw out the idea of hierarchy and marry for love alone.

One of the subtleties of *Emma* is that neither Emma Woodhouse nor Jane Austen ever abandons the idea that social status does matter; the plot development of the book tends to show that it matters very much indeed and, for all Emma's attempts at social engineering, is not easily modified. Emma's task is to find a way of integrating respect for social rank into an emotional and moral framework where it can take its proper – which is to say, significant but not primary – place. And that is easier said than done – in anyone's life, let alone the life of a high-spirited young woman, rather spoiled, determined to keep hold of her girlhood for a while longer.

Emma's solution for the time being is to deny that there is any problem that needs to be solved. Her pride and her playfulness are crystallised when Harriet wonders why Emma is not married. 'I must see somebody very superior to any one I have seen yet, to be tempted,' says Emma. 'I would rather not be tempted. I cannot really change for the better. If I were to marry, I must expect to repent it.' These are the words of a young woman in denial, but they are not necessarily the words of a bad person. They have the effect less of making one dismissive of Emma than fearful for her well-being, because such self-deceit in a beautiful and rich young woman must make her vulnerable to those more clear-sighted than herself. A person of lesser qualities than Emma, but with a cannier awareness of how things are, could take advantage of her.

When Frank Churchill, Mrs Weston's stepson, arrives in Highbury, our anxiety intensifies. Frank is dashing but clearly unreliable; we know this because he is too fond of dancing and goes up to London merely to get his hair cut (though he has also gone to buy a piano for Jane Fairfax, it later transpires). Yet at the same time that we fear for its outcome, we don't mind Emma having a flirtation with Frank; it might do her good. It's similar to Elizabeth Bennet's dalliance with Wickham in *Pride and Prejudice*; while it's pleasantly dangerous to our heroine, we back her intelligence and self-control to win the day and see off any young peacock. For a high-spirited girl who spends most of her time looking after her widowed father, Frank Churchill seems a harmless indulgence; and after the Elton–Harriet debacle, Emma climbs back a little in our esteem. She is not too lofty to play the game – even if it turns out that she is in fact being used by Frank as a decoy in his pursuit of Jane.

Her next problem is Jane Fairfax, an alarmingly beautiful but penniless orphan of middle-class origins. Emma just doesn't like her. She can't really say why not – though Mr Knightley obliges, as he often does: in this case by suggesting that it's because Emma is jealous of Jane, seeing in her the 'accomplished young woman that she wanted to be thought herself'. Mr Knightley is an exasperating man, so quick to chastise this motherless child sixteen years his junior, so slow to question his own judgements, and, in the case of his hostility to Frank Churchill, almost as deficient in self-knowledge as Emma herself. The tiffs between Emma and Mr Knightley are full of social and erotic tensions. Emma is a cleverer and more interesting person than Knightley, with access to a dynamic range of thought and feeling beyond his scope; when she is his age, she will be as wise as he is, but more engaged with life. For the time being, he uses his advantages of age and fractionally superior station in life to bully Emma, and the odd thing is that she does not really object. What makes the scenes between them so uneasy, so tense, is that they operate on so many levels. The reader has been made aware that Mr Knightley loves Emma, even if he barely knows it himself; we see that she respects him and, for all his crustiness, likes him as an old friend. Both are so aware of their relative social positions that they are to some extent prisoners of a sort of class destiny; a strong centripetal force is pushing them together, and that force is stronger at this stage than their personal feelings. The key element, though, is time. Knightley will not always be able to exploit his superior maturity. Emma needs to grow up, to become a woman and unite the different parts of her judgement and personality; Knightley needs to recognise the limitations of his self-satisfaction and confess the causes of his jealousy. But his window of opportunity is small. In order to clinch the deal – to win Emma – he will need to catch her when she has just grown into him but before she grows out of him. It is highly delicate.

When a piano arrives for Jane from an unknown donor, there is speculation that Mr Knightley has sent it. Emma dismisses the idea that he might secretly admire Jane, let alone to the point of planning to marry her. It offends Emma's ideas of social propriety (she calls it 'shameful and degrading') that the master of Donwell Abbey should consider allying himself – through marriage to Jane – to Miss Bates, the village chatterbox. It would also mean that Emma's nephew, Henry, son of her sister Isabella and Mr Knightley's younger brother, would no longer stand to inherit Donwell. All this – but nothing else – makes such an alliance unthinkable to Emma. Or so, at least, we are told; we are free to think that Emma's indignation is synthetic and that there is another reason why she recoils from the match.

One of the reasons we can forgive Emma for such a dislikeable thing as snobbery is that Jane Austen makes us complicit in the humour – the fun, even – of being snobbish. Looking down your nose at Robert Martin, the salt of the earth, is bad; but looking down your nose at Mrs Elton, the vicar's new wife, is not only amusing but seems the right thing to do.

There are some individuals in life whom everyone else feels entitled to laugh at, and those are people who gives themselves airs and put on genteel voices which, far from impressing others, merely reveal the ignorance and vulgarity of the speaker. Think of Linda Snell in *The Archers*. She turns out to have a good heart, but her bogus voice is a licence for her to be mocked. And in real life, or on television, there are people who try to seem refined and all-knowing, but whose phoney vowels and mispronunciations reveal their ignorance. Such people seem fair game, because by their pretensions they have forfeited their right to normal kindness. Mrs Elton is an example, with her would-be posh friends offstage in Maple Grove, her 'barouche-landau' (some sort of nouveau riche carriage, the Chelsea Tractor of its day) and the way she refers to her husband as 'Mr E' or her '*caro sposo*'. It would be wrong, Jane Austen implies, not to feel snobbish towards such a person, who is anyway quite able to look after herself; and the case of Mrs Elton acts as an extenuation for some of Emma's less acceptable snobbery – not least because Emma's own summation of Mrs Elton's character on their first meeting is incisive and truthful, needing only playful variation from Jane Austen's and other points of view in subsequent scenes.

In the potent cocktail of Emma Woodhouse's character, where faults can be glossed as oversights and misjudgement forgiven as impatience, there is another double-edged quality, and that is her eloquence. In an apparently trivial interchange, Mr Knightley's younger brother John, who is to deposit his two sons for a short stay with their aunt Emma, teases her that her social life has recently become so busy that she may not have time for the boys. Mr Knightley senior cuts in to say that the boys can easily come to Donwell if that would be easier. Emma stands between the brothers and plays one against the other, mocking both of them, and herself. She concludes, turning to Mr Knightley senior:

But you … who know how very, very seldom I am ever two hours from Hartfield, why you should foresee such a series of dissipation for me, I cannot imagine. And as to my dear little boys, I must say, that if aunt Emma has not time for them, I do not think they would fare much better with uncle Knightley, who is absent from home about five hours where she is absent one – and who, when he is at home, is either reading to himself or settling his accounts.

You can't command such eloquence without having access to a properly ordered mind. Emma's task is to make such access not intermittent, granted under the pressure of high spirits, but a permanent and defining aspect of her character.

In the third and final volume of *Emma*, the reader's fears for the heroine intensify. She notes that Frank Churchill seems less interested in her but ascribes this to his not being able to trust himself in her company. She is labile. Self-knowledge is beginning to dawn, but piecemeal, and with the potential for embarrassment or worse. When Mrs Elton's married status gives her precedence to Emma at the dance, 'it was almost enough to make her think of marrying'. Her mind is ajar. At the same time, she has her most friendly exchange yet with Mr Knightley, when she admits that he saw through Mr Elton before she did, and Mr Knightley for the first time acknowledges faults in his own powers of perception by admitting that Emma saw qualities in Harriet that he did not. They seal their new harmony with a dance, she hoping that they are not too much brother and sister for a dance to seem improper and he exclaiming, 'Brother and sister! No, indeed.'

Mr Knightley's self-deception is well on the way to being cured ('Nonsensical girl!' he calls Emma dotingly) and this grants him sleuth-like powers of observation. While Emma is toying with the idea that she could now match-make Harriet with Frank Churchill, Mr Knightley has somehow divined that Frank's real interest lies not in Emma, with whom his flirtation has been a screen or diversion, and certainly not with Harriet Smith, but has all along been in Jane Fairfax.

Emma, meanwhile, is ticking like an unexploded bomb. She visits Mr Knightley's splendid Donwell Abbey, rather as Elizabeth Bennet visits Darcy's Pemberley, but instead of thinking how well the house would suit her, she thinks only how much her nephew Henry will enjoy it. While increasing the tension, Jane Austen is pushing at the edge of the reader's credulity here: would any young woman truly not picture herself, just for a moment, as the mistress of such a house? The explosion duly comes at the famous picnic on Box Hill, when Emma jokingly insults the talkative Miss Bates and is reproved by Mr Knightley for thoughtlessness towards a poor spinster. Emma is mortified – 'vexed beyond what could have been expressed – almost beyond what she could conceal'. From this moment, what Mr Knightley calls her 'serious spirit' rather than her 'vain spirit' begins to dominate. When she hears news of Frank Churchill's secret engagement to Jane Fairfax, she chastises herself for having once again raised Harriet's hope in vain.

Then in a sudden volte-face, she is freed of her guilt – but dropped into something worse. Harriet had never understood that she was being ushered towards Frank; she had thought Emma was steering her towards Mr Knightley. The revelation breaks down all the walls in Emma's mind that have kept the 'serious' and 'vain', the intelligent and the snobbish compartments separated. 'A few minutes were sufficient for making her acquainted with her own heart … It darted through her, with the speed of an arrow, that Mr Knightley must marry nobody but herself!' She has become a woman. For Emma, it is a moment of empowerment – though also of trepidation, lest she is already too late; for the reader it is a joy and a relief, though also of course a sadness – the sadness that the youth of this flawed but wonderfully high-spirited girl is now over.

The warmth of Emma's remorse is deeply moving. No enemy could be more critical of her foolishness than she herself is. When at last she is alone with Mr Knightley again, we see, for the first time, the light of a sincere and desperate humility behind her words. And in what Mr Knightley himself says, Jane Austen lets us see, without describing them, the agonies he has endured since Box Hill, wondering if his blunt and bullying reproof has gone too far, if his pomposity and candour have dowsed the flame of love in Emma at the moment it flickered into being.

He rises to the occasion. 'If I loved you less, I might be able to talk about it more … I have blamed you, and lectured you, and you have borne it as no other woman in England would have borne it.' This is to my mind the most moving scene that Jane Austen ever wrote, and it is Mr Knightley's humble recognition of his own failings as well as of Emma's life-giving qualities that make it so. He has earned the right to love her and to be loved by her in return.

I closed this book with red and swollen eyes as I first closed it forty years ago. Nothing made by humans can be perfect, but surely *Emma* comes as close as any novel in English. Is there no flaw in this dazzling, Mozartian performance? Well, I suppose we might wish that 'liveliness' – the quality that Jane Austen so admires in her heroines – was not so much distrusted by her when it appears in men; we might think wistfully that Mr Knightley could do with a touch of Frank Churchill in his make-up, rather

as Edmund Bertram in *Mansfield Park* might profit from a hint of Henry
Crawford, and Darcy in *Pride and Prejudice* from a dose of Wickham …
But then again you might wonder whether the second violin needed a
semitone tweak at one moment in the Allegro in the Hall of Mirrors at
Versailles, or that the champagne was one degree too cold … And I'm not
sure that in the face of such rare happiness these are profitable thoughts.

'The wedding was very much like other weddings.'
– Emma marries Mr Knightley (1815 edition)

'A COMMON
LABOURING-BOY'

PIP

The story of *Great Expectations* (1861) is an upsetting one because it seems to lack a sense of fairness. It introduces us to Philip Pirrip, known as Pip, a village boy of the Kent marshes and, almost before we have come to know him and to take his side, it turns against him. A large sum of money from an unknown benefactor takes Pip from his simple home and thrusts him into London society, where he is all at sea. An embittered old woman trains a beautiful girl to break his heart.

Pip's worst enemies, however, are closer to home. They are, first, himself when older – the adult Pip who tells the story with a pitiless self-criticism – and, second, the author, who seems unwilling to extend his characteristic generosity of spirit to Pip's faults of snobbery and forget-fulness of old friends; neither narrator nor author seems able to admit that most people would have done little better than Pip. Into this vacuum of sympathy, the reader feels compelled to step. The young Pip we meet in the opening chapters is a lovable boy, and it apparently falls to us to keep the flame of his remembered goodness alive through everything that he, his author, accident and other characters can throw at him. It is a burdensome, at times dispiriting, responsibility.

It's important for us to be certain that the young Pip is worth fighting for. He is curious, we notice; he wants to know what 'There's another conwict off' means; there are signs that he is cleverer at his letters than Joe, his blacksmith brother-in-law (who isn't?), though not as good as Biddy, the village girl who becomes a schoolmistress. He suffers at the hands of his violent sister, Mrs Joe, but has developed a sort of stoicism and is affectionate towards Joe. He has a sense of tact in dealing with Magwitch, the escaped convict, managing not to use the word 'leg-iron', but saying only that a second convict has 'the same reason for wanting to borrow a file'. His most endearing quality as a child is that he is not ambitious; he loves Joe and sees no need for anything more. Like most children, he finds his life is governed by fear of the unknown as much as by love of what is most near or dear: Joe, the forge, the marshes.

The most significant moment in fixing the young Pip in our mind and in our affections comes when Joe explains why he doesn't rebel against Mrs Joe, his abusive wife: he has no wish for her to have to struggle, as his own mother did. Pip says: 'Young as I was, I believe that I dated a new admiration of Joe from that night. We were equals afterwards, as we had been before; but, afterwards at quiet times when I sat looking at Joe and thinking about him, I had a new sensation of feeling conscious that I was looking up to him in my heart.'

There is here a sense of moral order that overrides all social distinctions, and a clarity of judgement: the young Pip 'looks up' to the illiterate blacksmith, and rightly so. Only a child of naturally good judgement could have had this thought, and we can be sure that it was contemporaneous because Pip-as-narrator is a critic of, never an apologist for, his younger self. Touchingly expressed, it stays in the background of the book as a kind of lost touchstone that Pip must somehow find again.

When Pip is sent to play at Miss Havisham's and has his manners criticised by the chilly Estella, his reaction is to inspect the hands and boots that she has mocked. 'They had never troubled me before, but they troubled me now, as vulgar appendages.' The second half of the sentence shows how immediately Pip is affected by what he hears; but the first confirms what we need to have reaffirmed: that he had previously been unaware of such things.

Pip-as-narrator attributes his extreme reaction to Estella's mockery to the fact that his whole life thus far had been a 'perpetual conflict with injustice' – with his sister's unreasonable moods and violent thrashings. It now occurs to the young Pip that not only has he been brought up cruelly, he has also been brought up ignorantly. He walks the four miles home, reflecting that 'I was a common labouring-boy; that my hands were coarse, that my boots were thick; that I had fallen into the despicable habit of calling knaves Jacks; that I was much more ignorant than I had considered myself last night, and generally that I was in a low-lived bad way.'

The odd thing is that we as readers find this more heart-rending than Pip in retrospect appears to. There is a degree of irony in the older Pip's narrative detachment that intensifies our sense of protectiveness towards the child he was. This is a boy against whom the world is conspiring cruelly, and while this injustice makes it painful to read it also makes it thrilling. Within the first sixty pages, Dickens has presented three of the greatest scenes in Victorian literature: Magwitch and Pip in the graveyard; the Christmas dinner and the convict chase across the marshes; Pip's first visit to Miss Havisham and his meeting with Estella. It is a rare moment in a novel when the reader thinks that on balance he might prefer the next scene to be slightly less overpoweringly brilliant; something that would not sear itself for ever into the memory might instead be welcome – a little domestic development, perhaps; a comedy visit from a distant cousin; or the passage of a few uneventful months plainly recapitulated …

In a way, our wish is answered – most of the other unforgettable scenes of *Great Expectations* will be towards the end – but there is little remission of the pain we are required to undergo. This is a relatively short novel by Dickens's standards, and thematically it is tightly focussed. The conflicting claims of status and of home pull Pip this way and that on almost every page. When he asks Joe whether he is 'common' or not, Joe understands the word in a different, and purer, context. 'And as to being common, I don't make it out at all clear. You are oncommon in some things. You're oncommon small. Likewise you're a oncommon scholar.'

Pip is assailed by another, related fear. He is not merely frightened of appearing socially inadequate; he is worried that he has become, by his chance meeting with Magwitch, the escaped convict, a criminal by association. After he steals a file and a pie for Magwitch, he dreams that cows pursue him and denounce him as a thief. He feels he is an imposter before he becomes one. In Pip's mind the idea that he is not a 'gentleman' is entangled with a boyish fear of being exposed as a bad'un and a fraud. One reason that he is so susceptible to snobbery, so keen to 'improve' himself socially, is to rid himself of this fear of crime and prison, to make himself in some way unimpeachable. Yet through the pages of the novel a sort of shadow world

'Bullying, old' Mr Pumblechook and Mrs Joe quiz Pip about
his day with Miss Havisham (*Harper's Weekly*, 1860)

stalks him. Not only do the cows pursue him, but a wandering character called Orlick comes to the forge and seems to be Pip's evil twin, a lesson in what happens to people who up sticks and stray from their village. In the local inn, the Three Jolly Bargemen, Pip meets a 'strange gentleman' who gives him two pound notes, an incident which increases his sense of being unworthy and reminds him that he is on 'secret terms of conspiracy with convicts – a feature in my low career that I had previously forgotten'. With a narrative sleight of hand, Dickens lets the two fears bleed into one another. Pip is afraid not just of being eaten alive by the fiendish 'young man' Magwitch refers to; he is worried that having kept low company will disqualify him from Estella's love. 'What I dreaded was, that in some unlucky hour I, being at my grimiest and commonest, should lift up my eyes and see Estella looking in at one of the wooden windows of the forge. I was haunted by the fear that she would, sooner or later, find me out'. When Estella does let him kiss her, 'I felt that the kiss was given to the coarse common boy as a piece of money might have been, and that it was worth nothing.'

So confused and overwhelmed is Pip that finally he commits the sin of being ashamed of Joe when he dresses in his Sunday best to take him to play at Miss Havisham's. At the end of a harrowing day, Pip knows that his life is spoiled beyond redemption. 'Finally, I remember that when I got into my little bedroom I was truly wretched, and had a strong conviction on me that I should never like Joe's trade. I had liked it once, but once was not now … It is a most miserable thing to be ashamed of home. There may be black ingratitude in the thing, and the punishment may be retributive and well deserved; but, that it is a miserable thing, I can testify.' As an adult, looking back, Pip stresses the 'black ingratitude'; and it's left to us to feel the misery.

No wonder that when Mr Jaggers, the lawyer, arrives from London, bringing wealth and a means of escape, Pip will greedily accept the offer.

His awful exchange with Biddy – 'If only I could get myself to fall in love with you' – follows his revelation to her that he wants to become a 'gentleman' to make himself worthy of Estella. Pip is a snob in embryo before the money comes from Jaggers, and his treatment of Biddy as he prepares to leave for London shows him at his worst. The fact that Pip-as-narrator piles on the scorn for his younger self does not help at all; this is one of the most agonising passages to read in an altogether painful book. The end of the first part is almost unreadable, as Pip, walking alone on the road to the London coach, stops and breaks down. 'Heaven knows we need never be ashamed of our tears, for they are rain upon the blinding dust of earth, overlaying our hard hearts … If I had cried before, I should have had Joe with me then.' The worst thing is that we feel that this unhappy situation is not really Pip's fault.

Joe famously comes to visit Pip in his smart London lodgings, and Pip admits that 'If I could have kept him away by paying money, I certainly would have paid money.' He consoles himself with the thought that at least Joe will be seen only by friendly Herbert Pocket, who shares his rooms, and not by the odious Bentley Drummle, his rival for Estella. 'So,' he concludes, 'throughout life, our worst weaknesses and meannesses are usually committed for the sake of the people whom we most despise.' While acute and painful, this reflection of Pip-as-narrator is not fair. Pip does not commit a meanness to Joe by seeing him at one place rather than another; it is in fact Joe, through a letter written by Biddy, who has chosen the meeting place, and of course he wants to see Pip in his new home. The most shameful part of the incident is Biddy's letter, which silently reveals that Pip has not written home in all his time in London. Joe makes a fool of himself in Pip's rooms and Pip is mortified. But which of us has never been ashamed of a relation – a parent at a teenage party, a bigoted aunt or gauche sibling? When Pip's embarrass-ment has subsided he does run out and scour the neighbouring streets for Joe; but Joe has gone. The most interesting aspect of this famous scene is that we can see that Pip-as-narrator is actually unfair to Pip-as-character; what he asks us to see is not what is before our eyes, and consequently we feel the need to increase our emotional investment in defence of Pip.

On his return home, Pip finds himself on the same coach as two convicts, one of whom is the man who unaccountably gave him two pound notes in the Three Jolly Bargemen. He does not recognise the grown-up Pip, but Pip overhears him tell the other that the notes were given him by Magwitch to pass on to the boy who'd brought him the file and the pie. Far from wondering at this act of beneficence, Pip simply shrinks from the convict's closeness. 'It is impossible to express with what acuteness I felt the convict's breathing, not only on the back of my head, but all along my spine.' At home, he sees Estella, who is unimpressed by his new status, though tells him, 'I have not bestowed my tenderness anywhere. I never had any such thing.' In town he is mocked for his new airs and graces by the formerly sullen tailor's assistant; the other townspeople are taken in by Pip's fine clothes, but Trabb's boy can see at once that he has not become a gentleman, merely an imposter. Unhappily, he returns to London without even seeing Joe, though 'As soon as I arrived, I sent a penitential cod-fish and barrel of oysters to Joe (as reparation for not having gone myself).'

When Mrs Joe dies and Pip returns for the funeral, there is another excruciating scene with Biddy. Although he does manage to see Joe this time and even sleeps at the forge, Pip comments that Joe 'was much pleased by my asking if I might sleep in my own little room, and I was rather pleased too; for I felt that I had done rather a great thing in making the request'. By this stage, the weight of liking someone who does not like himself is becoming almost intolerable for the reader; we look for help increasingly to Herbert Pocket, a good if feckless young man who clearly does like Pip (he gives him a nickname, which is usually a sign of affection), and Mr Wemmick, a shrewd and loving man who also has time for him. The one person we are missing in our support team is Pip's as yet undeclared bene- factor, the man or woman whose gifts of money have been more curse than blessing but who at least must have the highest possible opinion of our man.

It is difficult to write interestingly about Dickens. Sometimes it's hard to think of much to say beyond, 'Isn't this unbelievably good?' Jane Austen's formal ambiguities always seem to yield something interesting, even to an A level student, but Dickens's effects sometimes seem inexplicable or other- worldly. We know that *David Copperfield* was his favourite of his books and the most autobiographical; we know there was a boy at the blacking factory called Bob Fagin; we know that William Dorrit was modelled on his own father, a debtor in the Marshalsea prison; but most of the time you wonder when you look at Dickens's novels: where did these things – these *people* – come from? What fever threw up the idea of Miss Havisham in his mind, what restless night gave him Magwitch springing out from behind a headstone? From what void did he pluck these fully imagined creatures, then make it seem by the conviction of his writing that we had always known them?

And what an extraordinary novel *Great Expectations* is, so powerfully confident from its opening sentence, so swift and sure; it has all the char- acteristics of Dickens's genius, yet displayed with almost disdainful ease. Scenes around which other novelists might have built a hundred pages are slotted precisely into the story and made to work their passage in both narrative and symbolic terms; the characters inhabit a strange hinterland between archetype and realism, forcefully alive, always believable, yet fraught with the menace of a dream. Miss Havisham, Magwitch, Estella, Joe Gargery ... it seems hard to picture the year 1859, a world in which these people did not exist. The secondary characters, Mrs Joe, Biddy, Jaggers and Wemmick, are all organically connected to the main plot; the minor, comic characters such as Mr Pumblechook, Trabb the tailor and Mr Wopsle don't outstay their welcome; the whole book has a remorseless onward drive.

Structurally, it works on all levels. The opening scene in the churchyard remains of primary importance to the plot, and Magwitch is reintroduced at the moment that his appearance can have maximum impact. On a stormy night he climbs the stairs to the twenty-three-year-old Pip's rooms in the Temple. 'I could not recall a single feature, but I knew him! If the wind and the rain had driven away the intervening years, had scattered all the intervening objects, had swept us to the churchyard where we first stood face to face on such different levels, I could not have known my convict more distinctly than I knew him now, as he sat in the chair before the fire.' No other English novelist has been able to make dramatic incident work for him in this way; no one else has been able to remove the ground beneath the reader's feet so that he feels himself falling through time. No other writer has orchestrated plot and symbol with quite such a sure symphonic touch; and while this is partly because Dickens has a grander architecture in mind than his fellow novelists, it is also because he always seems able to find a rhythm in the prose to make these effects work. In the first sentence, the exclamation mark, disdained by prose purists, goes through you like an electric shock. In the second sentence, the rhetorical triple condition is like a crescendo roll of the tympani, yet the climactic revelation of identity is couched in a negative ('could not have known'), while the word 'convict' is hidden deep inside the sentence so that the climax hits our ear not as a triumphant or assertive brass note but as strings remembered from an earlier movement might sound, with a subtler, troubling reconnection that asserts something inevitable; and the sentence ends, as such sentences in Dickens almost always do, with a domestic diminuendo that anchors it in reality. He uses the same ending in the drowning of Steerforth in *David Copperfield*: 'I saw him lying with his head upon his arm, as I had often seen him lie at school'. The key word in the Magwitch sentence is of course 'my'. It takes us straight back to the boyish distinction Pip made between 'his' convict, Magwitch, and the second one at large on the marshes. It is an acknowledgement and an identification; it is an admission that he has not been able to escape the shadow world of crime; but the drama lies in whether the possessive adjective can also lead to a proper sense of what belongs to him. For Pip, 'my' must also contain his wealth and the answer to who he truly is, the marsh boy or the London gentleman. He must understand his inheritance, in both senses of the word. No wonder Pip locks Magwitch, and his pistol, into the bedroom before he spends a sleepless night on the living-room floor.

Finally, Pip does begin to help our work in keeping alive the idea of him as a decent person. He uses his money to find Herbert Pocket a place in a finance house. Then he tells Miss Havisham plainly that by encouraging him to love Estella she was cruel to him. He is starting to acquire clarity in his view of others, at least, even if he persists in loving Estella despite her telling him, 'When you say you love me, I know what you mean, as a form of words; but nothing more.' When he next returns, Miss Havisham asks his forgiveness and Pip responds magnanimously, 'I want forgiveness and direction far too much to be bitter with you.' This is what we have been wanting to hear for a long time; Pip is starting to repay what we have invested in him, and he burns his hands in trying to rescue Miss Havisham from the fire that kills her.

The strands of the plot are brought together in broad loops. Estella is Magwitch's daughter. The second convict, Compeyson, is the man who left Miss Havisham at the altar. Jaggers's housekeeper is a murderer saved from the scaffold by his eloquence; she is also Estella's mother. These revelations don't strain our credulity, however; they emerge from the mist with a certain inevitability, as though we knew that these connections had all along been underlying the superficial action in its rapid but mysterious movement. The main reason that we find them satisfactory, not far-fetched, is that the leitmotif of the shadow world that has pursued Pip since the cows in the pasture first called out 'Stop thief!' is shown now not to be hallucinatory, but a real part of a society in which the law-abiding and the criminal are intimately joined at all levels – a precarious world in which only the smokescreen of respectability and social advancement has obscured that connection.

In the climactic scene, in which Magwitch is taken in a boat down the estuary with a view to being put aboard a steamer to escape the police who would arrest him for having left Australia, Pip finally vindicates our faith in him. Critics have noted how for the first time the narration loses its ironic second level: the gap closes as grown-up narrator and the young protagonist become one person in their swift practical repayment of a debt to the man who has crossed the world at risk of his own life merely to thank a little boy who once helped him. Pip no longer recoils from Magwitch. 'I only saw a man who had meant to be my benefactor, and who had felt affectionately, gratefully, and generously, towards me with great constancy through a series of years. I only saw in him a much better man than I had been to Joe.'

As the novel began with a firework display of unforgettable scenes, so does it end, with the drowning of Compeyson after his fight to the death with Magwitch; the revelation by Pip to Magwitch on his deathbed that his child, Estella, lives: 'She is living now. She is a lady and very beautiful.

And I love her!'; Pip's reconciliation with Joe: 'O God bless him! O God bless this gentle Christian man!'; and then the deep but powerless remorse shown by Pip on the occasion of Joe and Biddy's wedding. It is hard to know whether you weep at the sadness of the events described and the words uttered by the characters or whether the tears spring from simple admiration and gratitude for the genius that conjured these immortal people out of nothing and offered them to us for the price of a paperback or a library ticket.

Dickens was left with the question of how to finish his book. He decided to send Pip to Egypt to work for the same counting house as Herbert Pocket; Pip ends up unmarried and unmarriageable, a man whose life has been spoiled by unforeseen wealth and by the impulsive kindliness of his own actions as a child. Many years later in London, accompanied by young Pip, the child of Joe and Biddy, he sees Estella by chance. She imagines that the child is Pip's and goes her way; Pip's consolation is to know that 'suffering … had given her a heart to understand what my heart used to be'.

It was the perfect ending to what probably comes as close as anyone in Britain contrived in the nineteenth century to the perfect novel. It is sad, it is merciless and unyielding, but in those respects it is all of a piece with the novel that it concludes, which, among other things, is a refutation of the criticism that Dickens is sentimental. *Great Expectations* is one of the least sentimental novels imaginable; in some of its harsher moments one sometimes yearns for something like sentimentality to palliate them.

Dickens, alas, was persuaded to change the ending and to have Pip meet Estella again in the grounds of Satis House. The second version, which is the one used in most modern editions, is by no means a disaster. We know that Estella cannot love Pip; she has made it clear that she is incapable of such an emotion. But I think it is conceivable that they could have a future together because his obsession with her could blind him to the lack of real feeling on her part; she in turn might discover something in herself, some slight warmth that might respond to the better parts of Pip. It is also persuasively written, as Dickens acknowledges the difficulties that surround the relationship: there is the rhetorical rise, the invocation of lost time in the subordinate clauses, and a minor chord in the qualification implied by the final phrase: 'I took her hand in mine, and we went out of the ruined place; and, as the morning mists had risen long ago when I first left the forge, so, the evening mists were rising now, and in all the broad expanse of tranquil light they showed to me, I saw the shadow of no parting from her.'

It is moving and persuasive; but true lovers of this book will, I think, always prefer Dickens's own first instincts – unflinching to the last – for how it should end.

'WE ARE NOT SWELLS'

CHARLES POOTER

The easy way for novelists to deal with snobs – the one that pays quick dividends – is the comic one. The pretensions of Lady Catherine de Bourgh or Mrs Elton are something all readers can laugh at with an easy conscience. Most novelists are instinctively democratic in their views; a desire to validate the experience of the neglected or the downtrodden seems to be part of the temperament that leads most people to want to write in the first place. However, when the writer is himself a snob, it becomes more complicated. Evelyn Waugh is acute at catching nuances of speech and behaviour in people who are not as smart as they might wish to be. In *Brideshead Revisited*, the different social positions of Charles Ryder and Sebastian Flyte generate both comedy and a life-changing dissatisfaction for both men; but there is no sense that Waugh has done anything other than exploit the differences in a clear-eyed way. At the end of the Sword of Honour trilogy, however, at the funeral of Guy

Crouchback's father, Waugh's mask seems to slip, allowing us a glimpse of him rubbing his hands over the details of the grand Anglo–Catholic funeral that appears to embody everything he loves and personally aspires to be. I'm not sure that it matters if sometimes we laugh at the author as well as at his creations; but some readers are quick to recoil if they scent snobbery in the author rather than in his characters.

The Diary of a Nobody treads on this delicate ground. It has divided readers by raising the delicate question: can you laugh at Mr Pooter without looking down on him? To put it bluntly, can you enjoy the book without being a bit of a snob yourself?

Like the other great comic novel of its era, *Three Men in a Boat*, it was conceived as a parody; we weren't meant principally to laugh only at or with Pooter but also at the self-important diarists his journal is guying. Yet after a couple of early episodes in which he finds his fictional feet, Pooter suddenly takes flight. It may well be that we are meant to laugh at the genre, but in fact our sympathy for Pooter means that we quickly care about him too much to be bothered with any literary consideration; what happens instead is that we find ourselves rooting for this ridiculous bank clerk in the travails of his daily life, with its small indignities and bursts of odd domestic happiness. He is a man of his time and of his class, pinned down with lepidopteric precision and not always with kindness; but his vitality keeps throwing off the satirical bonds by which his author would imprison him. The more George Grossmith tries to identify the nature of Pooter's pettiness, to place and limit him by social definitions, the more easily he transcends them; the more we are required to see Pooter as 'other' and ridiculous, the more warmly we seem to identify with him and to cheer on his goodness of heart. It is possible that in his first incarnation, in the columns of *Punch*, Pooter was more of a clown,

'My first thought was that I was bleeding to death.' – Charles Pooter
accidentally dyes himself red with enamel paint (1892 edition)

but that the novel form into which the pieces were gathered gave him
more sympathetic substance.

Mr Pooter knows his place. We may be asked to view that place as
absurd, but we are more inclined to think it charming; to be satisfied with
your position in life can be a symptom of small-mindedness, but it can be
a manifestation of modesty. Having said all of which, we must admit that
Mr Pooter is an ass. His lugubrious neighbour Cummings and his off-
colour friend Gowing are united in their disdain for him. Often Pooter is
too humourless and too straight-laced. He gets shut out of the pub where

his friends are drinking because he is too prim to tell the fib that would open the doors to him. At other times his bursts of heavy-handed humour seem to his friends to be in poor taste, as when he makes a pun on their names. None of this stops them dropping in as they please and making free with Pooter's food and drink, and nor does it stop the reader adopting a defensive attitude to our narrator – as well as worrying about how much his hospitality may be costing him.

Some of the delight of the book, I suppose, is in the anthropological detail of how such a family lived. There are tradesmen who come to call to offer their services: Horwin, a butcher with a 'nice clean shop', Borset a butterman whose eggs turn out to be 'simply shocking'. The Pooters have a live-in servant in their small house. It seems an enviably ordered society in which all these tradesmen are likely to make a fair living, and their world begins to take on a nostalgic burnish. Our great-grandparents may have lived like this.

There are strikingly odd details that only a contemporary chronicler can deliver. A novelist of today, creating such a respectable character, would not have imagined that he drank champagne – even if the 'Jackson Frères' marque sounds dodgy. I like the detail about the pub bye-law, which meant that on Sunday walkers could be served out of licensing hours if they had come from far away as 'bona fide travellers'. The Pooters drink quite a lot of alcohol, in fact: port, Madeira and whisky as well as champagne, though Pooter can never connect his booming headaches and raging night thirsts with anything he has drunk the evening before.

Pooter is a snob, but he is not a social climber. 'We are homely people, we are not swells,' he tells a visitor; but the crucial thing is what he says before: 'You must take us as you find us.' Mr Pooter has found a rung on the social ladder that suits him, and it is his life's work to hold on to it. When the grand Mr Perkupp, his boss, comes to visit, he worries that 'The Laurels' should look clean and attractive and proper; but when the thespian friends of his son Lupin come to call, he is much less concerned for appearances. When Lupin suggests he should wear 'dress boots' not ordinary boots with evening dress, he grandly dismisses such trivial concerns as being beneath him. Likewise, his wife Carrie's rather 'fast' friend, Mrs James of Sutton, holds no terrors for Pooter with her silly fads and fashions; he is confident enough to recognise nonsense when he sees it. His only worry is that Mrs James will lead Carrie into unnecessary expense.

Mr Pooter's snobbery consists in an obsession with appearances, which stems from a fear that he might lose a position in society which previous generations of Pooters have worked to achieve. His boring work as a bank clerk, his modest pay, short holidays and continuing self-discipline (with a few lapses) are the prices he pays for what he treasures: stability. He is a man who knows – and whose fairly recent family will have experienced – what it is to be poor; and what he knows has scared him. It also worries him that his son Lupin is in danger of risking all that has been saved from the chaos of slum London by two or three generations of diligence. Respectability is precarious – though, like all parents, Mr Pooter knows that he must allow Lupin to learn from his own mistakes where paternal lectures have clearly failed.

If snobs suffer from a defect of vision, then Mr Pooter's blindness is a partial and touchingly simple one: in his anxiety to preserve his status he sometimes loses sight of just how happy he is. He has a very good relationship with his wife, Carrie. She values his steadiness but is not so indulgent that she can't be exasperated by his pomposity. They have outbursts of affectionate laughter; they dance round the parlour; he tells her how much he loves her and she calls him a 'spooney old thing'. This looks like a pretty good marriage. He has, for someone who claims to be a stay-at-home, a remarkably active and varied social life – which turns out to be his trump card when someone he has met through his dining out puts an important client his way. He has friends who, if rather cavalier towards him, are capable of being entertaining. He has a son whom he loves anxiously and who may or may not carry on the Pooter tradition of respectability before all things. He has a boss who – and this would not always be the case – values his good qualities and long service to the firm. Above almost all, Pooter has The Laurels, Brickfield Terrace. When Mr Perkupp at the end rewards him for his loyalty by buying him the freehold of his house, red-painted bath, dodgy boot scraper and all, he first asks him if he likes it, to which Pooter replies: 'Yes, sir; I love my house and I love the neighbourhood, and could not bear to leave it.'

Mike Leigh's famous 1977 television play *Abigail's Party* depicted a group of people who were perhaps of a similar social standing to Pooter, but almost a hundred years later. Whatever the author's intentions, it seemed to me impossible to laugh at his characters without being snobbish oneself. What else was funny about Abigail proposing to put the red wine in the fridge?

Charles Pooter, by contrast, may be a mockable fool, but he gets plenty of things right. There may have been snobbery in the conception of the character, and there is condescending comedy in some of the social detail, in the useless knick-knacks, the parlour games and the piano on the hire purchase; but, happily, there is more to Pooter than that. The great pleasure of this book is in the way the character so exhilaratingly defeats his author's satirical intentions and becomes his own man.

'THE MOOD WILL PASS, SIR'

JEEVES

One of the odd things about Jeeves is how seldom he appears in the stories that immortalised him. While P. G. Wodehouse never used anything as vulgar as a formula, there is an elegant pattern to Jeeves's exits and his entrances. He is on hand when the story begins, which is first thing in the morning, as stories should. He usually enters bearing a cup of tea, though it may be something stronger if Bertie's state of health requires it. At this stage, Jeeves acts principally as a messenger. There has been a telephone call, a visit, a telegram or a development. It brings a complication or a dilemma that invariably entails Bertie making a visit to a country house.

Relations between master and servant are strained. A moustache, a soft-bosomed evening shirt, a pair of purple socks ... Some faux pas has been committed by Bertie, and Jeeves is in a dignified sulk. Usually, this stops short of warfare, though in the case of *Thank You, Jeeves*, Bertie's attachment to the 'banjolele' leads to Jeeves's resignation. Normally, the resentment is left on a low heat. When Jeeves is first consulted for his advice he usually regrets that he is 'unable to offer a solution'. Naturally the plot could not develop the necessary complications if Jeeves were able to cut through all difficulties in the first act, but whether help might have been more swiftly forthcoming had he been feeling less affronted is something we can never know for sure. The suspicion, however, adds piquancy to the master–servant relationship.

The arrival at the country house is my favourite moment in a Jeeves novel. It might be Totleigh Towers, Sir Watkyn Bassett's Wiltshire house, where although the man is vile, every prospect pleases. Brinkley Court in Worcestershire, home of Aunt Dahlia, is a destination of choice, with the prospect of dinner from Anatole, the resident wizard of the roasts and sauces. Rolling up at a large stately home without knowing one's host can still intimidate even such a seasoned boulevardier as Bertie – as is the case at Deverill Hall in Hampshire (somewhere off the A3, it appears), home of the Haddock family, inventors of a patent headache remedy. It can hardly help Bertie's spirits as he approaches the massive front door to have Jeeves whisper in his ear, 'Childe Roland to the Dark Tower came, sir.' I suppose it's the 'sir' that makes this so excruciating. I doubt whether any character in English has managed to get more work on that monosyllable than Jeeves did; on his lips it can go from respectful via quizzical to insolent. There is no need for Wodehouse to flag the tone with adverbs; it's all in the rhythm of the dialogue.

Jeeves is often sent on ahead by train with the heavy luggage, leaving Bertie free to give a lift to a young popsy, such as Nobby Hopwood, or simply to tool along solo in the old two-seater, all cylinders purring sweet as a nut. On arrival at the stately h, Jeeves, having presumably acquainted himself with the layout of the place and the whereabouts of his master's lodgings, makes himself scarce. There is some sponging and pressing of Bertie's suits to be done and the evening wear to be laid out in due course. There is intelligence to be gathered, either from the servants' quarters or by some judicious eavesdropping among the 'quality' in the library or the smoking room, where he frequently acts as an auxiliary butler, pushing round the cucumber sandwiches and the lapsang. Such teatimes are invariably fraught, the cup that cheers doing anything but, with sundered hearts sighing, aunts expressing themselves forcibly and a surprisingly high breakage rate of china ornaments. These gatherings also offer a rare moment for the whole cast, including troublesome small children, usually boys, to be brought together in one place.

In the central part of the book, Jeeves is seldom present, but allows Bertie to take 'control' of events himself. In this Act Two, Jeeves may offer a word or two of solace to Bertie, but is more often bent on helping others, and Bertie hears lavish praise for his man from Stephanie 'Stiffy' Byng, Tuppy Glossop or some other lovestruck youngster who has benefited from that fish-fuelled intellect. Bertie generally greets these encomia coolly, though not without a quiet pride.

What is Jeeves's own accommodation like in these fine houses? Austere, one imagines. A bareish bedroom reached by an uncarpeted back staircase smelling of lime wood and polish. Jeeves's personal packing would be economical and meticulous; he would never find himself without the needful, thanks perhaps to a mnemonic inherited from his uncle Charlie Silversmith or similar error-eliminator of his own devising. A spare pair of spongebag trousers, black jacket and waistcoat; a shirt for each day; stiff collars and studs; spare tie; the complete works of Spinoza and, if he is in skittish mood, perhaps a volume of the poet Herrick. A woollen dressing gown would be essential for the excursion down a cold corridor to the shared servants' bathroom, where hot water would roar from brass taps at Brinkley or trickle from a gas geyser at Totleigh Towers. As for Jeeves's slumberwear, it would perhaps be an act of lèse-majesté to picture it.

As we know, Jeeves does not walk anywhere, he oozes, drifts, or otherwise soundlessly materialises. The trick is in knowing when he might be needed. Bertie is frequently *persona non grata* at the luncheon table and requires a plate of sandwiches and a half-bot of something to be brought to him in the shrubbery. This is followed by a moody gasper and a cup of black coffee, which he may in his anguish have forgotten to stipulate – but with Jeeves, you don't need to ask for such essentials.

At some point in the day, Jeeves presumably has time to himself. Fishing is one of his favourite pastimes – rod and line in a Hampshire chalk stream, or a shrimping net with his aunt at Herne Bay both seem to provide the necessary relaxation. He also 'lets it be known' that he is reluctant to miss Ascot, and Bertie is indulgent about this, even when it means heading off alone to the Riviera, where he makes the ill-advised purchase of a white mess dinner jacket with brass buttons. Presumably Ascot would be one of the few race meetings where the dress conventions would meet with Jeeves's approval, though of course formal attire is as fraught with potential solecism as weekend clothing. The other reason that Jeeves might like Ascot is that he is in receipt of information that enables him to place bets with a reassuring degree of certainty. Asked by Bertie if he has given the bookies a hiding, Jeeves concedes that he has made 'a quite satisfactory sum, thank you, sir'.

One of the more ticklish duties in Jeeves's day is ministering to Bertie's alcoholic requirements. Like many avid users of the grape and grain, Bertie is under the impression that he is the soul of moderation. A brace of cock-tails before dinner, a glass of wine with it, and perhaps a trickle of port when the ladies have retired … That is all he will admit to. Experience will have taught Jeeves, however, that a whisky and splash is something that needs to be accessible at all times, as does a decanter of brandy for its fast-acting restorative effect. There is something called a 'pre-lunch snifter', which appears to have a set hour attached to it, as well as the half-bot that goes with the sandwiches in the garden or a late-night omelette; though if a larger lunch is taken indoors a little more fluid might conceivably be necessary. Before Bertie has changed for dinner or even contemplated the brace of cocktails, there is the longed-for tug at his sleeve from the host and the muttered invitation to a whisky and soda in the gunroom. It is difficult to imagine such a clandestine yet convivial gathering confining itself to a single glass. While many novels and stories begin with Bertie suffering from the effects of the previous night (Pongo Twistleton's birthday at the Drones seems to be a particularly exacting event) we seldom see Bertie the worse for wear. The electrifying exception to this rule is the night of his arrival at Deverill Hall in *The Mating Season*, though in his mitigation it must be pointed out that he is impersonating the teetotal Gussie Fink-Nottle and has spent a long dinner among deaf or intimidating aunts sipping orange juice, Gussie's preferred potion. When Bertie is left alone with his host, the magnificently well-built, yet inhibited, Esmond Haddock, something in the way that Bertie eyes the port decanter gives Esmond pause.

'I say, I suppose it's no good offering you any of this?'
I felt the table talk could not have taken a more satisfactory turn.
'Well, do you know,' I said, 'I wouldn't mind trying it. It would be an experience. It's whisky or claret or something, isn't it?'

'Port. You may not like it.'

'Oh, I think I shall.'

It is not long before Bertie is standing on a chair with the decanter in his hand conducting Esmond Haddock in a series of increasingly successful hunting songs. If I were to be quite honest, I suppose I would have to admit that this is probably my favourite scene in the whole canon of English literature.

Jeeves, meanwhile ... Well, meanwhile, what? All is leading to his triumphant intervention in Act Three. At the climax of *Right Ho, Jeeves*, Bertie is despatched on a bicycle without lights to ride nine miles from Brinkley[11] to Kingham Manor to retrieve the back-door key from Seppings, the butler, when all the guests find themselves locked out on the lawn after the fire alarm has been set off (by Bertie). It is Jeeves who ensures that Bertie is selected. 'Yes, madam, Mr Wooster would perform the task admirably. He is an expert cyclist. He has often boasted to me of his triumphs on the wheel.' This is completely untrue, but characteristic of a hint of sadism in the Jeeves of the third act. Jeeves is a man who knows how to wait for his revenge, and Bertie pays a high price not only for sartorial errors but also for imagining he can manage better without Jeeves during his stay. In this case, Jeeves has already taken the matter of the white mess

---

[11] Or 'Bingley' as it momentarily appears in a 'Homer nods' moment. Perhaps the most notable of these is when the Rev. Aubrey Upjohn, Bertie's private-school headmaster, a canonical figure in the Wooster history, appears in a late book as the 'Rev. Arnold Abney'. It is odd that publishers' editors have not corrected these few but painful slips.

jacket in hand ('I am sorry to say, sir, that while I was ironing it this after-noon I was careless enough to leave the hot instrument upon it'); but Bertie is so relieved that he does not have to marry Madeline Bassett that he can tolerate any amount of retributive cruelty.

It is the exact balance of the sweetness of revenge for Jeeves and the vast relief that Bertie feels that makes the endings of the novels so satisfactory. If there is a little zest of lemon in the mixture, that seems only to help the flavour. At this point, I should acknowledge that criticising Wodehouse, as Evelyn Waugh remarked, is like taking a spade to a soufflé. You are likely to end up with egg on your face. Even writing a wholly uncritical thank-you letter can make you look an absolute ass. There is nothing serious about the books except their gossamer artistry. To say more is to gild the l.

As to whether Jeeves is a snob, however … Well, I think he probably is. He is a reactionary snob, because he likes the world the way it is. As Bertie says in *Right Ho, Jeeves*: 'In the matter of evening costume, you see, Jeeves is hidebound and reactionary.' One of the extra-textual questions people sometimes ask about him is: If Jeeves is so clever, why doesn't he make a lot of money and stop having to clear up after Bertie? If he can make a quite pleasing sum at Ascot, possibly on the basis of a few tips, why not the same, in spades, on the stock market? There is a dull answer about a lack of capital, but the more interesting one is that Jeeves doesn't want to change his happy life.

I think Jeeves enjoys visiting these lovely houses. He's probably one of the few in the servants' hall who appreciates a plate of Anatole's *Timbale de ris de veau à la Toulousaine*. The kitchen maid wouldn't like offal. He probably enjoys a kippered herring for breakfast, too, followed by a slice of toast, with honey made by contented bees. I doubt whether he drinks much, but a glass of Margaux from the remains of the decanter brought back from the dining room to accompany a knob of cheese would bring his own supper to a satisfactory conclusion. Bertie is a generous employer; holidays are good; and Jeeves is able to manoeuvre the master into a round-the-world cruise, for which he receives a free ticket. His tastes in literature are not so much highbrow as austere, though I think it quite possible to imagine Jeeves enjoying a tasteful comedy in the theatre. As far as music is concerned, I don't see him as a Wagnerian, but someone who would enjoy Gilbert and Sullivan, Handel – or Schubert at a push. (Not the Russians, though: Jeeves and Tchaikovsky … An awful thought.) Presumably the Junior Ganymede club gives ample opportunity for indoor entertainments, such as bridge, whist or draughts (hard to imagine a fellow–valet giving Jeeves much of a game at chess), as well as a full selection of newspapers in which he can read the financial pages to keep abreast of takeovers and mergers that might impinge on his employer's circle. His room in Berkeley Mansions is quite well appointed, one imagines, with its own bathroom and comfortable armchair for getting to grips with some of the more trying Germans.

The point is, though, that this happy world must not change. The principal threat is from marriage, and Jeeves makes it clear that he would not continue to work for a married Bertie. The danger is a real one. Bertie is young, has the stuff in sackfuls, is kind, has a weakness for female good looks and is a serial fiancé. One does not bandy a woman's name, but Florence Craye, Honoria Glossop, Roberta 'Bobbie' Wickham and Pauline Stoker have all, so far as I remember, been engaged to him; and so has Madeline Bassett. Even though Bertie can't stand the sight of her, he feels obliged to concede to an engagement as a matter of honour because Madeline has misunderstood his intentions.

It's important for the romance and jollity of the plot that we believe these girls are attractive, though for realism's sake, they must all be flawed, or Bertie would be lost. Most of them rule themselves out by being too high-spirited. The prettiest of them all is probably Cora 'Corky' Pirbright in *The Mating Season*. After all, she is an actress in Hollywood and does well there; but she has a large hound called Sam Goldwyn, who is such a menace that he is impounded by the local constabulary. And, mercifully, she is in love with Esmond Haddock. 'Stiffy' Byng, niece of Sir Watkyn Bassett, is another lively and attractive proposition, who features in what is arguably the most perfectly made of the Jeeves novels, *The Code of the Woosters*, in which Bertie is required to steal a silver cow-creamer from Sir Watkyn Bassett. Stiffy, however, is also ruled out by dog ownership – a savage Scottie – and her preference for another.[12] Roberta 'Bobbie' Wickham gets 'right in amongst' Bertie, requiring emergency intervention from Jeeves, who counsels against alliance with a young lady with hair of 'quite such a violent shade of red'. Bobbie is the Nietzsche of the fiancée world – fundamentally unsound.

'It might be judicious if you were to attempt to persuade his lordship that the spirit in which you embraced Miss Stoker was a purely brotherly one' (1933 edition)

---

[12] My old Penguin has the binder's title abbreviation at the foot of every sixteen pages 'C.O.W' 1, 2, 3 etc. I like that. In a memorable article ('Beyond a Joke: The perils of loving P. G. Wodehouse', the *New Yorker*, 19 April 2004), Anthony Lane recalled buying an expensive American first edition of *Uncle Fred in the Springtime* 'not because it contained any textual variants but because I wished to calibrate, if possible, how different the prose felt in an unfamiliar typeface'.

I have always had a very soft spot for Pauline Stoker ('one of the most beautiful girls I had ever met,' says Bertie), daughter of the American tycoon J. Washburn Stoker, whom (Pauline, I mean, not J. Washburn) Bertie discovers in his bed one night in a cottage in Chufnell Regis wearing his heliotrope pyjamas with the old gold stripe. I was never wholly convinced by Bertie's disavowal of his earlier feelings: 'But of the ancient fire which had caused me to bung my heart at her feet that night at the Plaza there remained not a trace'; though Pauline's grim father is a problem. Angela Travers, Aunt Dahlia's daughter with Tom Travers, her second husband, is perhaps the most suitable mate for Bertie, though he invokes biblical problems about teaming up with a cousin, while Angela reveals a certain hard side to her character when Tuppy Glossop mocks her story of having been attacked by a shark in the Bay of Cannes. I also have a deep *tendresse* for Zenobia 'Nobby' Hopwood, a 'girl liberally endowed with oomph', though inexplicably enraptured of Boko Fittleworth and, conclusively, the ward of Aunt Agatha's husband, Lord Worplesdon. Marriage to Nobby would mean visits to Steeple Bumpleigh, Aunt Agatha's lair.

Bachelorhood for Bertie is the deal-breaker for Jeeves, but there are other – more recondite – elements of Jeeves's enchanted world that he must fight to preserve. There are rules, conventions, habits, customs, rights and wrongs; they may seem trivial, but not to him: someone must ensure that it all remains the same, and the task falls to Jeeves. All of us were brought up to know that there was a right and wrong way of doing things: in some houses the book of rules amounted to little more than a nodding acquaintance with the criminal law; in others, there was a whole encyclopaedia of etiquette. Oddly enough, the number and ferocity of the rules has never been in proportion to wealth or social status; rich or 'smart' people seem more carefree about such things – and Bertie Wooster is a case in point, quite happy to break the conventions of dress, at least.

Someone, somewhere, once invented these 'rules', however. I am still aware, dimly, of trying to walk street-side of a woman when on the pavement, to guard her from the mud splashes of the passing horse-and-cart traffic; but it was news when my father told us one Christmas that only a cad keeps billiard chalk in his waistcoat pocket. The children of an hereditary peer may style themselves 'The Hon.'; those of a life peer may technically also do so, though it is apparently considered 'not on'. A gentleman's trouser bottoms should 'shimmer, not break' on the instep of his shoe, according to Jeeves. To wear a made-up bow tie is obviously the mark of a bounder; but did you know that only a Pierrot or Sinbad costume is considered acceptable at a fancy-dress party?

It's not possible to keep a straight face about these things. Put others' comfort before your own, the weak before the strong … Beyond that, it becomes whimsical. When Nancy Mitford and Evelyn Waugh drew up their snobbish lists of what was U and Non-U, it turned into a joke. There did seem to be one decent rule: in language, prefer Anglo-Saxon to French; so you 'should' say 'napkin' not 'serviette', 'what?' not 'pardon?' and so on. Beyond that, it quickly degenerates into a farce of petty invention and caprice. Is it permissible to wear a gardenia buttonhole before the Saturday of the Lord's Test? I don't know; but I know of a man who did, who gave much of his life to studying such things and who resigned from the employment of Lord Worplesdon on account of that gentleman's eccentric evening wear. '"There are moments, Jeeves, when one asks oneself 'Do trousers matter?'" "The mood will pass, sir."'

When I was a child I imagined there existed, somewhere, a book of all such rules; and I think that Jeeves perhaps believes so, too – though in which magnificent library it resides he 'could not say, sir'. Not in Lord Worplesdon's, obviously, and not in any of the castles of the Royal Family, since they have not lived long enough in England. Perhaps in Mr Knightley's study, though, in Donwell Abbey, such a priceless vademecum could be found – though even putting such sacred things in print might, in Jeeves's eyes, devalue them. The important things in life are handed on by subtler methods, by 'breeding' or instinct; and it is the life's work of a gentleman's personal gentleman to see that it remains so.

'JUST A SPINSTER'

JEAN BRODIE

Muriel Spark's slender novel *The Prime of Miss Jean Brodie* was published in 1961, when John F. Kennedy was president of the United States and the Beatles were playing in Hamburg. It opens, however, in quite another era: in the pivotal year of 1936, when France had a socialist government, Hitler invaded the Rhineland, Mussolini established Fascism in Italy and civil war broke out in Spain.

Marcia Blain School, the private academy in Edinburgh at which Jean Brodie teaches, would appear to be far removed from such turbulence. Most British politicians in 1936 still trusted Hitler's good intentions, and the greatest shock in Britain was the abdication of Edward VIII. The key events for women of Miss Brodie's generation, meanwhile, were already twenty years in the past: the First World War had so reduced the number of living men that many women were spinsters of necessity.

Miss Brodie is different. She believes she is a citizen of the world, awake to its history and its cultural excitements. In her mythology of herself, the death of her fiancé in Flanders has debarred her from marrying. She has – heroically, she thinks – accepted the blow that fate has dealt to her womanhood and has managed to turn it into a kind of liberation. While she bows the knee to the parts of history she cannot change, she will be a free, modern and controlling agent in the rest of the life that lies before her; if history has pre-empted the great choice of her life, she will make all the other decisions herself – and they will be of such an idiosyncratic hue, so utterly Brodie, that the world will look at her and see not a saddened Edinburgh spinster but a magnificent woman who has risen on the steps of necessity to a higher plane, where 'goodness, truth and beauty' radiate from her suffering but triumphant face. Miss Brodie's project is to make of herself an icon: an image of transcendence to be looked at with wonder and respect. Her tragedy is that she turns out not to be a leader in the ranks of an enlightened culture, but the victim of self-delusion and of forces she has not understood.

Muriel Spark was an instinctive writer, a poet as well as a novelist, and this extraordinary little novel sometimes reads as if handwritten in a notebook, unrevised. Yet for all its home-made, anti-academic quality, *The Prime of Miss Jean Brodie* has the suggestiveness of a folk song or ballad; it is not the lightweight thing it may at first appear, but a work of eerie resonance – an almost miraculous book.

Each of the girls in the Brodie 'set' is assigned one quality for which she is 'famous' and is seldom allowed to appear without this quality being mentioned, whether it is being good at maths, sex, gymnastics or just having small eyes. The result is a helpful jog to the reader, but, more than this, gives a comic-Homeric aspect to the story, in the same way that Hector is always the 'tamer of horses' and Odysseus repeatedly 'wily'. The idea of legend is increased by the sudden leap forward in time in the second chapter. In one scene we have looked back at the girls aged only ten, and the next we are hearing how one died in a fire aged twenty-three and one became a nun. We also learn how Miss Brodie herself died, at the age of fifty-six, 'betrayed' by one of her girls and sacked from Marcia Blain. The shocking effect of this is to make the girls' lives at ten and sixteen (we see both academic years) acquire the glamour of an old ciné film – poignant and almost unbelievable.

In 1936, Jean Brodie, a little marginal arithmetic tells us, is actually forty-six; her prime, she decided, began in 1930, at the age of forty. She warns her girls that they must be alert when grown up and be sure not to miss their prime, but 'live it to the full'. She marks the start of her own prime by 'renouncing' the love of Teddy Lloyd, the married art teacher, and beginning an affair with Gordon Lowther, the singing master. Of the rejected Teddy, she says, 'I am his Muse ... But I have renounced his love in order to dedicate my prime to the young girls in my care. I am his Muse but Rose shall take my place.' We already know that it is in fact Sandy who becomes his lover, so Miss Brodie is wrong. One of the extraordinary things about the narration is the way Spark fearlessly anticipates events, so that we often know more than the characters; so when little Mary is panicked by magnesium flares in a chemistry lesson, we already know that as a grown woman she will die in a hotel fire.

Miss Brodie can only reprove Sandy for sleeping with Mr Lloyd: it was to have been Rose's destiny because she is 'famous for sex'; and in any case Teddy Lloyd is a Roman Catholic. There is something of Emma

Woodhouse in the way Miss Brodie presumes to matchmake Rose with Mr Lloyd. Sandy says that Mr Lloyd 'interests' her; but it turns out that it is, of all things, his religion that she's interested in: 'She left the man and took his religion and became a nun in the course of time.' Sandy's mind has all along been 'as full of religion as a night sky is full of things visible and invisible'. Mr Lowther also proves to have a mind of his own. An elder of the church, he wants to marry a jolly woman he can sing to and play golf with; the sinful arrangement by which Miss Brodie sleeps with him – in the very bed in which he was born – begins to appal him. He finds himself a more suitable bride.

The Brodie set are no longer the 'crème de la crème', 'old heads on young shoulders' or any other such thing within their teacher's control. At sixteen, they start to do what they want – and none more so than the marginal Joyce Emily who, inspired by Miss Brodie's admiration for Franco, goes off to fight in the Spanish Civil War, where she is killed. It is Jean Brodie's admiration for Mussolini, Franco and Hitler – enthusiastically disclosed to her girls – that proves her nemesis. By letting her admiration of things Italian spill over into a regard for Fascism, Jean Brodie awakens in Sandy, at least, the critical, doubting spirit that makes her question her teacher. It is ironic that while the creation of such an inquiring mind is agreed to be the end of good teaching, it has never been the aim of Miss Brodie's instruction – the purpose of which has been to control her girls and make them admire her. It is as though she has unconsciously acknowledged that the true snob cannot abide a sceptical questioner.

Jean Brodie is a cultural snob, whose love of European culture seems to spring partly from a displaced sexuality (she thrives 'abroad', away from

Calvinist eyes, and once falls for an Egyptian tour guide), but more urgently the expression of a need to be seen as different from, and superior to, other Edinburgh spinsters of her age and background. Muriel Spark, in a passage of simple exposition, makes it clear that there were plenty of middle-class women in Edinburgh in 1936 whom the war had deprived of husbands:

> They went to lectures, tried living on honey and nuts, took lessons in German and then went walking in Germany; they bought caravans and went off with them into the hills among the lochs; they played the guitar, they supported all the new little theatre companies; they took lodgings in the slums and, distributing pots of paint, taught their neighbours the arts of simple interior decoration; they preached the inventions of Marie Stopes; they attended the meetings of the Oxford Group and put spiritualism to their hawk-eyed test.

What they did not do was teach. That calling was reserved to more religious women from poorer backgrounds. Had Miss Brodie been willing to accept the position that society had assigned to her – not such a bad lot, to consort in comfort with the 'great talkers and feminists' – no harm would have come to her or to any girls. The interesting complication is that Miss Brodie, for all her free love and 'progressive' instincts, does have a streak of traditional piety in her. She ought, says Spark, to have been a Roman Catholic because that church might have 'embraced, even while it disciplined, her soaring and diving spirit, it might even have normalised her'. However, she takes a whimsical stance against the Church of Rome, indulging a 'rigid Edinburgh-born side of herself ... although this side was not otherwise greatly in evidence'. Every Sunday she goes to a different Low Church Protestant service; and although she has an affair with a married man and as good as lives with a bachelor, she forbids Eunice to do cartwheels on Sunday, 'for in many ways Miss Brodie was an Edinburgh spinster of the deepest dye'.

Jean Brodie is a monster. She is an egotist who has no right to be a teacher – to take the impressionable minds of the young and fill with them silly prejudices that are designed to create an aura of tragic glamour about her 'dark Roman profile', like a halo, and make the girls look up to her. She pays a terrible price for her vanity and self-obsession when she has to accept responsibility for Joyce Emily's death in Spain. She loses her job as a teacher when, in 1939, she is 'betrayed' to the headmistress by Sandy, her best pupil, for teaching Fascism. She dies young, unattached and unmourned.

Yet she has vitality. 'Everyone thought the Brodie set had more fun than anyone else ... And indeed it was so.' Some of her shortcomings are no more than exaggerations of common human faults. Most worthwhile and interesting people invent a 'narrative' of their own life; it is just that few of them are as colourful, nonsensical and fundamentally dishonest as Miss Brodie's. Her rejection of the traditional way of learning is not altogether wrong-headed; it is the fact that she takes it to such extremes that raises a problem: 'All of the Brodie set, save one, counted on its fingers, as had Miss Brodie, with accurate results more or less.'

And in grey Calvinist Edinburgh, she does bring colour and laughter. 'Whoever has opened the window has opened it too far ... Six inches is perfectly adequate. More is vulgar.' Muriel Spark doesn't tell us if Jean Brodie is smiling inwardly when she says such things; perhaps by the age of forty she no longer recognises how ridiculous she is. If you are allowed to get away with things for a long time, the division between the serious and the absurd becomes unclear. She asks her class who was the greatest Italian painter and they answer 'Leonardo'; she tells them they are incorrect: 'The answer is Giotto. He is my favourite.' In Miss Brodie's world, whim has become dogma. It is misleading, and potentially damaging, for the pupils to be enlisted into this personality cult; it is an apparently – but only apparently – harmless variation of the cults being developed in Weimar, Madrid and Rome.

Jean Brodie can 'get away with things' in front of children; her fantasy of herself would not pass among fellow adults, and this is the heart of the case against her. When, after the end of the war, Sandy meets Miss Brodie 'shrivelled and betrayed in her long-preserved dark musquash coat', she has no time for her old teacher. 'The whine in her voice ... bored and afflicted Sandy. It is seven years, thought Sandy, since I betrayed this tiresome woman.'

Even as a teenager, Sandy's small eyes are open to the core of Jean Brodie's self-deceit. As Sandy walks about the poorer parts of town, hearing the 'unbelievable curses of the drunken men and women', she 'began to sense what went to the makings of Miss Brodie, who had elected herself to grace in so particular a way and with more exotic suicidal enchantment than if she had simply taken to drink like other spinsters who couldn't stand it any more'.

This perception is brutal, but telling. What is unforgivable is the way Jean Brodie makes a passion play and a psychodrama out of her simple disappointments, thus dragging others into her solitude and her factitious martyrdom. The phrase 'exotic suicidal enchantment' is the key. The 'exotic' side of Jean Brodie is undeniably attractive; the 'suicidal' nature of her choice is amply shown by her early death; and 'enchantment' suggests her power over others as well as the fact she is herself labouring under the spell of self-delusion.

In middle age, the gymnastic Eunice, who has become a nurse and married a doctor, comments: 'She was full of culture. She was an Edinburgh Festival all on her own.' But when pressed for more detail by her husband, Eunice reflects: 'She was just a spinster.'

'THE UNLIKELY FEAT'

JAMES BOND

I had a call one summer day in 2007 from my literary agent, Gillon Aitken, who also represented Ian Fleming's estate. The Fleming family wanted a new James Bond story to mark the centenary of Ian Fleming's birth; Gillon had been asked to approach me and see if I would be interested in writing such a book.

We met at a safe house to discuss the proposition. My first response was: why me? There were plenty of expert thriller writers to choose from, while I had evinced no interest in James Bond or in the genre. It was true that I had been excited by Bond and Alistair MacLean as a twelve-year-old, but that was a long time ago. On the other hand … Like it or not, Bond was, with Sherlock Holmes, the most famous British fictional character of the twentieth century, and that film theme music had always sent shivers down me as a teenager. After five years researching the history of psychiatry for my novel *Human Traces*, I was drawn to the idea of something light-hearted. Cecil Day Lewis, I remembered, wrote detective stories; Julian Barnes had written a series of stylish private eye novels; Kazuo Ishiguro wrote jazz songs in periods between books. And Ian McKellen, my wife pointed out, spent each New Year playing Widow Twankey.

The first Bond book I read at the age of twelve was *From Russia With Love*. I had the Pan paperback film tie-in edition with a picture of Tatiana Romanova on the back cover in a slashed turquoise dress with black stockings. I had found the jacket rather more exciting than the contents, which made heavy weather of the bureaucracy of the Russian secret services. I remembered odd bits from the other books as well, such as the end of *Live and Let Die* when Bond and the girl (what was her name?) had been tied to the back of a motorboat and towed as living bait over shark-infested reefs.

Eventually, I decided I would read all the Bond books in the order in which they had been published. If I liked them and had an idea of how I could add another one to the body of twelve, then I would do it. I didn't expect them to have lasted at all well, but I think I was only about forty pages into *Moonraker* when I knew that I wanted to say Yes. What impressed me about the books was a single thing: jeopardy. You feared for the safety of the hero, all the time. Here was a man with a single underpowered handgun (the Beretta, which, as a gunsmith told Fleming, was a 'lady's gun – and not a very nice lady at that'), soft shoes, a short-sleeved shirt and really only his wits and fists to defend himself against enemies more numerous, better armed, more cynical and more powerful than himself. But he had one other thing: cruelty. While blindly patriotic and essentially fair-minded, Bond would, if necessary, do ruthless things to protect himself and the national interest. There was the thrilling sense that we were being given a privileged look into the world of those nameless men who unofficially made it safe for us to sleep at night. We did not approve of what Bond did, necessarily, but it was not his or our fault that other people were so schem-ing, so power-crazed and so murderously hostile towards us. If Bond had occasionally to be a bastard, then we would grimly acquiesce, because we lived in troubled times and he was our bastard. It didn't occur to me at this stage that I would end up one day writing about Bond as a snob. Hero, yes; villain, if he had to be; lover, with relish. But snob?

Once I had decided to say yes to the Flemings' offer (with the self-imposed proviso that I must first come up with a robust story), the next question was whether my book should be set in the twenty-first century, as the recent and impressive *Casino Royale* film with Daniel Craig had been, or whether it should be in period. I asked the Fleming family what they had had in mind, and they said they were divided, so the choice was mine. This was a relief because I already knew that the only way I could do this was not as a film-related updating but as a literary homage. As a project, the former not only looked opportunistic, it lacked romance. But for me the challenge of slipping back into another period (one I half-remembered) was exciting; and the idea that I could inhabit Fleming's way of writing and try to create 'the one more novel he would have written' had he lived – that seemed to me worthwhile, and challenging in a technical way. It could be a wreath laid on his grave to say thanks for all the harmless fun that Ian Fleming had given me and millions of other schoolboys, of all ages.

The last novel, *The Man with the Golden Gun*, was published in 1965 and the last stories, *Octopussy*, in 1966. This suggested 1967 as the likely year for my 'added' Fleming book. The Summer of Love. I couldn't see Bond liking that very much, but that in itself could give me some comic mileage. His flat, after all, was just off the King's Road, so he would inevitably bump into some drug-smoking hippies and hear some loud rock music (the Beatles, we already knew, could in Bond's view only be endured through earmuffs).

Having chosen a year, I tried to isolate the essential building blocks of the Bond novel: setting, villain, villain's field of expertise, girl, home set-up, regular characters, gadgets. The setting was easy. While you might think that Ian Fleming had left no atmospheric corner of the world unvisited, there was a large area he had disdained: the Middle East. In his companion, *James Bond: The Man and His World*, Henry Chancellor wrote:

> James Bond never disappears into the souks of North Africa, or gets lost in the deserts of the Middle East ... Fleming ... had little enthusiasm for Tangier ... 'The paint is peeling off the town and the streets are running with spit and pee and worse and its inhabitants, the Arabs, are filthy people and hate all Europeans.' He took a similar view of Beirut ... There was something about Arab countries that Fleming never liked. In *Thrilling Cities* he dismissed the whole region, right through to India, as 'the thieving areas of the world'.

Fleming's loss was my open goal.

Beirut was a great playboy city in the 1960s, but the Lebanon seemed to lack resonance for today's reader. While I wanted a period piece, I also wanted settings that still had a fearful or unsettling ring. Iran had the advantages of being one of the then President Bush's 'axis of evil' countries, of bordering the Soviet Union/Russia and of having been in a liberal period under the Shah in 1967, so Bond would get to meet girls not dressed in hijab. Iran and Russia ... It sounded good to me. While Bond had given his life to war against the Soviet Union, I wasn't sure that he had ever been inside its borders, and that could give a creepy scene, behind enemy lines.

The Bond novels seemed to me to divide into spy books, in which SMERSH or some other Cold War agency was the enemy, and adventure stories (*Live and Let Die, Diamonds are Forever*) where Bond is more like an international policeman. In the second category, the spy's involvement in gang-busting is explained with a quick line from M that 'the PM is worried' about the price of diamonds, gold or whatever. The adventures had a much better pace, but the spy novels did have an extra dimension of menace. So the obvious thing to do was grab at both.

A good villain needed a creepy speciality (creepier by far than Dr No's bird-guano racket), and it seemed odd to me that although drugs were mentioned in passing in a story in *For Your Eyes Only* and at the start of *Thunderball*, they had never been the villain's main occupation. Opium is the king of drugs and could tie neatly into the Iranian setting since eastern Iran bordered on the poppy fields of Helmand. In 1967, the use of recreational drugs was becoming an important issue for the first time in the West, and, like Iran and Russia, drugs seemed to be a hot period item that still resonated in 2008.

I had long been interested in the 1953 CIA coup in Iran (then Persia) that had removed the prime minister Mohammad Mossadegh, who had nationalised the oil wells and cleared out British and American interests, and replaced him with the restored shah. The CIA officer in charge, Kermit Roosevelt, had helpfully written an account of the coup. Then there was the question of American involvement in the Far East, particularly French Indochina, that I had first come across in *The Quiet American* by Graham Greene. The point of these peripheral things would be to add some – but not too much – political background. The last thing I wanted to do was to slow down the pace of the story, but it seemed a good idea to borrow a little extra menace, a few frissons, from reality.

Such morally grey historical events could also help me create a villain who was not too much out of pantomime. I had been struck by an article I had once read about the businessman Rupert Murdoch, which attributed much of his anti-British zeal to the fact that some unwise student had teased him at Oxford and thus precipitated a lifelong hatred of what Murdoch thought of as 'the British Establishment', or some equally lazy construct. I thought it would make the villain more interesting if much of what he said was not paranoid or megalomaniac but had a real – or fairly real – political basis. Even its admirers concede that the story of empire is not all mission schools and railways, and a hatred of Britain inspired a part of my villain Dr Gorner's character; I gave him the book of empire nasties and let him invent a couple more.

On the other hand, I didn't want to lose the expected broad-brush grotesquerie of Ian Fleming's villains. Political ambiguity was fine, maybe, but only up to a point. I liked those villains who had some kind of physical quirk, such as the one in *Live and Let Die* who was effectively a zombie – undead, and harder still to bump off with a lady's gun. My father once told me he had been at university with a man who had a monkey's paw in place of his right hand and I wondered if this might work. And if a villain, why not a sidekick? Oddjob in *Goldfinger* was a hugely successful character, with his passion for karate and eating cats. Oddjob was in. Or rather, Chagrin, a Vietnamese with an ex-Communist speciality of torturing French Catholic nuns and Vietnamese children, was in. I forget where I found his pencil-in-the-ear torture. Perhaps I made it up.

Other characters who were indispensable were M, Miss Moneypenny and May, the Scottish 'treasure' who keeps house for Bond in Chelsea.

Felix Leiter also seemed to work well and I had had a weakness for him since I was first introduced to Bond at the age of eleven by my school friend Fali Vakeel. Fali was always Bond in our make-believe, but I was allowed to 'be' the shark-maimed CIA man Leiter. I also liked the character of Karim Bey in *From Russia With Love*. He is the worldly head of station in Istanbul, and my character Darius Alizadeh in Tehran plays a similar role – and meets a similar end. At a party in Winchester in July 2009 I was reprimanded by an MI6 officer for having a foreign national in this role, but I think he had not understood that the 'Service' Bond works for is not the same thing as MI6. We know this because M and Co. refer to MI6, or SIS, as a different organisation. If Fleming's Service had a foreign national as head of station, that was good enough for me.

Then the girl. I was a bit worried about her, because to create a full-on bikini bird might grate in 2008; on the other hand it would be pointless to produce some politically correct schnauzer. Although Scarlett is a swinging sixties girl in an open-top car and a short dress, she is much better educated than Bond, trilingual, musically gifted and working for a Paris investment bank. Ian Fleming's women turned out to be more interesting than I had expected. Each has a mind of her own (even if, as in the case of Honeychile in *Dr No*, the height of her ambition is to become a hooker in Miami). Most of them are in some way damaged by fathers, lovers (Tiffany Case in *Diamonds are Forever*) or by the repressive state itself in the case of Tatiana Romanova – and how lazy a surname was that for a Moscow cipher clerk, causing Fleming to have to throw in a justificatory paragraph of how she is distantly, and improbably, related to the tsars. In *Moonraker*, it turns out that the girl is not only a serious career civil servant, but is engaged to another man and won't even sleep with Bond (though luckily her clothes get blown off when a bomb is dropped down a cliff). The chastity route, however, was not one that Fleming cared to travel again. And if one girl, why not two? If Scarlett, why not Poppy? When it came to Bond and Scarlett having sex, I thought I might write it in a more realistic, less stylised way than Fleming. This was a disaster. It was – embarrassingly – as though there were three of us in the room. I tore it up and vowed to stick closely to Fleming's style of describing Bond on the job – rough, abrupt and, in its way, quite innocent. It clearly wasn't my place to be teaching Bond new tricks in this department.

I noted that many of Fleming's books seemed to gain by the use of a prologue – starting somewhere unexpected with louche characters whose involvement only later becomes clear. Since I had decided that Bond's French opposite number René Mathis was also well worth a scene or two, it seemed to me that a Paris slum was the obvious place for a prelude, where we see the end of the drug trail and the violence and misery it causes. The last set-piece element I really wanted to copy was a game. There are cards in *Casino Royale* and *Moonraker* and the round of golf in *Goldfinger*. But what game had Ian Fleming not used? Football? Cricket? Rugby? The only other sport that seemed to work – requiring few people and the chance of cheating – was tennis. It could easily take place in Paris, in a swanky suburb before a huge lunch on the Seine. Tennis might not be everyone's idea of a glamorous game, but it was certainly less naff than golf.

This left the style. If I was going to do a real homage to Ian Fleming, I would have to write like him. I like doing parodies of other writers, and had published a loo-side book of them called *Pistache* (including, as it happened, a pastiche of Fleming). The trick with parody is to find the characteristic elements of a writer and exaggerate them, so your version is roughly 120 per cent of the writer's own style. With the Bond book, though, I thought it would be crucial to pull up well short of this line (after all, the films had dipped into self-parody and Austin Powers and others had gone further). So my idea was to create a style that was about 80 per cent Fleming: reminiscent, but not a duplicate – and certainly not an exaggeration. Understanding the style itself was not too hard. Fleming had learned to write as a newspaperman, for Reuters in Moscow, and it showed. Short sentences predominated. Active verbs were preferred to passive, and Anglo–Saxon roots to Romance; adjectives were few and adverbs fewer. Semicolons were a rarity. The only time Fleming's prose became engorged was, oddly enough, when he wrote of machinery – Bond's Bentley, the motor yacht in *Thunderball* or the steam locomotive in *Diamonds are Forever*. Style is one thing, tone (the author's implied attitude to the words) is another; and this was where Fleming had been at his shrewdest. I would describe his tone as elitist but inclusive. His descriptions of international air travel, casinos, beautiful women, guns and hair-raising drinks said to the reader: this is Bond's world, known also to me – now come on in and feel a part of it; you, too, are by nature one of our exclusive threesome.

And talking of locomotives and motor yachts reminded me of one other thing I had to do: find an exciting vehicle. I noticed from the books that Bond wasn't much interested in gadgets, which were largely the addition of the films. This was a relief; but there was no getting away from the need for some impressive mobility. It was while looking online for an Iranian summer retreat on the Caspian Sea that I came across a URL devoted to the 'Caspian Sea Monster'. This turned out to be the Ekranoplan – a daring Russian amphibious vehicle of the Cold War which even the website described as 'Bond-like', while lamenting that no more than six had been built and no one had ever heard of it. For all the days of bad luck and toil as a writer, pushing heavy boulders uphill, you sometimes get an unexpected break.

*

James Bond himself posed me some problems. He had been left as a shell of a man by Ian Fleming – brainwashed, exhausted and not fit for much. So to start with I had to rehabilitate him. This turned out to be helpful, as it allowed me to feel my way into the character slowly. I had noted all Bond's consumer choices while reading the books: the Morland cigarettes with the three gold rings, the short-sleeved shirts of Sea Island cotton and so on. The gun changed in due course from the lady's Beretta to a sturdier Walther PPK. Fleming had written a magazine article entitled 'How To Write a Thriller' in which he explained why he had begun specifying brand names. They did not start out as showy connoisseurship or brand snobbery, but as a way of bringing our man back to earth after some barely credible exploits. So if Bond had swum a crocodile swamp and defeated five machine-gun-wielding goons with his bare hands, what better aftermath than a piece of toast with Cooper's Oxford marmalade? Soon, however, Fleming began to have more fun with the selection of brands, becoming more outré, specifying what vintage of champagne Bond preferred and at what temperature it should be drunk. His editor at the publishers Jonathan Cape, a fastidious man called William Plomer, tweaked some of the details and suggested others, with the result that in the later books Bond has arguably developed from connoisseur to fusspot. Cyril Connolly thought he had gone yet further and that there was something not altogether heterosexual in Bond's pickiness. In a parody called 'Bond Strikes Camp', Connolly had M require 007 to go to a transvestite bar in Chelsea, dressed as a woman, and accost a suspicious stranger who turned out to be none other than M himself in drag.

I followed all the brand details faithfully because they are important to the man, and to readers' expectations. Some people queried the number of eggs my Bond consumed, but I can only say that Fleming's ate

more, since Fleming himself believed that breakfast was secretly everyone's favourite meal. Bond's drinking habits did give me a slight case of
heartburn, however. Before the crucial game of cards against Hugo Drax
in *Moonraker* he consumes a large vodka martini, a carafe of Wolfschmidt
vodka from Riga, a bottle of Dom Perignon 1946 champagne and half a
packet of Benzedrine. Later, he absorbs a large brandy and another bottle
of champagne. Like Mr Pooter, Bond is reluctant to blame his hangover
on volume consumed, and is suspicious only that Benzedrine and champagne don't mix. I was keen to have René Mathis lure Bond into drinking
at least some wine – if only for his health's sake. Mathis selects Château
Batailley, a structured Pauillac, not too girly, and Bond is impressed
enough to order some of his own volition in his final bedroom feast with
Scarlett in the George V in Paris. Drinks of all kinds were happily available
in the Shah's West-loving Tehran.

Much has been written about Bond's brand snobbery. The key point is
that being able to distinguish small details, and caring about them, could be
a lifesaver for a spy. Thus Bond's fussiness is to me a credible by-product of
his professional powers of observation. There is also an argument, made by
Ben Macintyre in *For Your Eyes Only: Ian Fleming and James Bond*, that
'Much spycraft is boring, dangerous and uncomfortable, and spies tend to be
self-interested people, fascinated by material things. Perhaps because of this,
human comforts and luxuries assume a disproportionate importance when an
agent is off duty.' Ben Macintyre's chapter 'Shaken, Stirred and Custom-
made: Bond's Life of Luxury' is definitive on these matters. Read this, along
with Henry Chancellor's chapters 'A Man in his Time' and 'The Right Way
to Eat', and you will know more about Bond's brands and consumer choices
than I did even when in the heat of writing *Devil May Care*.

*

James Bond's consumer snobbery was attractive to readers in post-war Britain because it reminded them that there was a life beyond rationing and blancmange. Some of them can hardly have known what all these exotic things were; sometimes even Ian Fleming didn't seem too sure, as when he gives Bond an avocado pear for dessert, while the 'half-measure of Kina Lillet' specified in his dry martini recipe would apparently have given a disgusting taste of quinine to the drink.

In Dr No's headquarters, Bond notes that 'the soap was Guerlain's Sapoceti, *Fleurs des Alpes*' and this suggests some cruel precision in the villain's attention to detail in the bathroom of his prisoner, even if few readers, including this one, knew what he was on about. The Fleming legacy in this matter has been unhelpful. Lesser writers – airport novelists – failed to spot that the details usually served a purpose and just threw in all the brand names they could think of; the effect was not much more than 'Look at my heroine. Isn't she rich?' Even in such an enjoyable novel as *The Bonfire of the Vanities*, it's hard to think that Tom Wolfe, such an acute social critic, gained much from pointing out that Louis Vuitton luggage is vulgar. The brand-name thing was brought to a logical and bloody conclusion – you would have thought – by Brett Easton Ellis in *American Psycho*, where the main character, serial killer Patrick Bateman, insanely lists the maker of every piece of clothing worn. Sadly, however, the airporters kept going with their names. Perhaps they hadn't read *American Psycho*.

What is ultimately important about the character of James Bond is that he is – almost unbelievably – believable. Kingsley Amis, who wrote an official James Bond book called *Colonel Sun* in 1968, under the pen name Robert Markham, put it like this: 'Mr Fleming has brought off the unlikely feat of enclosing this wildly romantic, almost narcissistic and (one would have thought) hopelessly out-of-date persona inside the shellac of a secret agent, and so making it plausible, mentally actable and, to all appearance, contemporary.' This is not one of Kingsley Amis's clearest sentences, but I think it does suggest his sense of amazement that, having had a go at it himself, he found such an 'unlikely' character was ultimately 'plausible'.

My Bond was necessarily slow off the mark, as I built him up to fighting fitness, but I suspect there is also a sense in the early scenes of my trying to probe his mind, his mood, his melancholy – and coming up against a brick wall. I think there is melancholy in Bond – and Fleming said as much when he talked about the colours he wears – but it resists the novelist's searchlight. I wasn't too worried about this to begin with, though later, when the story speeded up it became more problematic. In the novels I usually write there is not much in the way of incident or dramatic disclosure; when there is, I normally slow down the narrative so that the reader can take time to assimilate the development. If it were a film, you would linger on a shot or go into a slow dissolve; in a book you must have words, and this is therefore a good moment for the character to take stock, to analyse his motives or to look back at his life. Then, when you return to your story, the reader has had time to absorb the impact of the earlier incident.

There were many moments in the action of *Devil May Care* when I wanted this slowing-down and deepening-out process, but I was never able to write satisfactory descriptions of Bond's mental processes. He tended to emerge from them as fussy, or mathematical, or just slow-witted. I could get him to clarify the significance of a previous piece of action, but that was about all the introspection he would permit me. So I threw these sections out. I achieved some variation of pace by bringing in another character, usually Scarlett, and at least taking the focus off Bond for a moment. But the truth is that he really came alive for me when he was in action: drinking, fighting, running, flying. In the less active scenes in Paris, Moscow and Tehran I relied on his continuously critical awareness – whether of other characters such as Taylor, the shady CIA man, or of food, drink, cars, girls – to give us a sense of the man, and this too seemed to work better.

This may sound as though I thought Bond was a hollow or not fully realised character, but this was not in fact the case. The more I came to know him, in the course of attributing thoughts, judgements and actions to him, the more I came to think that Ian Fleming had actually – and however 'unlikely', in Kingsley Amis's word, it seemed – created a real person. James Bond is a man whose character is defined by his relationship to external reality in all its guises, from the life-threatening to the comic. This is a recognisable psychological type in real life, even if, for obvious reasons, not much favoured in mainstream literary fiction. If you cared to be pretentious, you could track through *Devil May Care* a subtext in which I am courting the character of Bond, trying to bend him a little more to my will, and in that process – which consisted mostly of rebuffs – finally decoding, with any luck, a little of his DNA.

'A PRINCE AMONG PEASANTS'

CHANU AHMED

Monica Ali's *Brick Lane* was warmly received on its publication in 2003. Readers admired the author's breadth of understanding and her apparent ease in the form, which were remarkable in a first novel. Many expressed a sense of gratitude that a writer had sent a despatch from a field that was felt to be under-reported: the immigrant experience. Enthusiasts used the word 'news' when talking about the book because they felt it brought them a report of what people were thinking – though, as we will see, this later led to difficulties in the bear pit of cultural correctness.

What *Brick Lane* really had going for it was flair, humour and a great character called Chanu Ahmed. Chanu is a forty-year-old immigrant from Bangladesh who has been living in East London for more than sixteen years when we find him – just married to a young woman called Nazneen, who has been flown in from a semi-literate rural family to be his bride in an arranged marriage. Nazneen occupies the central position of the novel and most of the action is seen through her eyes; but by far the most interesting character is Chanu.

He is an intellectual snob, proud of his degree from Dhaka University and of the certificates he has collected from various British colleges of no great distinction. He can quote Chaucer and Dickens; he has read David Hume and other Scottish philosophers as well as having some knowledge of the great poet of his homeland, Rabindranath Tagore. Chanu sees himself as an intellectual, a pearl among the swine at the local council office where he works. He is contemptuous of the Sylhetis, his fellow immigrants from Bangladesh, because they are peasant farmers without a university degree among them. When he sends off an autobiographical story to the *Bexleyheath Advertiser* he calls it 'A Prince Among Peasants'. His rival for promotion is a man called Wilkie, who goes to the pub at lunchtime and returns half an hour late to his desk. Chanu, an intermittent Muslim, despises Wilkie less for his Brit booziness than for the fact that he has only one, or maybe two, O levels.

Chanu is a Mr Punch figure; like Mr Pooter, he probably has his ultimate origin in the *commedia dell'arte* – the sixteenth-century itinerant Italian drama that so influenced French and English playwrights. In the *commedia*, the Pulcinella character developed into the bully who beats his wife and is beaten, in return, by life and circumstance. If you subtract the actual violence, you can see in Mr Punch, his English descendant, the outline not only of Pooter and Chanu, but most of the heroes of British television comedy: Tony Hancock, Captain Mainwaring, Alan Partridge, David Brent and so on. It is significant that one of the first things Nazneen thinks is that Chanu had not beaten her … yet.

While a towering Enlightenment figure in his own mind, Chanu is poor, lives in a dingy council flat, is overweight and requires Nazneen to apply the razor blade to his troublesome corns. When the local council, predictably, overlooks his claim to promotion in favour of the uneducated Wilkie, Chanu becomes a minicab driver. There is comedy in the way that he can't understand why the world refuses to take him at his own high estimation of himself; he can't see that while his attachment to reading and education may be admirable it has not stopped him from appearing to others a ridiculous man. 'These people here didn't know the difference between me, who stepped off an aeroplane with a degree certificate, and the peasants who jumped off the boat possessing only the lice on their heads.'

This raises, in its playful way, some serious questions about society and how the individual fits in. Chanu has the wit to understand why the white working class in the East End are frightened of their Muslim neighbours: it's because they fear the immigrants may rise above them in the pecking order, as previous newcomers to the East End – Huguenots from France, Jews from Eastern Europe and others – have done; they like to feel there is a safety net, a more despised group, below them. Touchingly, however, Chanu expects the 'traditional' British people in positions of authority – those higher up in the council offices, for instance – to make the nice discriminations that he makes between himself, a man of learning and substance, and the Sylhetis, peasants only good for driving rickshaws. In fact, the council officers and others make no such distinctions; to them, Chanu is just another 'Paki', an immigrant like all the others. Wilkie will have the job, when he gets back from the pub; Wilkie won't rock the boat or want to have days off at the 'wrong' time for Ramadan.

The skill of Monica Ali's characterisation of Chanu is that she makes him simultaneously ridiculous and poignant. Because he is the beneficiary of the arranged marriage, we expect to dislike him; but our expectations are not met. We laugh, but we feel indignant at the same time on his behalf. Chanu's values, we feel, are good ones. Education is indeed the most important thing that humans have, and the only sure way for poor children to find better lives. But is book knowledge on its own enough? Billions of pounds of government budgets annually say Yes. Entire postgraduate departments of Cambridge and Harvard, where scholarship is pursued for its own sake and needs no practical application, are based on this belief. British politicians have decided that over half the young population must have university degrees, even though the number of jobs requiring education to tertiary level is barely 10 per cent. In Chanu we see one of those graduates with knowledge to burn, with a degree and no job worthy of it; a man with nowhere practical to place his passion for learning.

What Locke and Hume and Thackeray have failed to give Chanu is self-awareness. He is idealistic in the way that he expects high-mindedness among the native British and tends always to think well of his fellow man (except the Sylhetis). Yet for all his reading he is ignorant of the ways of the world; he understands some of the motivation of the white working class, but he does not see the depth of cynicism in the country he has lived in, by the end of the book, for thirty years. He has little insight into the husband-figure he presents to Nazneen. He expects her simply to be the bride he has ordered and barely seems to imagine that she has an inner life. While he is kind enough to her in his way, it never occurs to him that a non-English-speaking woman from a Bengali village will respond to the challenge of life in the urban West in a way quite different from his own. Chanu assumes universal values that override culture and religion; monoglot Nazneen works closer to the ground, quick-witted, adaptable and increasingly practical in the struggle for survival. Her first child, a boy, dies in infancy and is buried swiftly in the Muslim way, reminding her of the many child deaths back home, 'of cousins who came into the world and left again promptly, as if they had wandered into a room by mistake, apologized and turned back'. She ends up with two anglicised, stroppy, 'assimilated' daughters and a young, politically active lover. It is all too sad.

Monica Ali herself has a Bangladeshi father and English mother, was born in Bangladesh and brought up in Bolton. When residents of Brick Lane protested at a feature film of the novel being shot there, Germaine Greer disputed Ali's right to speak for Bangladeshi Britons, and criticised Chanu as an irresponsible creation who would become 'a defining caricature'. Monica Ali, Greer wrote,

> is on the near side of British culture, not far from the middle. She writes in English and her point of view is, whether she allows herself to impersonate a village Bangladeshi woman or not, British. She has forgotten her Bengali, which she would not have done if she had wanted to remember it. When it comes to writing a novel, however, she becomes the pledge of our multi-ethnicity ... [Ali has created] her own version of Bengali-ness. As a British writer, she is very aware of what will appear odd but plausible to a British audience ... An author may say she loves and respects the characters she has created. But what hurts is precisely that: she has dared to create them.
>
> Ali did not concern herself with the possibility that her plot might seem outlandish to the people who created the particular culture of Brick Lane. As British people know little and care less

about the Bangladeshi people in their midst, their first appearance
as characters in an English novel had the force of a defining caricature ... English readers were charmed by her Bengali characters,
but some of the Sylhetis of Brick Lane did not recognise themselves
... For people who don't have much else, self-esteem is crucial ...
Bangladeshi Britons would be better off not reading – or, when it
comes out, seeing the film of – *Brick Lane*.[13]

This article prompted a reply from Sir Salman Rushdie. He called Professor Greer's argument 'philistine, sanctimonious and disgraceful'.[14] 'There
is a kind of double racism in this argument', wrote Sir Salman. 'To suit
Greer, the British–Bangladeshi Ali is denied her heritage and belittled for
her Britishness, while her British–Bangladeshi critics are denied that same
Britishness, which most of them would certainly insist was theirs by right.'

What might Chanu have made of such a rumpus? Would he begin by
questioning the ethnic and/or citizenship status of Greer and Rushdie,
his native Australian and Indian critics? Or would he think such ad
hominem/feminam questions undignified? Whatever you may think of the
tone of the argument, the questions it raises are not unreasonable. Is Chanu
a good Muslim? A proper Briton? A true Bengali? A corking snob? Or
just a man?

He is certainly full of human frailties. When he has been revolted by
the antics of the extremist white youths he proudly makes his daughters
dress in hijab, but when he is irritated by the 'peasant' separatism of some

---

[13] Germaine Greer, 'Reality Bites', the *Guardian*, 24 July 2006
[14] Salman Rushdie, letter to the *Guardian*, 29 July 2006

of his community he tells Nazneen to put the girls in skirts without trousers. His greed and sedentary life give him gastric troubles, though this leads to a much-needed weight loss, which he shows off proudly. '"Willpower," he said. "And ulcer," he conceded.' He's worried, however, that too much weight loss will make him look less like a factory owner than a rickshaw wallah.

Monica Ali introduces another vein of snobbery in Nazneen's attitude to her husband. 'If Chanu was awake, he was thinking, and his thoughts were written on his face. He is like a child, thought Nazneen, who has learned to read but must mouth the words.' She observes how he uses the television, never watching it but keeping it on like a fire in the corner of the room, occasionally stirring it up into different colours by changing channel. She notices that, like Emma, Chanu doesn't stick at things and suspects that his latest degree will never be finished. One day Nazneen catches him sitting in a friend's house with his knees apart, ankles crossed and his coat still on, 'like a gardener who had come in to collect his wages'. So there is something of the snob in Nazneen, too, and a trace of Tess Durbeyfield and Elizabeth Bennet in being one of 'nature's ladies'. Her rapturous sex with Karim, her young lover, is proof that she has transcended the bounds of a rural, religious upbringing. The interesting question with Nazneen is the extent to which her upward social mobility relies on her adopting western morals and manners. She adapts, changes her behaviour and begins to flourish, or at least to manage, in London. Chanu, who takes a more absolutist view and clings to the standards he believes are universal, is rejected by his adopted country and chooses to go home, where he hopes that people will recognise his superior qualities. It is not their religious faith in either case that is the decisive factor, nor is it really a question of culture. Chanu speaks better English and is much better read in English literature than Nazneen, yet it is she who ultimately begins to feel more comfortable. In the end, the life-changing factor for these two people is not culture, religion or gender, but personal temperament. The novel's epigraph, taken from Heraclitus, states: 'A man's character is his fate'; it does not say 'A person's nationality is culturally normative.'

Chanu and Karim, the men in Nazneen's life, are of different generations, and some of the tension and comedy springs from this. But while each to a minor extent represents the changing attitudes of immigrants – from first-generation deference to second-generation antagonism – neither is typical. Karim is an Islamist activist, which puts him in a minority among young men of his age, while Chanu is too much defined by his idiosyncrasies, too contradictory, too vain and too universal to do the menial novelistic turn of being a cultural symbol.

'There was in the world a great shortage of respect and Chanu was among the famished', writes Ali, as she starts to extend the remit of her character. He has read Warren Hastings on the glories of Bengal and imagines himself to be in a coalition of the enlightened; Nazneen hasn't heard of Warren Hastings but does point out that Bengal's two great national heroes were Sylhetis. There is something heroic in Chanu's largeness of spirit: he will not be dragged down by such detail into revising his opinion of the lice-ridden Sylhetis; nor is he a slave to his religion, pointing out to his wife the pair of them are Muslims only because of the Moguls, and that Bengal was Buddhist and Hindu, twice, before it was Muslim. He would like to draw on the wisdom of other religions – Buddhist thought, Christian parables, Hindu philosophy.

It is also crucial to our understanding of Chanu that Nazneen never knows whether he has found out about her affair with Karim. Monica Ali skilfully lets Nazneen and the reader suspect that he has – and that he has generously decided to remain silent. So Chanu is kind and subtle – large-hearted as well as foolish; and such a man is more than a cipher or symbol for a cultural news update.

It's true that Chanu resembles other immigrant characters in fiction, notably Samad in Zadie Smith's equally admired *White Teeth*, published in 2000, who also has a higher view of his intellectual status than others do, and V. S. Naipaul's Mr Biswas, in *A House for Mr Biswas*, published in 1962, from whom Chanu may have inherited his half-comic dignity. In the end, though, Chanu's multiple contradictions and inexhaustible self-delusion give him an almost Dickensian grandeur; he reminds you less of a 'defining caricature' than of your own uncle – and sometimes even of yourself. Monica Ali takes us into the lives of people we may think we've never met before; but then, by the patient accumulation of detail, she begins to uncover subtler mechanisms, to show the inner reality of her characters so that the more particular the details, the more resonant the people seem to become. At some point, the circle is squared; the weight of individuality produces – paradoxically – a man who speaks to all of us, a universal character. This is what good novelists, uniquely, can do. 'News' is probably best left to journalists.

PART FOUR

VILLAINS

To a large extent the villain, like the hero, is out of place in the novel. While the hero came from epic poetry, the villain sprang from the theatre. As realism became the dominant form in fiction, however, his histrionic ways began to become an embarrassment; that he survived at all is a testament to how useful he could be.

In a novel, the villain is the one who knows what's going on; he has the gen; he holds the keys to the plot, in both senses of the word. Barbara Covett in Zoë Heller's *Notes on a Scandal* not only manipulates her victim, she literally controls the story for the reader: 'The task of telling it has fallen into my hands'. Fosco in *The Woman in White* demonstrates the glamour of superior knowledge; the challenge for Wilkie Collins was to retain or release the details of what Fosco alone knows in a way that kept his readers agog. Fosco is also a foreigner, which lends him extra mystery: he may have weird Continental powers (chemistry, Mesmerism …) that will be beyond his English adversary, Walter Hartright. What's more, Fosco is a count – a title that doesn't exist in Britain but was much favoured for villains, including Bram Stoker's Count Dracula and the villain of Ann Radcliffe's Gothic novel *The Mysteries of Udolpho*, Count Montoni.

The villain is a seducer. Sometimes, as with Fagin, this is in an asexual way – he seduces Oliver Twist with laughter, food and occasional kindness. Long John Silver in *Treasure Island* seems to be a kind of hypnotist: 'He fixed his unfathomable gray eyes on me, with that cold, clear, irresistible glitter in them ... An unutterable suspicion that his mind is prying into mine overcomes me at these times ...'. With Fosco, it is the sexual fascination he has for his most worthy adversary, Marian Halcombe, that prevents her from seeing his deviousness more clearly. In Robert Lovelace, Richardson's villain in *Clarissa*, sex is the explicit driving force for a million words of seduction and rebuff. However, Lovelace's schemes for sleeping with Clarissa Harlowe so thrilled the readers of the novel that Richardson had to rewrite the book to underline Lovelace's immorality. There is always the danger that the villain will be so attractive to a reader hungry for intrigue that he will suspend his moral judgement and so thwart the high-minded author. It was quite a coup, I always felt, that Howard Kirk, the apparently irresistible seducer of Malcolm Bradbury's novel *The History Man*, remained in all ways repulsive to the reader.

Villains often have not only the power of knowledge and sex but of language, too. Lovelace is high on poetry for much of the time. Richardson consulted an anthology of verse to keep the quotations coming, and it sometimes seems that Lovelace needs this rhetoric to maintain the heat of his desire. Humbert Humbert in Nabokov's *Lolita* relies on his high-flown language to make his illegal urge seem tenable. Barbara Covett uses tart phrasing to expose the vacuity of her colleagues and of her prey.

When I wrote a novel called *Engleby* in 2005, I didn't know when I began it that Mike Engleby, the narrator, was going to be a villain. I knew that his voice was not quite right, like a radio turned slightly off-station, but I had no idea where he was taking me. Readers' reactions brought home to me the different standards they apply to people in books. One reader told me she loved Mike Engleby. I said, 'Well, it's fine to sympathise until you find out what he's done.' 'No,' she said. 'Even when I found out, I still liked him.'

At the start of the twentieth century, the dramatic inheritance of the villain became more cumbersome, as a value system emerged that was based on new ideas of psychological exploration. If every human motive could be explained, the idea of villainy could look clumsy. In France, Emile Zola's novels adhered to a dogma of character determined by social circumstance, and this made moral distinctions marginal; while in Emma Bovary, Flaubert had already presented a day-dreaming adulteress as a person to be viewed not as a caution but as a fascinating and suggestive case. Zola's *Thérèse Raquin* in 1867 told the story of a woman who, with her lover, murders her husband, but tried to present her as a 'scientific' case study. Mauriac's Thérèse Desqueyroux, in the 1927 novel of the same name, tries to poison her husband, but the stifling nature of her marriage and the dreaded life of the bourgeoisie[15] were presented as exculpation. In some ways these are post-moral books; they are certainly post-religious.

The idea that a criminal should be explained found few takers among British novelists, which is puzzling when you consider that the natural drama of such a situation – the tension between outer and inner life, between social norm and personal reality – was elsewhere the mainstay of the serious novel. For British writers, the villain tended to remain the

---

[15] What Henry James witheringly called 'the puerile dread of the grocer … which has sterilized a whole province of French literature'.

servant of the plot, the instigator of the action par excellence. In Paul Scott's Raj Quartet, Ronald Merrick is a post-Freudian villain. He is a bad man, but he is bad for given reasons; he has, in fact, a complete psychopathology and is presented to us as someone wholly explicable in these terms. This is clearly quite different from Fagin or Fosco, where we are not given any childhood experience or analysis of motive. The shape of Merrick's darkness is not ours, but it finds an echo. We all know that the distinctive shapes of our personalities – our strengths as well as our desires and weaknesses – could, in the wrong circumstances, become deformities. The interesting thing about Merrick, however, is that although he is a modern character in the *tout comprendre, c'est tout pardonner* sense, Paul Scott does not actually ask us to forgive. Merrick, for all the scrupulousness with which Scott makes his unconscious and conscious desires known to the reader, remains a villain.

Barbara Covett is Merrick taken one step further. She is our contemporary, and her circumstances are much less bizarre than Merrick's. With Merrick you feel that, with a flex of your imagination, you can understand him; with Barbara you feel that, had the cards of your life fallen a little differently, you could *be* her.

The trajectory of the British villain is complete. Lovelace is so indebted to the theatre that sometimes his letters to his friend Belford include stage directions. The highpoint of the villain, as with so much else, is in the work of Dickens, where the stage background is fully assimilated into novelistic plot, as in Quilp, the dwarfish villain of *The Old Curiosity Shop*, who, with a liking for hot brandy, has a way of 'making himself more fiery and furious … heating his malice and mischievousness till they boil'. By the end of the Victorian period, the theatrical inheritance is starting to unbalance the villain again, leading to such melodramatic creations as

Bram Stoker's Dracula and Stevenson's Jekyll and Hyde; the secondary villain of *The Woman in White*, Sir Percival Glyde, seems to have strayed out of pantomime. Freud and his followers, though at first ignored in Britain, eventually gave a helping hand to novelists by stressing – scientifically or otherwise – the universal knowability of motive.

You can argue that the principal difference between a twenty-first and an eighteenth-century villain is that the modern one is much harder to spot. You would look askance at Lovelace and run a mile from Fagin, but you wouldn't give Barbara Covett a second glance – which is a large part of her awful charm.

Clarissa refuses the advances of Robert Lovelace (1748 edition)

'BUFFETING THE MOON'

ROBERT LOVELACE

Clarissa is the longest novel in English and Robert Lovelace is its dominant character. Over the space of a million words, twice the number in *War and Peace*, his high spirits, erotic ambition, wit, stratagems and manic determination overshadow all else – including the eponymous heroine. The book is a battle of wills that ends with the death of both combatants. Lovelace is a criminal villain in deed because he rapes a woman; he is a villain in the conception of his Puritan author because his lustful urges embody the low nature of the fallen human being. But in his own eyes, he is a villain only for his 'contrivances' – the word he gives to his deceits and trickery. He is inclined to excuse himself even these, however, because they are no more than a slightly unpalatable means to an end – the seduction of Clarissa – in which he sees no shame. He is a villain in the literary sense, in that he has all the traits that novelists who followed Richardson would incorporate into such characters: he alone is in charge of the plot and its momentum; he is dynamic, charming and superficially attractive; and his sense of his own superiority finds an expression in his delight in language, which he uses more effectively than the other characters. Most villains are good with words, as Humbert Humbert noted in *Lolita*: 'You can always count on a murderer for a fancy prose style.'

Yet there is a paradox at the heart of Lovelace: is he really a villain to the reader? It is a matter of historical fact that many of Richardson's readers responded sympathetically to Lovelace, arguing that he was not that bad, that he was clearly capable of reform and that if Clarissa had had a greater degree of self-knowledge she could have avoided the violence that befalls her. Richardson was appalled by this response, and extensively revised the book between editions to underline Lovelace's villainy, trying to remove any instances of behaviour where he might establish a sympathetic foothold in the reader's imagination. Some of the additions strike an odd note, as for instance a plot to trick Anna Howe (Clarissa's friend and correspondent), her mother and maid on to a boat and have his way with them – a plot that lacks any of Lovelace's tense poetry and seems shoved in merely to blacken his name.

What we have as a result is a very conflicted character, a man who appears at times so nervously driven as to be unstable, perhaps almost unwell. For all his intellect and his charm, there is a void in Lovelace. He is good at using other people, but seldom understands them. There is a trace of the sociopath. This seems to be partly because of internal stresses as imagined by the author, but may also derive from a tension between what Richardson moralistically required of Lovelace and the effects that the character's autonomous energy, once unleashed, begins to generate in the open-minded reader. The genie is out of the bottle, and one sometimes has the sense of an author running a step or two behind his creation, trying to limit the damage of his exuberance.

Richardson builds up the expectation for Lovelace's delayed entrance into the novel by having Clarissa quote the opinions of others in her letters to Anna Howe. If Richardson had been trying to write a romance, he could hardly have made his hero sound more raffishly attractive. He is spendthrift, but generous; he is capable of financial self-control and jealous of his independence from family financial ties. He is sexually dangerous – to the extent that his tenants lock up their prettier daughters when he visits – but has no single mistress, preferring 'newelty' or constant challenge. He has a group of close male friends, some 'as bad as himself'; he has a good head for drink and a great way with words. While he is an inveterate plotter, he is also good-humoured and loves 'as well to take a jest as to give one'. He would be a challenge for a romantic heroine as formidable as Jane Eyre or Elizabeth Bennet, but, alas, Clarissa Harlowe is only eighteen years old. She lacks the sparkle, wit or maturity to be a match for Lovelace; such gifts for flirtation and friendship as she timidly displays in the early part of the book are withdrawn as she becomes reduced to a single position – that of resilience under siege. While this process seems psychologically sound – it is probably how a girl of her age and background would react – it robs the novel of a dynamic complexity and throws the spotlight more and more on to Lovelace to provide the narrative energy.

Spotlights are what he likes, and he has a theatrical heritage in Jacobean and Restoration drama (plays which Richardson as a Puritan may not have seen – though there is evidence he had been to see tragedies – but as a professional printer would have read). Lovelace's first appearance at the

Harlowe household involves him wounding Clarissa's brother James in the arm with a sword after James has attacked him. The Harlowe family, embodiments of a new and powerful middle class made rich by 'trade', close ranks against Lovelace, the decadent aristocrat, and steer their prized Clarissa towards a repulsive but respectable local landowner called Roger Solmes. Lovelace is delighted by the Harlowes' response, as he knows that such parental clumsiness can only inflame Clarissa's interest in him.

When we first meet Lovelace in his own words (not until Letter 31), we see how conniving, nervous and brilliant he is. 'All my fear arises from the little hold I have in the heart of this charming frost-piece', he tells his fellow rake, Belford. Clarissa represents the greatest challenge woman-hood has yet held out to him; he will take her and have her as his revenge upon the only woman he loved, who was unfaithful to him. 'To carry off such a girl [as Clarissa] in spite of her watchful and implacable friends; and in spite of a prudence and reserve that I never met with in any of the sex; – what a triumph! – What a triumph over the whole sex!'

As Clarissa fights off her family and their plans for her, Lovelace offers her hope, escape and vague offers of marriage. He writes to her from the 'Ivy Cavern in the Coppice', at the end of the Harlowes' garden, where he spends the night outside. He signs himself 'Your ever-adoring, yet almost desponding Lovelace', and you would think that any eighteen-year-old's head would be a little turned. And indeed, his little 'frost-piece' does melt a fraction. She agrees to meet him in the garden and is tricked away with him in a coach to St Albans, where the gravity of what she has done sinks in. She writes to Anna: 'You will soon hear … that your Clarissa Harlowe is gone off with a man!'

Now we hear much more from Lovelace, as he gloats over his prize. 'She is in the next apartment! – Securely mine! – Mine for ever!' He can't quite believe his good luck, particularly in the way the Harlowes have unwittingly fallen in with his plot: 'The whole stupid family were in a combination to do my business for me.' With Clarissa, he now becomes a model of earnest delicacy, undertaking to 'reform' himself by a study of religion, to make himself worthy of her. In his letters to Belford, however, he is triumphalist: 'In short, my whole soul is joy. When I go to bed I laugh myself asleep; and I awake either laughing or singing … For why? – I am not yet reformed enough!'

The awful thing is that this is really quite funny. Clarissa is a nice enough girl, but can hardly remain a virgin for ever. What would be so dreadful in becoming another of Robert Lovelace's 'conquests'? Clarissa's problem is that she has been manoeuvred into an impossible position. She can face neither the prospect of returning home and being compelled to marry the absurd Roger Solmes nor that of becoming Lovelace's travelling mistress. Lovelace's famous plotting is not quite as good as it seems. Clarissa might very well 'give' herself to him if it were not under such duress; he needs to contrive a choice for her in which sleeping with him would not be the lesser of two evils, but something the natural woman in her could choose freely.

By now Clarissa is confused. 'What concerns me is that every time I see this man, I am still at a greater loss than before what to make of him … He looks with more meaning, I verily think, than he used to look; yet not more serious; not less gay – I don't know how he looks'. Words fail her – but not him. Lovelace has 'never had a more illustrious subject to exercise my pen upon': he is a writer if not by profession at least by occupation; and he does it well. 'How it swells my pride, to have been able to outwit such a vigilant charmer! I am taller by half a yard in my imagination than I was. I look down upon every body now. Last night I was still more extravagant. I took off my hat, as I walked, to see if the place were not scorched, supposing it had brushed down a star; and before I put it on again, in mere wantonness and heart's ease, I was for buffeting the moon.'

With no indelicacy, Richardson takes the reader close to the workings of desire. 'Many a one have I taught to dress, and helped to undress', Lovelace reflects. He talks about Clarissa's clothes a great deal, as a true womaniser would; men less devoted to the chase tend not to notice such things as shoes and dresses. By having Lovelace talk about Clarissa's clothes, Richardson can, without indelicacy, invite the reader to think of her body. Not that Lovelace is shy to talk about her skin, too, and the veins he sees beneath. 'Oh Belford! What still more inimitable beauties did it [a handkerchief over the cleavage] not conceal!' He apparently sees her heart beating beneath her dress …

Lovelace is convinced, almost quoting Alexander Pope's *Epistle to a Lady*, that every woman 'is a rake in her heart', and that 'what they *think*, I *act*'. In other words, the demure female exterior is a sham, put up for social reasons; women are as lustful as men. His reason for thinking so is that while rakes prefer a woman with the appearance of modesty, such women 'generally prefer an impudent man'. And, he argues, 'Whence can this be, but from a likeness in nature?' Later, in Letter 228, he writes, 'Show me a woman and I'll show thee a plotter.' He thus projects his own two dominant qualities, rakishness and plotting, on to the female sex as a whole; he really *identifies* with women, and this is one thing that makes him so convincing as a womaniser. Yet he can also be a professional seducer, detached and opportunistic. He recounts how he tries a risqué joke in female company or even shows a lewd picture and gauges from the reaction of the women present how deep their sensual knowledge is and thus how easy a prey they may turn out to be. He loves their clothes, their hair, their manners in a devoted way. It reminded me of Mickey Sabbath, the main character of Philip Roth's extraordinary novel *Sabbath's Theater*. Sabbath does not have a job because he cannot spare the time from chasing skirt; it is far too serious and time-consuming a business to leave room for something as petty as *work*. What Sabbath and Lovelace have in common is the ability to identify with women, really to adore their femaleness, and yet, when necessary, to stand apart and view them as the polar attraction.

What an extraordinary man Robert Lovelace is. Excess appears to be his norm. He thinks little of spending the night in a bleak coppice adjoining the Harlowes' grounds, where, with his wig and linen frozen, kneeling on the 'hoar moss' on one knee, he writes a letter to Clarissa with frozen fingers, resting the paper on the other knee. His feet lose their circulation so badly that for some minutes they won't bear his weight when he tries to stand again. But 'love and rage' eventually get his circulation moving. The neurotic, obsessive detail of his descriptions of Clarissa's clothes and skin, and the manic longing of his imagination for 'what lies beneath' combine to make him appear at times quite seriously unbalanced. Yet he never allows his undoubted good nature – which lies in a commingling of judgement, wit and generosity – to get the better of him. When he has managed to persuade Clarissa to flee with him by telling her she will be discovered in a compromising situation by her parents, having met him in the garden, he begins to laugh at the thought of his triumph: 'Flying from friends she was resolved not to abandon to the man she was determined not to go off with? ... I must here lay down my pen to hold my sides.' There is something diabolic in this laughter because the hilarity has become detached from circumstance; it is what psychologists call 'inappropriate'. Yet the reader cannot quite condemn a man with the ability to reflect à la Wilde: 'I fancy, by her circumspection, and her continual grief, that she expects some mischief from me. I don't care to disappoint anybody I have a value for.'

He moves Clarissa to lodgings in London, though the house is, unknown to her, a genteel brothel. One night, a fire breaks out, and Lovelace flies to Clarissa's room to 'save' her; he discovers her 'with nothing on but an under-petticoat, her lovely bosom half-open, and her feet just slipped into her shoes'. There is something comic in this carry-on, as the seducer is defeated by the chill of his 'frost-piece' while simultaneously surprising her in increasing stages of undress: 'This assemblage of beauties offered itself to my ravished sight', he writes, where the word 'ravished' pleads for sympathy, yet seems sinister in context. He 'spares' her, though he believes he had a 'right' not to. Then he is ashamed to go downstairs without having made love to her for fear of the mockery that his failure will excite in the madam of the house, two of whose whores are previous 'conquests'. The ebb and flow of feeling, from dark to absurd and back again, is precisely caught by Richardson in this scene, which evokes some sympathy for Lovelace and looks hard at the complicated machinery of desire.

As if this tension were not enough, there is sometimes a sense in which Lovelace's breadth of reference and facility with words make him seem enslaved not just by sex but by rhetoric. He compares himself to Hannibal and Clarissa to a doe or bird, likely to be caught in a snare; he is a word-driven man, and we are free to wonder whether someone who had fewer of Rochester's poems by heart would be able to keep himself at such a pitch of passion. He uses flighty verbal constructions to avoid facing uncomfortable judgements. ''Tis a plotting villain of a heart; it ever was and ever will be, I doubt. Such a joy when any roguery is going forward! – I so little its master! – A head likewise so well turned to answer the triangular varlet's impulses.' By portraying his impulses as organs of the body (head/heart) and then personifying one into a 'varlet', he distances himself from them, as though they were somehow independent beings, not subject to the control of a unified personality. Lovelace's life is lived by the lights of the much-quoted poetry of others, so much so that he sometimes seems estranged from his true self. The critic Ian Watt suggested that Clarissa is equally divided, unable to locate or trust her warmer feelings for Lovelace because of externally acquired restraint. But even were it otherwise, even if she had grown up in a less middle-class and Puritan family, with some of the laissez-aller of her social superiors *or* inferiors, would she specifically have warmed to Lovelace? It seems a large presumption, though there are many suggestions that she is, to use a Wildean phrase, 'far from indifferent' to him. When Lovelace is apparently taken ill in London with a 'vomiting of blood in great quantities', Clarissa finds herself concerned and tells Anna Howe that this new feeling for him 'has taught me more than I knew of myself'. In this letter (212), she seems on the point of 'falling in love' with him. 'I hope my reason will gather strength enough from his imperfections ... to enable me to keep my passions under— What can we do more than govern ourselves by the temporary lights lent us?' The break in the sentence after the word 'under' gives a graphic idea of how close she is to 'succumbing', and this letter as much as any in this huge book gives a sense of the DNA of the eighteen-year-old girl and makes her seem interestingly more than the 'frost-piece' of Lovelace's jibe or the flirt-in-denial of Anna Howe's projection. (Clarissa's surname, with its uncomfortable suggestion of 'harlot', meanwhile, seems chosen to complicate matters – to suggest subliminally that there could be a price for which she would comply – the name of that price being, in my view, independence: in other words, the option of sleeping with Lovelace of her own free will, without the thought that it is a choice between the Scylla of sex with him and the Charybdis of life with Roger Solmes.)

The reason we keep reading this immensely long story of a deadlock is that we sense there is room for manoeuvre. Dr Johnson remarked that 'there is always something [Clarissa] prefers to the truth', but we feel she could yet recognise it. Clarissa may well be almost 'in love with' Lovelace at the beginning, but is not aware of her own emotions because her self-knowledge is clouded by her fear of sex. By the time she can admit such feelings, Lovelace's behaviour has disqualified him from being loved. There may also be a moment at which Lovelace's feeling for Clarissa stops being a mixture of lust, challenge and contempt, and purifies itself into something close to love; but by then Clarissa can no longer reciprocate. It is this sense of emotional harmony destroyed by time that gives the novel a tragic dimension.

When the pulse of Lovelace's rhetoric gives him peace to confront his own moral position reasonably, he exonerates himself of bad faith or evil intent. His 'contrivances', he admits, are deceitful, but his aim is a single seduction – and think of all the girls he has not seduced while working on Clarissa. Furthermore, she is an unmarried girl; so he is not cuckolding anyone. He suggests that far from being a bad man, he is merely an honest and self-aware one; most men, if they were truthful, would like to do what he is attempting – to sleep with Clarissa Harlowe.

Such intervals of calm are rare, however, and become more so when Clarissa escapes from Mrs Sinclair's. Lovelace is demented to think that 'some villain, worse than myself, who adores her not as I adore her, may have seized her' (Letter 228). He tracks her down to Hampstead and visits her (in a scene complete with stage directions that shows much of Richardson's theatrical conception of the character), disguised as a gouty old man. Clarissa is tricked back to Mrs Sinclair's bawdy house, where Lovelace reveals to Belford that he is considering the use of force. 'But would I not have avoided it if I could? – Have I not tried every other method? And have I any other recourse left me?' He convinces himself that once he has taken her virginity, she will be too ashamed to tell how it took place but will be content to marry him. Again, he is not quite the plotter he believes himself to be. In a formidable moment, Clarissa later tells him, 'That man who has been the villain to me that you have been shall never make me his wife.'

The detail of what takes place is, to put it mildly, slight. When I first read this book at the age of nineteen, I was only aware of a change in the attitudes of the characters some pages after the event. Had I missed something? Yes. It was Letter 257, which reads in its entirety: 'And now, Belford, I can go no farther. The affair is over. Clarissa lives. And I am Your humble servant, R. Lovelace.' I was probably not the first reader, dizzy with nearly 900 pages of intermittently feverish prose, to blink and miss an understated climax. I was annoyed with myself. It was like reaching the summit of Mount Everest in the dark and only finding out that one had passed over it when almost back at base camp.

Yet reading the letter again this time, I thought its brevity effective. It may have been imposed by reasons of propriety and by Richardson's religious scruples, yet how eloquent it is. All post-coital tristesse is in those few words. Lovelace's passion, wit and erudition have been inflated by the great bellows of his rhetoric; and now the air has all gone out of him. One senses his disappointment, not perhaps so much with the sexual experience itself, but with the fact that he has wrongfully obtained something whose unobtainability had given shape and momentum to his life.

'SOME LOATHSOME REPTILE'

FAGIN

The first thing you notice about *Oliver Twist* is the mock-heroic style, indebted to Fielding, and the slight lack of confidence – by Dickens's standards – it suggests. It is an early book, Dickens's second, and started to appear in serial form, in 1837, before *The Pickwick Papers* had finished its periodical publication. Some of what he learned from writing *Oliver Twist* may have made its way into the later parts of *Pickwick* so that, as one critic wittily remarked, there is the remarkable phenomenon of an author whose second book influenced his first.

While hesitant in some ways and mechanical in others, the novel shares with the best of Dickens the odd sense of portraying something that was always there. The workhouse, the child at large on dusty roads, the gang of thieves, Bill Sikes swinging from a rope on a chimney pot … It is as though these people and scenes were part of a collective memory, needing only the brilliant beam of Dickens's imagination to illuminate them. Of course, we sigh, Dodger, Nancy ... How are you? The character who seems most archetypal, the figure who has outgrown and outlived the rattling machinery of the inheritance-based plot, is Fagin.

This is odd, because Fagin is not an archetype at all; it is merely the conviction and ferocity of Dickens's presentation that makes him seem so. He runs a gang of boy thieves who pick the pockets of rich gentlemen for watches and handkerchiefs; he is also the agent for a housebreaker, Sikes, and a prostitute, Nancy. He is part uncle to the boys, part pimp, part fence – and all Jew. This last aspect of him is the oddest. It is not shown in any religious devotion or dietary observance – indeed, the very first glimpse we catch of Fagin is of him frying sausages, which we presume are made of pork. He is a Jew only in that Dickens repeatedly and insistently calls him one. There is no evidence to suggest that pimping and thieving were particularly Jewish occupations in the mid-nineteenth century, though the historic denial of full voting rights and citizenship to Jewish people would certainly have meant they were over-represented in crime figures. But Dickens's conception of Fagin as a Jew seems impulsive, almost random. Perhaps it sounded exotic or colourful; maybe it stood as a contrast to the older London of Bill Sikes. The odd thing is that it adds nothing to Fagin; his religious and cultural background is probably the only part of him that has no bearing on how he behaves.

This is not all that surprising. Novelists who work at the pitch of imaginative frenzy that Dickens enjoyed for most of his creative life, publishing serially, don't always plan out all the implications of every creative decision, even those primary, character-creating ones. Fagin seems Jewish just because he *is*; that's the way the idea of him burned itself into Dickens's mind: scraggy beard, long greasy unkempt hair, uncertain avuncularity, intermittent kindness, cunning, lack of sexuality and Jewishness – all seem to have come together, all of a piece. It's possible that, consciously or otherwise, Dickens wanted to tap into people's idea of Jews as money-lenders when they see Fagin's avaricious love of what has been stolen for him by the boys. Usury, unlike thieving and pimping, was an area of activity in which Victorian Jews were indeed prominent; by sneering at Fagin as he fondles his stolen goods, the reader might discharge some anger at the high rate of interest he was paying to a real-life Jewish money-lender. My sense of it, however, is that Dickens was not interested in Fagin's Jewishness, and that to become obsessed by it is like entering into a long debate about the breed of Sikes's dog. It doesn't matter. Dickens couldn't even be bothered (as later he would with Riah in *Our Mutual Friend*) to give him a Jewish name. Fagin is an Irish name. It was also the name of a boy Dickens had known when working in his famous blacking factory. The important thing – and, I think, the only thing that mattered to Dickens – is that the name works so well for the character; it could be forename or surname, and it pulls together all the disparate parts of him. It works, it's how he was; and being a Jew is as intrinsic yet ultimately random to Fagin as are plentiful teeth to the villainous Carker in *Dombey and Son*.

There were, however, protests from some readers. Dickens's repeated use of the phrase 'the Jew' rather than 'Fagin' to identify him, particularly at his worst moments, seemed to some people an attempt to suggest that his villainy was representative of a whole people. It can't have been helpful to Dickens's position that there is a second Jew in the book, Barney, a tapster in a grimy tavern, 'younger than Fagin, but nearly as vile and repulsive in appearance', who speaks through his adenoids and in answer to Sikes's question 'Is anybody here?' replies, 'Dot a shoul.' It is a documented fact that in the second half of the novel, Dickens, responsive to the criticisms, stopped calling Fagin 'the Jew' so often and called him instead by his proper – albeit Irish – name. It is possible that the kindly Riah in *Our Mutual Friend* was offered as an olive branch to offended readers, but your guess is as good as mine as to what Dickens 'really' felt or intended in Fagin; mine, for what it's worth, is that he was simply carried away by the exuberance of his own creation and intended no racial slur. That does not mean to say that what he wrote is inoffensive: it does grate; and he must have thought so, too, in order to change at least the nominal way in which he refers to Fagin. It is also reported that in the last public readings of his life, Dickens dropped any hint of an East European or Yiddish inflection when he did Fagin's voice.

Dickens's usual way with villains was to present them as long-distance plotters who deceive the upright characters. He elicits our moral condemnation by first mobilising our anger. We gloat and exult over the ultimate fall of Uriah Heep in *David Copperfield* or Casby in *Little Dorrit* because we have seen the suffering their hypocrisy has over the years inflicted on people we like, such as Dora's trusting father or the poor tenants of Bleeding Heart Yard.

Fagin is not like that. His opening words constitute the first civility ever shown to Oliver Twist – 'We are very glad to see you' – and, still better, his first actions are to provide Oliver with sausages, hot gin and coffee. He is also the first person in the child's life actually to play with him, and, while it's only a game of steal-the-handkerchief, it's hard to overstate how touching this scene is. By its presence, it suggests a previous world of absence: the workhouse full of children with no games, ever. We learn that Fagin can be a hard master, though, sending Dodger or

Charley to bed with no supper or even knocking them downstairs if they have returned from the streets empty-handed. Even here, though, Fagin has a kind of charm because he presents his plight not as that of a criminal with no loot to sell, but as that of a poor home bird dependent on the unforgiving world outside to make ends meet. If there is anything of the Jewish stereotype in Fagin, it is of the mother.

The reason Fagin works so well for Dickens is that he is unstable and unpredictable. There is something warm in him – he, not the 'good' characters, is the only provider of real laughter in Oliver's life – but he is a coward. We don't know which of these two qualities, if it came to it, might prevail, though we have a cold premonition from an early exchange with Sikes about how to deal with any leak of information Oliver might make while at large. Sikes is of the view that Oliver must 'be taken care on'. And Fagin agrees. 'If he means to blab us among his new friends, we may stop his windpipe yet.'

At other times, it seems that Dickens is forcing himself to make Fagin appear more villainous than he naturally is. 'It seemed just the night when it befitted such a being as the Jew to be abroad ... The hideous old man seemed like some loathsome reptile, engendered in the slime and darkness ... crawling forth by night in search of some rich offal for a meal.' It is not just a sense of anti-Semitism that makes this passage troubling, but the feeling that the novelist-as-controller is forcing a predetermined shape on a living character. We almost dare to feel that we know Fagin better than Dickens does.

However, the evidence mounts against Fagin. He gives a sly kick to the sleeping Sikes. He has a plan to 'own' Oliver, to make him his own creature – 'Once fill his mind with the idea that he has been a thief, and he's ours – ours for his life!' He gives him reports of true criminal cases, 'Tyburn tales', to read, as though he will be impressed by their glamour. He conspires with Oliver's half-brother, Monks. He has moved Nancy from thieving into prostitution, and there are even suggestions that the young thieves may be more than pickpockets. In real life such gangs would probably also have been rent boys, drawing custom from the West End; though in Fagin's defence we should say that Dickens is not able to make this suggestion explicitly. Worst of all, Fagin inflames Bill Sikes to do what is necessary to keep Nancy quiet after she has been heard interceding on Oliver's behalf. His half-hearted plea as the enraged Sikes stalks off murderously into the night only makes matters worse. '"You won't be – too – violent, Bill?" … "I mean," said Fagin, showing that he felt all disguise was now useless, "not too violent for safety. Be crafty, Bill, and not too bold."' He is like a version of the apparition who tells Macbeth to be 'bloody, bold and resolute' – but a cowardly one.

Fagin is a bad man, though there is not much effort by Dickens to understand why or how he is bad. There are social and political questions raised by the lives of Fagin, Sikes and Nancy that Dickens does not care to examine. Nancy is given the chance to reform by Rose Maylie and by Mr Brownlow, but chooses to return to the life she knows ('I am too chained to my old life') as though it is fated – as though she hardly wants to better herself or be happy. Perhaps 'happy' scares her; perhaps she doesn't know what happy is. 'When such as me,' she tells Rose, 'who have no certain roof but the coffin-lid, and no friend in sickness or death but the hospital nurse, set our rotten hearts on any man, and let him fill the place that parents, home and friends filled once, or that has been a blank through all our wretched lives, who can hope to cure us?' Here is a deterministic view of society so deeply embedded that even its victims embrace it; though here, too, is the profound instinctive sympathy that Dickens would develop in his later books; here, in fact, is the exhilarating sight of a writer discovering his genius. Whatever Dickens's reputation as a social reformer, it is always in the anger of his compassion not in the detail of his politics that he is most compelling. Historians have pointed out that in any case the repressive aspects of child and poor laws depicted in *Oliver Twist* had already been repealed by the time Dickens wrote it.

In the novel, meanwhile, goodness seems to exist only outside the structures of society. The law and its officers, the state and its workhouses, are as unfair and unkind as the outlaws Sikes and Fagin. The magistrate Fang, Mr Bumble the beadle or the workhouse madam Mrs Corney are state civil servants, but are as bent as the freelance criminals. The only way to justice is to bribe the Bow Street Runners, bribe Mrs Maylie's servants and kidnap Monks to make him confess his plots. Goodness must use criminal means to prosper, and in the London of *Oliver Twist* it is not possible to be happy, and good, and law-abiding. In this anarchic world Fagin must find his way, and the reader is left with the sense that life is a dreamlike Grand Guignol, in which states of degradation such as those inhabited by Sikes and Fagin flash alternately with states of perfect virtue chez Maylie or Brownlow. In both worlds, law and morality are separate.

Fagin is a character who in some senses overpowers the novel he appears in. He carries not only the narrative of the book – both in its day-by-day momentum and, simply by knowing it, the complicated backstory – but also the heart, the spirit, the flavour of *Oliver Twist*. Even while Dickens was meant to be taking a rest from writing it, he admitted: 'I have great difficulty keeping my hands off Fagin and the rest of them.' Not 'off Oliver', one can't help noticing or 'off Rose Maylie' … It can't have been hard to resist the idea of writing another scene with Mr Brownlow being kindly.

Novelists tend to feel warm towards the characters that perform best for them in books; and Fagin is in this sense by far the most successful character in *Oliver Twist*. Dickens's own morality is not that of the Victorian church; in fact, the last sentence of the book makes a plea for Oliver's spurned mother, even though she was 'weak and erring' in having a love child. Because Dickens can be generous and flexible, it sometimes seems to us that the distancing effects he uses when dealing with Fagin are exaggerated. In the tale of an orphan lost in the criminal underworld it must have seemed important to Dickens the public man to keep the moral lines clear – even if it was sometimes against his own novelistic judgement to do so. The harshness with which he feels obliged to deal with Fagin makes for an unhappy tension in the reader, and arguably shows Dickens's inexperience. In *Our Mutual Friend*, at the other end of his career, Eugene Wrayburn and Bradley Headstone are allowed to develop under the same passionate impulses, free of authorial manipulation, to the extent that either could turn 'villain' under his own steam.

Dickens seems to have had trouble when he came to terminate Fagin's story: 'The Jew is such an out and outer', he wrote, 'that I don't know what to make of him.' He therefore did what he always did when in a difficult corner: he summoned up an extra effort, he rose to the occasion – and the results of it are in the remarkable chapter 'The Jew's Last Night Alive'. For the first time in the book, Dickens uses Fagin's point of view, as we witness the scene in court, the details of which Fagin, with hours to live, picks out with hallucinatory sharpness of detail. He sees a young man making a sketch of him; the point of his pencil breaks and he sharpens it with a knife. Fagin wonders if the likeness is any good. When he looks at the judge, he speculates how much his clothes cost, and how he put them on. These are among the last sights his eyes will see on earth. The guilty verdict is a popular one in court, and Fagin can only plead in mitigation that he is 'an old man'. What charge he is guilty of is not quite clear, and the critic John Sutherland has pointed out that none of his crimes carried the death sentence. But Dickens takes the law into his own hands, so when Fagin is taken down, his fellow convicts treat him not as a sad old fence, but as evil incarnate, rattling their bars as he passes, screeching and hissing at him.

Alone in the condemned cell (a scene unforgettably depicted by Cruikshank), Fagin thinks of those he has seen hanged. Their ghostly presence oppresses him and he beats the door and walls with his hands. A warder brings a light; another is to spend the night with Fagin, presumably to make sure he doesn't kill himself. Wounded in the head by a missile thrown by the mob, he passes an interminable day on his wooden bed, while Dickens turns the rhetorical screw. People come to the gates of Newgate prison, not to demand a reprieve but to make sure there will be none! Mr Brownlow and Oliver visit him in his cell. Oliver asks him to say a prayer, but we already know that Fagin has no religious belief because 'Venerable men of his own persuasion had come to pray beside him, but he had driven them away with curses. They renewed their charitable efforts and he beat them off.' Angrily disowning his own faith, he is not much of a Jew in the end.

The book closes with the revelation that the local church of Oliver's new home with his foster-father Mr Brownlow has a simple tablet on the wall that bears the name of Oliver's mother, Agnes. The closing lines take the novelist's traditional view of morality in the case of Oliver's mother –

that human love and goodness override social norms and religiously determined ethics. The comforting liberal glow of the words is somewhat diminished by the ruthless despatch with which the novel's largest character has just been sent to meet his maker on the Newgate scaffold.

Fagin in the condemned cell (1910 edition)

'HIS PRIVATE ROD'

COUNT FOSCO

In the twentieth century, plot-driven novels fell from critical favour. Even Dickens was viewed suspiciously, not only on the grounds that his novels were sometimes sentimental, but also that they had simply too many events; F. R. Leavis, the most influential mid-century critic, was prepared to admit only *Hard Times* into his canon of English novels. The anti-plot tendency seems to have begun with the high reputation of the late novels of Henry James, where the interest lies in the thought processes that shape motive – two steps, in other words, away from action itself. It must have seemed logical that if this was high art, which it was, then the opposite – anything with story in it – must be low. The tendency had picked up speed by the time of Virginia Woolf and James Joyce. One of the obvious points about *Mrs Dalloway* and *Ulysses* is that nothing much happens; the underlying aim of both these novels was to reproduce on paper the experience of being alive and their secondary aim was to refashion those sensations into something less molecular and more shapely. Such impulses had previously been the territory of poetry, but the insight of Woolf and Joyce was to see how prose could do the job as well or better, provided the narrative was freed from the tyranny of plot. There was a further dividend, as all literature students were taught, in that a non-linear structure seemed appropriate to a world broken by war; it imitated the poetic fragmentation of *The Waste Land* and the breaking up of the picture plane by modernist painters in Paris before 1914.

Through the twentieth century, the stock of plot-based novels continued to fall. Story seemed to become the preserve of 'lending library' authors such as Charles Morgan, Hugh Walpole and J. B. Priestley, then to be taken further downmarket by genre writers, into thrillers and detective stories, until, by about 1970, few 'literary' novelists allowed incident of any serious kind to put its big foot on their lawns. The uneasy reputation of John Fowles is an example of this consensus. Fowles's great talent as a writer, despite a certain literary tricksiness, lay in his feel for narrative. Sometimes, as he himself admitted, this was so intoxicating that he could barely control it; he cited *The Magus* as an example. The gift made him no friends in British mainstream critical opinion where, in the 1960s and 70s, the whole idea of story was considered dubious, though American universities took a different view of Fowles's standing.

It's hard to say when plot began to be rehabilitated. Perhaps when more thoughtful writers looked again at Tolstoy, where the 'idea of things happening', as Virginia Woolf called it, is central to the artistic purpose. Some of the great moments in Tolstoy are events or anticipation of events: Prince Andrei in *War and Peace* lying wounded at Austerlitz, looking up into the eyes of Napoleon; Pierre setting off in peasant disguise to assassinate the French emperor; Levin in *Anna Karenina* glimpsing the face of

Kitty through the carriage window as she is driven past; Vronsky break-ing his horse's back during a race; the death of Anna at the railway station ... though of course such incidents only become powerful if they are part of an orchestrated whole. Thus in many ways the most effective plot moment is not in one of these big scenes but in a prefiguring of them, as when Prince Andrei on the balcony of a hunting lodge happens to over-hear Natasha and Sonya chatting in the warm evening below him and a thrillingly muted drumbeat of future connections is sounded.

Or perhaps the reconsideration of plot came with a second look at Proust, and with the acknowledgement that, although it may take a very long time to happen, an awful lot does get done in *A La Recherche du Temps Perdu*. Zola's most widely admired novel for a long time was *L'Assommoir*, because it has the least amount of plot and seems to develop more 'organically' than his other novels; but by the end of the century there was a growing admission that not only were *Thérèse Raquin* and *Germinal* very thrilling books, but that their achievement lay in the way that event was handled. Flaubert was almost as much a modernist model as Proust, but again reflection showed that not only does a good deal happen in *Madame Bovary*, but some of it is of a sensational kind. So by the end of the twentieth century a rough new consensus was emerging among writers, if not necessarily critics, that event was not necessarily vulgar per se; it was a question of how it was handled.

In the hands of a master, such as Tolstoy, plot development can be more than just event, it can be symbolic; it can dramatically embody the inner life. An English example of this is in *David Copperfield*, when the body of Steerforth is washed up on the beach at Yarmouth after Ham, the noble-hearted fisherman, has died in trying to rescue him from a shipwreck. What Dickens achieves in this heart-stopping scene is something Proustian: he makes time disappear. As he does so, we see through the events of the present and deep into the past, into the connectedness of all things and into the transitory nature of human affection. Steerforth has run off with Little Emily, the child of the fishing family, and brought disgrace on them all. David's own relationship with the Peggotty family, a source of such life-sustaining joy to him in childhood, now brings deep remorse, because it was he who introduced Steerforth to them. Steerforth was the object of David's hero-worship at school and David misjudged and indulged him because he had lacked a father of his own to admire; he should never have allowed the dangerous Steerforth into the world of these decent people and their adored, pretty daughter. Eventually David stands above the drowned body of his friend washed up on the sand, 'among the ruins of the home he had wronged – I saw him lying with his head upon his arm, as I had often seen him lie at school'. The ground seems to open up beneath one's feet as all the terrible inevitability of past and present is laid bare. But it is important to accept that the way the effect in one of the most sublime scenes in Victorian literature is achieved is not by a direct or psychological approach to the abstract questions in hand, but by the tightly controlled use of a violent event.

Dickens's friend Wilkie Collins was less ambitious in his use of narrative, in that he seldom uses it to resonate beyond the event it relates; but *The Woman in White* is a tour de force of storytelling, almost pure and almost simple. It was viewed at the time as a 'sensation novel', a pejorative term for stories designed to give regular shocks at the end of each published instalment. As a piece of plot design, it was nevertheless mould-breaking at the time of publication, in 1860, because of the way it pieced together the contributions of different narrators from letters, formal statements and diaries. Yet there is clearly (too clearly for Trollope: 'The construction is minute and wonderful. But I can never lose the taste of the construction') a single storytelling intelligence with overall control, and the book never loses its strong forward momentum. As a child of anti-plot twentieth-century literary education, I had not read this book before 2009, and what a treat I had missed. It is a thrillingly enjoyable novel, and there is just enough repressed sexuality and twisted psychology to add a sense of something darker at work beneath the hectic rush of events.

Count Fosco does not appear until more than 200 pages into the story, though his entrance has been much anticipated. To build up a character in such a way – to tell the reader how fascinated he is going to be – is something more often done by airport novelists. For a writer of Collins's skill to risk anticlimax in this way argues a great confidence in the character and trust in the attention of his periodical readers. There is a sense of relief in Fosco's appearance because the main villain up to this point, Sir Percival Glyde, is a disappointment. There is too much of the vaudeville baronet about him, with his moustache and walking stick. And although he is there to disrupt the central romance of the book by exercising his agreed right to marry beautiful Laura Fairlie in place of the man she, and we, prefer – the drawing master Walter Hartright – Sir Percival fails in two villainous essentials: although bad-tempered, he does not seem very clever; and although we flinch at the thought of him in bed with Laura, he exudes little sexual danger.

For the task of introducing Count Fosco, Collins uses the most reliable of his many narrators – Marian Halcombe. Marian is Laura's half-sister and is one of the most compelling of Victorian heroines, being loyal, quick-witted, passionate, ugly and surprisingly hairy. She has a swarthy complexion, an incipient moustache, a low forehead, a manly jaw and thick black hair – all set on a trim, feminine figure. She has all the qualities of vigour and intelligence that are lacking in the aptly named Laura Fairlie (blonde, insipid) and Walter Hartright (honest, dull). This is more like it, we think. Sir Percival, Walter and Laura can play their parlour game like cut-out puppets in a Pollock's Theatre; but Marian is operating on a different level and requires a worthy counterpart.

Enter Fosco. 'I am becoming anxious to know the Count', Marian reflects. 'I wonder if I shall like him?' Fosco in prospect interests Marian 'infinitely more than his wife', though Laura, who knows them both, won't say what Fosco is like; she wants Marian to form her 'own opinion first'. We are grateful for this reticence, since Laura's opinion would almost certainly be anodyne. All we know is that Fosco and his wife are friends and travelling companions of Sir Percival, the baronet who is to steal away pretty Laura and who seems in some way implicated in a plot to keep Anne Catherick, the eponymous woman in white, locked up in a county lunatic asylum.

When Fosco finally appears, the practical Marian is bowled over. 'This, in two words. He looks like a man who would tame anything. If he had married a tigress, instead of a woman, he would have tamed the tigress. If he had married *me* I should have made his cigarettes as his wife does'. The first thing sensible Marian does is imagine being married to him – this despite the fact that he is old enough to be her father, that he is 'immensely fat' and she has an admitted prejudice against corpulence. Unable to confine herself to 'two words' on the count, Marian gushes over almost ten pages.

Fosco is portrayed by Collins, chiefly through Marian's eyes, as a character who embodies polarities. This is what makes him attractive; this is what makes him untrustworthy. He is obese, yet very light on his feet. He looks like Napoleon, yet is a creature of the salon – a fancy man with a sweet tooth and no Grande Armée to command. He is Italian and a count (a doubtful title to English Marian, since it does not exist in British society), but he speaks English so well that it is 'almost impossible to detect, by his accent, that he is not a countryman of our own'. He is 'foreign' but familiar. His hair is dark brown, but his complexion is fair: no swarthy Neapolitan he. Is his hair dyed? Or is he just of 'superior' breeding in some way? He wears fancy waistcoats of effeminate display, yet emits a heterosexual charge to Marian. And as for his eyes … 'They are the most unfathomable grey eyes I ever saw; and they have at times a cold, clear, beautiful, irresistible glitter in them, which forces me to look at him, and yet causes me sensations, when I do look, which I would rather not feel.'

Fosco's contradictions mirror Marian's. She is ugly, yet attractive. We like her mind, her character and her trim figure. What is in her hormones that makes her so feminine yet so mannish? Her attractiveness is literary, because in real life that low, hairy brow would be a killer of lust. But on the page we don't see it; we hear her voice and follow the movement of her clever mind; we remember her slim hips as first seen from behind by Walter. A sensualist such as we believe Count Fosco to be might well contrive a way of making love to Marian that excluded her swarthy face from view. It is almost as though she appeals to the latent homosexuality of the heterosexual man; but her allure is even more interesting, because less resolved, than that. Many aroused bachelors wrote to Collins asking if Marian had a real-life counterpart they might be introduced to.

Fosco is, Marian thinks, 'close on sixty years of age', yet active and virile; he swiftly establishes himself as the pack leader at his friend Sir Percival's house. He seems to have all that is needed to be a Lothario or a Romeo, yet is uxorious in the extreme, doting showily on his cold and repulsive wife, who in turn is like a servant to him. What must he be doing with her in the bedroom to maintain such control and such devotion? Or as Marian puts it: 'The rod of iron with which he rules her never appears in company – it is a private rod, and is always kept upstairs.' Marian thinks a good deal about the fat man's 'private rod' and, to judge from Collins's relaxed and playful attitude to sexual matters, he was probably aware of the double entendre.

For all his 'Napoleonic' qualities, Fosco appears as nervous as a filly. 'He starts at chance noises as inveterately as Laura herself does', says Marian; but anyone can fake a start. Is he really that nervy? He doesn't like it when Sir Percival beats his spaniel, and that is fine and noble of him, yet almost his first act is to put his hand on the head of a vicious chained blood-hound – to tame and humiliate the creature, as though by hypnotic force. He has the 'fondness of an old maid' for his cockatoo, to say nothing of the canaries that perch on him and the pet mice that crawl over his waist-coated folds of flesh. It is one thing to be kind-hearted towards our dumb friends, another to be sentimental. Late in the story, he indulgently gives most of his fruit tart to a monkey, but spurns the organ grinder's request for a penny. He does not know at that time that he is being watched, so we may assume that Collins wants this incident to show us the 'real' Fosco. A man who cares more for animals than for humans is not a good man.

More often, by a continuing use of half-reconciled polarities, Collins is underlining the question of un/trustworthiness. We don't know how much of Fosco is a show and how much is real. While he exerts a sexual power over his wife and over Marian, there is something in his love of fruit tart, cream and sugar plums, his weeping at the sound of music, that is meant to suggest a quality far from machismo. 'How much I seem to have written about Count Fosco!' says Marian after her initial descriptions. 'I can only repeat that I do assuredly feel, even on this short acquaintance, a strange, half-willing, half-unwilling liking for the Count.'

The reader does not share Marian's indecision. We dislike the count. He is pompous, condescending and bombastic. We are told by Marian how fascinating he is, but we do not really share this fascination. Little of what he says seems arresting or original. He is long-winded; he takes up too much space in the narrative as well as in the room. We want to know more about Anne, the woman in white, and about Sir Percival's unspeakable 'Secret'. Fosco vexes us; he is annoying. However, the feeling we do share with Marian is one of fear: he is successfully unknowable. Although we incline to the view that he is a villain, we don't know how his villainy will show itself.

The main reason we don't like the count is that he brings out the worst in Marian, whom we love. We need her at her forthright best to keep evil from prevailing; we don't like to see resourceful Marian succumbing to the 'charm' of this ridiculous count. She says that she 'distrusts the influence' he has on her. She talks of the pet mice creeping over his fat body, a sight 'for some reason not pleasant to me. It excites a strange, responsive creeping in my own nerves'. For some reason! The Marian we know and admire is cleverer than this.

Then Fosco gives a famous speech about how clever criminals are not caught by plodding policemen; and in 1860 the idea that the recently formed detective force could be outwitted was alarming to readers. Yet this is also Fosco at his most bombastic and obviously untrustworthy: 'Ah! I am a bad man, Lady Glyde, am I not? … I say what other people only think!' Honourable Marian, meanwhile, clings to the idea that so long as you don't antagonise him he will behave well towards you. 'Don't make an enemy of the Count', is her advice to Laura. Play fair by him, is her implication, and he will play fair by you. Her blindness towards the count is her only weak point, and Collins exploits it to add tension to his all-important plot.

It is not long before Marian records that Fosco 'permitted me … to make his acquaintance, for the first time, in the character of a Man of Sentiment' in a very fancy waistcoat, 'as if there was some hidden connexion between his showiest finery and his deepest feeling'. He comes upon her with his 'horribly silent tread' and asks: 'Surely you like this modest, trembling English twilight … Observe, dear lady, what a light is dying on the trees! Does it penetrate your heart, as it penetrates mine?' Modest English penetration is on his mind as well as hers.

There are times when Fosco and Marian seem to embody opposing principles: the effeminate man and the hairy woman, each proud of his/her intellect, each to be 'completed' in some odd or sadomasochistic way by the other. The battle they fight is over the liberty and life of Anne Catherick, the well-being of Laura Fairlie and the sum of £20,000. Yet it often feels – and this is where the novel seems more than mere storytelling – that their real battle is a personal one that touches on quite archetypal forms of gender and identity.

In a famous scene, Marian listens from an outdoor balcony to Fosco and Sir Percival as they plot in the room below, with the French doors open. Fosco praises her intellect and compares her to a man, though oddly enough his admiration for her makes him sound homosexual. He prefers Marian to Sir Percival's 'flimsy, pretty blonde' (Laura), but then, as one might almost warm to his robust judgement, he drinks Marian's health in sugar and water, there being, presumably, no sarsaparilla in Sir Percival's drinks cabinet.

The sexual tension reaches a breaking point when Wilkie Collins lets us see that Fosco has been reading Marian's private diary. Fosco handwrites a 'Postscript by a Sincere Friend', in which he comments on the journal approvingly, especially the depiction of himself. He regrets that they are on opposite sides as in another life 'how worthy I would have been of Miss Halcombe – how worthy Miss Halcombe would have been of ME'. In a novel whose fascination derives, first, from its multiple narrative strategies and, second, from the inverted sexual tensions between its two chief protagonists, this moment of inter-textual penetration is a masterstroke.

The highly intricate plot of *The Woman in White* turns on the resemblance between Laura Fairlie and Anne Catherick, who is on the run from a county lunatic asylum when Hartright first meets her. It turns out that she has been placed there by Sir Percival Glyde as part of a long-term scheme to get his hands on Laura's money – a scheme in which Fosco provides the brains and the finesse. Eventually, the identities of the two women are actually switched by Glyde and Fosco, so Laura finds herself locked up in the asylum after Anne's premature death. Sir Percival's great secret is revealed to be that he is illegitimate; and in an attempt to destroy the revealing marriage certificate in a church vestry, he is burned to death. Anne and Laura turn out, unsurprisingly, to have been half-sisters. Hartright, Laura and Marian live happily ever after in a *ménage à trois*, the intimate arrangements of which are left naughtily unclear.

As for Count Fosco, the rest of his story is grace notes and comedy. There is a scene narrated by Laura's valetudinarian uncle, Henry Fairlie, when Fosco visits him in Cumberland. First impressions are 'highly favourable', but don't last long. Henry, who is too self-absorbed to notice much, takes against Fosco. 'He looked like a walking West Indian epidemic. He was big enough to carry typhus by the ton … I instantly determined to get rid of him.' Later, 'He made another speech – the man was absolutely inexhaustible.' Though at lunch, where Fosco makes a pig of himself over his favourite fruit tart and cream, Henry is moved to comment, 'What a man! What a digestion!' Like a stopped clock, Henry Fairlie has his moment.

The cumulative effect of all the ambivalence that Collins contrives around the character of Fosco and of his long-windedness is to make us long for action – for the man to show himself in his true colours – in deed. In a proto-thriller, it is a good idea to make the reader crave more action – provided you can satisfy that craving, and Collins is well up to the task. Before he has finished his sport with Fosco, Collins has a few bravura touches left. There is a droll description of the count at the opera in London, displaying his superior sensibility to the music; it is enough to make one wonder if this is not a scene that inspired Stephen Potter to the idea of one-upmanship. Fosco's first sighting of the diminutive Pesca, Hartright's old Italian friend, shows him unsettled for the first time in the book – more than unsettled, in fact: terrified for his life. It is tremendously satisfying that it should be Pesca, a loose end from the first chapter, who should now be pulling the threads of the story together. Then there is the business of Fosco writing his 'confession' – a process that epitomises his self-importance, his reliance on ritual and the mysterious hold he has over his wife. His insistence on taking a 'power nap' halfway through is an acutely comic addition.

When Fosco lies dead in a Paris morgue, the sightseeing French women have only one comment to make: 'Ah what a handsome man.' Fat, scruffy, old and dead, he still has the magic. Fosco's power throughout the book has derived from sex. He is not really that clever, it transpires in the end, and not really that wicked; his membership of an Italian secret society is a schoolboy mistake from which no good could ever come. And if he was such a Napoleon, what is he doing involved in a petty scandal with a dim Hampshire baronet over a sum of money that will generate an income of £3,000 a year? What Fosco ultimately has is not guile or wickedness or sophistication, but sexual power; and *The Woman in White* is much concerned with this matter.

'Come back and sign.' – Count Fosco and Sir Percival
attempt to gain control over Laura's fortune (1860 edition)

'A PROBLEM CASE'

STEERPIKE

Mervyn Peake's Gormenghast series (1946–59), is, like Tolkien's *The Lord of the Rings* (1954–5), a three-book fantasy. Tolkien's territory is a natural landscape and his hobbits have human thoughts and feelings. Their names, except that of the faithful serving man, Sam, are from an invented stock, but in other ways, the world of *The Lord of the Rings* operates on the same natural principles as our own. It is like a child's game, in which dolls or teddy bears take the place of people, but in the child's very real house and garden. The otherness of the hobbits makes them cute, and occasionally able to do odd things, but the success of the game depends on its closeness to life.

Peake's fantasy is almost the opposite of Tolkien's. Peake's characters are human, but his landscape is surreal. Instead of Middle Earth, read the Kingdom of Gormenghast and its castle, home to the earls of Groan. At the time the book opens, the head of the family, Lord Sepulchrave, is the seventy-sixth earl. In what history-rich nation can there have been an earl-dom for more than 2,000 years? Sepulchrave's servants include Swelter, the cook; Flay, the loyal footman; a doctor called Prunesquallor; a wet-nurse called Slagg, and 'masters of ritual' called Sourdust and Barquentine. There is a headmaster called Deadyawn.

Tolkien has imagined creatures in a real universe; Peake has humans in a surreal world. In Tolkien, there is no blurring of the boundaries, and it is easy to accept his hobbits as behaving within predictable limits, as a child can accept the 'rules' of Enid Blyton's Toytown. Peake's world is less predictable, less delineated; it is not such a comfortable place as Middle Earth (for all its epic journeys and frightening Orcs); Gormeng-hast requires a more flexible attitude to the question of fictional reality, and for some readers, this has been too big an ask. Fantasy, they say, is for teenage boys; and it's true that the vehemence of Gormenghast's admir-ers, as with any cultish work, can be off-putting.

I read the first chapters with trepidation, not having ventured into fantasy land for some years. The moment that I was able to commit myself to the book was when Steerpike, a lowly kitchen boy in Swelter's hellish domain, takes centre stage and begins to inject some movement into the static world of the castle where everyone else is devoted to keeping things as they have been for centuries. In our needy, amoral way, we readers cling to Steerpike because he offers entertainment. We are initially not worried about what sort of person he is, partly because he seems motivated by a perfectly acceptable desire to escape from his kitchen servitude and partly because it is already clear that this is not a novel that will offer subtle moral or psychological distinctions for us to care about; its interests lie elsewhere.

Although Peake at once presents Steerpike as flawed and untrust-worthy, his drive to self-betterment does not seem villainous. The castle needs shaking up; the plot needs kick-starting, and Steerpike is the man to do it. Although he is someone who calculates, weighing the odds in any situation so that he can turn it to his advantage, there is nothing inherently despicable in his upward mobility (literally upward, as he ascends the floors of Gormenghast).

Peake's success with the character is to imbue him with a sense of danger. It begins with the name, which suggests control and movement, but also something predatory – either a sharp-toothed, flesh-eating fish or the weapon of the medieval foot soldier. He is introduced as a 'high-shouldered boy, who throughout the scene had preserved a moody silence. He loathed the figure above him [Swelter] and he despised his fellow apprentices. He leaned against the shadowy pillar, out of the chef's line of vision.' His eyes were 'hot with a mature hatred'. Something has been festering for a long time. He has 'an insipid moustache', and eyes that are 'small, dark red and of startling concentration'. His face is described as 'masklike', presumably to suggest that he needs always to conceal his thoughts, though it is also a symptom of certain neurological illnesses. His eyes are compared to those of the vulture or lynx, and this is apt, because sight-predators can spot their prey and focus on it from a great distance; natural selection has weeded out those who couldn't. What such creatures cannot do, however, is see the whole landscape. This is Steerpike's problem, and will ultimately be his downfall.

We are relieved to discover that Steerpike is clever – something he reveals in the way he is quickly able to exploit Flay's hatred of Swelter, a resentment that has led to a long-running feud. Although he is ugly ('his body gave the appearance of being malformed'), Steerpike is aware that he has some animal charm, and uses it to ensnare the earl's teenage daughter, Fuchsia, whose 'whole nature was a contradiction of his own'. At their meeting, Peake, for the first time, lets us inside Steerpike. 'His mind had been working away behind his high forehead. Unimaginative himself, he could recognize imagination in her ... He knew that behind her simplicity was something he could never have ... To win her favour he must talk in her own language.'

Certain types of 'personality disorder', to use the current medical term, make the individual unable to deal with the concept of 'the other'; such a person cannot 'empathise', cannot imagine the thoughts and feelings of another or may not understand that other people even have such things. This is characteristic of someone with 'antisocial personality disorder', or what used to be called 'psychopathy'. Steerpike, interestingly, is able to project himself into Fuchsia's mind. He doesn't understand what he sees there, but he knows how to profit from it: he knows that to win Fuchsia's trust he must do something theatrical, yet 'simple and guileless' – and this, the guilelessness, is what he finds difficult. Yet he manages. 'He was not the artist. He was the exact imitation of one', someone who could 'understand a subject without appreciating it'.

Steerpike's manipulation of the virginal Fuchsia throughout the book is subtly described. She is beguiled by his 'wonderful long sentences' and thinks that being with him is 'like watching someone from another world who was worked by another kind of machinery'. Peake tells us that he, meanwhile, was 'like a snake among the rocks' and has no emotional feeling for the girl: 'He admired beauty. It did not absorb him.' Peake has sharp phrases for the interplay between them. 'His simulation of embarrassment was exact'; or, 'Quick as an adder he was in her arms.' At one point Fuchsia weakens in Steerpike's embrace, seeing in him a simple human being she has upset, only to see that at that moment they are lying on the grave of her old nurse. Later, Steerpike is prepared to rape Fuchsia in order to bring her under his control; there is little lust in his design, only a power play.

With Fuchsia nominally on his side, Steerpike goes on to win over most of the inhabitants of Gormenghast, including the earl's 'half-witted' twin sisters Cora and Clarice. His aim is to acquire 'power', though what he will do with this power is not clear, chiefly because he has not considered the question himself. The sisters will be 'a gift' to his plans and 'that at the moment was what mattered'. It is the phrase 'at the moment' that will be his problem. 'Life was amusing', he thinks later. 'Everything, he thought to himself, can be of use. Everything.'

In his ascent to an unofficial position of eminence in Gormenghast, Steerpike goes through a brief political phase in which he appeals to the sisters' sense of equality. This is not a theme that Peake or Steerpike appear much interested in, however, and once a short-term gain has been achieved, the idea of political reasoning is swiftly dropped. It is possible that Peake was at this point thinking of the rise of real-life dictators of the 1930s and wished to make an allusion to them; but the character of Steerpike and the world in which he operates don't seem to me to be enhanced or explained by the suggestion that they 'refer' to history or have allegorical intentions. But while I take my Gormenghast neat, some readers have preferred to take it with a shot of Nuremberg. The first book was written during the Second World War, so it is not an outlandish preference; and nor am I saying that fiction never means to draw on real-life parallels. Writing at the same time as Peake, George Orwell was at work on two books, *Animal Farm* and *Nineteen Eighty-Four*, which depend on their closeness to fact for their impact. I personally don't believe that the Gormenghast trilogy needs such a connection to operate properly; but I think it's a matter of taste.

By the end of the first volume, *Titus Groan*, Steerpike has changed. At the start of the second, *Gormenghast*, he is introduced, in a sort of recapitulation of volume one for new readers, as someone beyond redemption. Power has corrupted him. 'If ever he had harboured a conscience in his tough narrow breast he had by now dug out and flung away the awkward thing.' Having tricked Cora and Clarice into setting fire to the castle library, Steerpike now immures them in their apartments and leaves them to die.

He has apprenticed himself to the librarian Barquentine in the hope that by learning the history and arcana of Gormenghast he can replace Barquentine in a position of real authority. When he feels he knows as much as he needs, he tries to murder the old librarian, but a fire breaks out and they fall together, in flames, into the castle moat. Steerpike survives, but is branded on the face. His last rational plan for power has failed, and from now on he becomes a sort of demon – hunted, demented and without fixed purpose. Steerpike's decline coincides with the rise to early manhood of Titus, the heir apparent. It is clear that Titus will play Macduff to Steerpike's cornered Macbeth; what is not predictable is the approval that Mervyn Peake gives to Titus in admiring genealogical phrases. It is not just that Steerpike has become a menace and a terror to be purged, it is more that the natural order of things is to be reimposed. All talk of 'equality' now seems quaint and absurd as Titus, the young master, comes into his earldom.

*

With a fantasy character such as Steerpike, you look in vain for psychological 'motivation'; there is no sense in which his calculation and cruelty can be seen as the result of previous experiences, still less of 'trauma', or of 'compensation' for something in his just-finished childhood (he is seventeen when the trilogy opens). There are aspects of him that are simply unexplained, most obviously his way with words – something that greatly impresses Fuchsia. There is no suggestion of how he came by this erudition. He is a character who is shaped by the literary needs of his creator; he is the plot-instigator par excellence, and without Steerpike and his ambition there would be no book.

The closest Peake comes to explanation is to suggest that Steerpike's problems begin with the limits imposed by his humble birth. In a psychological novel, one might point out that Steerpike's ultimate failing is therefore one of education – or breeding. To put it bluntly, he is too lowly to inherit and not well educated enough to plan on a grand scale. His cunning is of the street, not of the cloister. As Dr Prunesquallor asks, 'Are you a problem case, my dear boy, or are you a clear-cut young gentleman with no ideas at all?' The snobbish old retainer, Flay, is appalled by the thought of Steerpike with the Lady Fuchsia. 'What could it mean? The blasphemy of it! The horror of it! He ground his teeth in the darkness.'

But while he has no revealed or imagined past, Steerpike does have a narrative development over the 750-odd pages of his life. What changes him, what damages him and makes him interesting, is the fact that in the end, devious and cunning though he is, he is not calculating enough. 'He did what he wanted to do. He did what furthered his plans.' He does not see them in a larger perspective, but lives from one manipulable crisis to the next. It may be that in the end he stops having any goal or motivation; after all, he can't change his birth and 'become' the next Earl of

Gormenghast. In any event, after the death of Barquentine, Steerpike is no longer the driver of the action, the man who, like Lovelace or Fagin, holds the reins. On the contrary, he is overtaken by events; he is cornered by the rising flood water and by the advent of the rightful heir. His plight, though 'deserved' in the moral sense, has something of the universal nightmare about it; he is caught in a situation in which 'returning were as tedious as to go o'er'.

'His face was pale like clay and save for his eyes, mask-like' – Steerpike by Mervyn Peake

'A DARKNESS
OF THE MIND'

RONALD MERRICK

Ronald Merrick is the main character of Paul Scott's Raj Quartet, set in British-ruled India between 1942 and 1947. It was televised in fourteen hour-long episodes by Granada in 1983 as *The Jewel in the Crown*. The scale would be unthinkable today. Fourteen hours! Two years of filming divided between locations in India and the Granada studios in Manchester ... The cast included Rachel Kempson and Dame Peggy Ashcroft, but the main parts were played by less well-known actors: Tim Pigott-Smith, Art Malik, Susan Wooldridge and Geraldine James. As well as reading the book, I watched all fourteen episodes again on video. It has its longueurs, and you can't help feeling that ten hours, twelve at most, might have covered it, but the main performances are still convincing; Ken Taylor's script is respectful yet dramatic in its own right; and Christopher Morahan's direction catches the symphonic construction of Paul Scott's books.

Its moments of transcendence mean that it still remains unmatched by anything I have seen on television.

As for the books themselves, there was a rumour when the series was being broadcast that they were stodgily written and not worth the investment of reading time, especially after fourteen hours of viewing. This turns out to be untrue. The four novels have more detail about the political struggle for Indian independence than will probably be of interest to most modern British readers; the character of Barbie Bachelor, the spinster missionary, though serenely well done, arguably takes up too much room. A sensitive but determined editor could reduce the number of pages (2,000 in paperback) by between ten and fifteen per cent. Yet what extraordinary ambition the quartet has, what richly understood characters, what steely invisible construction, what great human sympathy, what thematic harmonies and what moving resonances.

The story of the quartet is simple. A gauche English volunteer nurse, Daphne Manners, is raped by several drunken Indian peasant youths in the Bibighar Gardens in the fictional British garrison town of Mayapore. The local superintendent of police, Ronald Merrick, who has proposed to, and been rejected by, Daphne, takes into custody a young English-educated Indian called Hari Kumar. Merrick tries to frame Hari for the rape by leaving Daphne's bicycle outside his house, and while Hari is in custody Merrick tortures him for his own sadistic sexual satisfaction. The British in general are inclined to think that while Merrick may be a bit off-colour, such rough 'justice' is sometimes necessary for the maintenance of law and order in a huge and politically troubled country. Hari's political allies, and one or two British liberal sceptics, are not so sure. Questions remain; the case will not quite go away; doubts fester.

That is really it. The four books are constructed in concentric rings that circle the rape and its aftermath. New details of the night of the crime and of the interrogation are added at intervals of hundreds of pages, so that the narrative moves in two ways: one linear, one circular. Time passes. The story deals with the lives of people not directly involved with the event in question, most importantly the Layton family. The paterfamilias is an infantry colonel on his way back to India and his unfaithful wife after having been a German prisoner of war. Sarah, their older child, is a dutiful daughter of the regiment but with a poignantly evoked inner romantic life; Susan is the neurotic younger sister whose husband is killed in action and who goes on to marry the man who was burned and disfigured in trying to rescue him – Ronald Merrick. The political situation develops, the lives of the characters go on; people die, children are born; but still, like a vulture hanging over a hill of corpses, the plot continues to circle, round and round, reinspecting from new perspectives, reinterpreting the question of what happened in the Bibighar Gardens and of what Ronald Merrick did to Hari Kumar. History moves on, but there is no escape from the past.

Ronald Merrick, from the moment he steps into the plot, is all wrong. He is a man too much dedicated to his work, and his job is not a rewarding one. He is not a pukka solider or even a 'box-wallah', or businessman; he is a cop, and has to deal with local miscreants – drunks, agitators, thieves. He is very good at keeping order, but this does not win him the respect he craves. The officers look down on him because he has no king's commission in the army and because he was educated at a state grammar school. He is the only child of elderly parents, we learn later; they ran a corner shop and his grandparents were 'in service'. Merrick's is the sort of solid education most people today would regard as hopelessly desirable, but in the top echelons of British India of the 1940s it has stigmatised him. He has not been to a public (i.e. private) school, like the army officers, most of whom have been to Chillingborough – an imagined establishment that exerts a strong, if slightly comic, pull over its old boys in this corner of the empire.

This snobbery draws us to Merrick's side, but then we find that's not a good place to be. There is something cruel, denied and mechanical about him. We may not be put off by his 'background', but we are repelled by almost every other aspect of him. Paul Scott uses many narrators and viewpoints in the course of these four books, but none of them, except the unbalanced Susan Layton, is really sympathetic to Merrick. Each, however, seems to have a piece of that awful broken jigsaw to contribute.

Merrick is at first the 'most eligible bachelor on the station. He was quite good-looking if a man with a permanent sneer in his eye can ever be called that.' Other young women are envious of Daphne when Merrick asks her out, and Daphne, who is a 'galumphing' girl, is flattered by his attentions. Yet there is something about him she can't quite overlook: 'It's his manner that's against him (and something behind his manner, naturally)'. Sister Ludmila, an Eastern European who runs a medical mission in Mayapore, puts it much more sharply: 'There was nothing straightforward about Mr Merrick. He worked the wrong way, like a watch that's wound up backwards, so that at midday, for those who knew, he showed midnight'.

It is in Sister Ludmila's compound that Merrick has his first sight of Hari Kumar, half naked, washing under a pump. Merrick feasts his eyes – rather as Lady Chatterley does on first watching Mellors at his ablutions. He addresses him in Hindi, but Hari, it turns out, speaks no Indian language: he has been educated in England, at Chillingborough. Merrick knows that Hari has been seeing something of Daphne, though he does not know how close they are. Merrick is repelled by Hari because he thinks that people with brown skin are inferior to those with white; he is also intimidated by him because Hari has the polish and the manners that he lacks. The anguish for Merrick is that he is attracted to a man he wants to look down on. He has not yet admitted to himself that his desires are for men, not for women, and is a long way from being able to confront the nature of his feeling for this half-naked Indian man whom he wishes to despise, but by whom he feels threatened and ashamed. It is entirely in keeping with the time and the place that Merrick should look to his job and to the structures of the Raj for help. These at least are safe and secure; they are greater than any individual. He will take Hari in for questioning; then he may be able to get his own desires under lock and key.

Sister Ludmila, though, sees what is happening. Merrick 'had long ago chosen Hari Kumar, chosen him as a victim ... to observe more closely the darkness that attracted the darkness in himself ... On Kumar's part, a darkness of the soul. On Merrick's a darkness of the mind and heart and flesh ... For Merrick was a man unable to love. Only he was able to punish. It was Kumar whom Merrick wanted. Not Miss Manners.'

Much of what Merrick does to Hari Kumar lies within the bounds of normal – if not acceptable – behaviour. A senior army officer, Brigadier Reid, recalls that Merrick told him that if he 'sometimes bent the rules and paid [Indian criminals] back in their own coin, he believed that the end justified the means. He said he was almost "off his head" at the thought that a decent girl like Daphne Manners, with every advantage civilised life had to offer, should have been taken in by a fellow like Kumar who had the benefit of an English public school education.' Reid believes that 'Merrick was obviously acting in the heat of the moment, believing [Hari and others he had arrested] guilty of attacking a girl he was obviously fond of.' A charge of rape 'simply wouldn't stick', but the men's record of political activities was such that they could be 'dealt with' under the Defence of India Rules.

Reid sees a procedural problem, but registers no distaste for Merrick's attitude. And herein lies another conflict for Merrick. Those who agree with his view of the world are people, such as Brigadier Reid, that he fears (for their status) and despises (for their stupidity). Those that he wants to respect him – people such as Daphne Manners – recoil from him. Daphne's journals give a moving account of her trying hard to like a man who has been kind and attentive to her, but she cannot bear being lectured about her friendship with Hari. When she says she doesn't care what colour or nationality Hari is, Merrick replies, 'That's the oldest trick in the game, to say colour doesn't matter. It does matter. It's basic. It matters like hell.'

Daphne's journals reveal a loving, independent spirit, something much more complex and intriguing than the conventional memsahib we at first encountered. Paul Scott's inhabitation of his women characters is one of the wonders of these four books; the sustained flight of sympathetic imagination seems flawless. Daphne dies after childbirth, and the first volume closes with a description of her daughter Parvati, who may or may not also be Hari's child. She is dressed in a pale pink saree and is practising her singing lessons in the garden of the house where Daphne had been happy. 'Her skin is the palest brown and in certain lights her long dark hair reveals a redness more familiar in the north'. The first book ends with the morning raga that she sings – Parvati, this offspring of love and violence, of chance and history. It is one of the most haunting fictional images I have ever encountered.

In *The Day of the Scorpion*, Merrick agrees to be best man to a simple young officer called Teddie Bingham, who is to marry Susan Layton in

Ranpur. Merrick has been seconded to the army and has been promoted to the rank of major, but a stone is thrown at him at the wedding and it transpires that this is not the first incident of harassment. Even though Merrick has left the police force, the friends and political allies of Hari Kumar, who is still in prison, are pursuing him. The truth is closing on Merrick in other ways. Count Bronowsky, a homosexual White Russian with an administrative role in Ranpur, tricks him with a remark about a handsome officer into revealing his true sexual preferences. Merrick admits that he was the 'worst possible choice' as Teddie's best man.

Moreover, Lady Manners, Daphne's aunt, has managed to have the Kumar case reopened. A young officer called Rowan interrogates Hari in prison, and Hari tells how Merrick first lifted his genitals with his swagger stick to examine them, then rubbed blood into them from the wounds on Hari's buttocks where he had been beaten. Hari believes that Merrick wanted Hari to strike him. 'He invited me to hit him. I think he really wanted me to.'

The most important human emotion, Merrick tells Hari in prison, is not love but contempt. 'He said a man's personality existed at the point of equilibrium between the degree of his envy and the degree of his contempt'. It is in this scene that Paul Scott takes the reader into the heart of Merrick's darkness. Here is a man who, while appearing tightly disciplined, has lost all control of himself. The dividing line between his public duty and his private passions has completely disappeared; yet he uses the full force of the colonial bureaucracy to license and conceal his own sadomasochistic impulses. One of the most upsetting aspects of this powerful scene is the fact that Hari does not know that Daphne Manners is dead, or that she had a child.

Merrick goes to fight in Burma with Teddie Bingham against Indian nationalist insurgents who have joined the Japanese. Bingham foolishly tries to show Merrick how to be a pukka officer by attempting to win back an Indian patrol to its former imperial masters. But by calling out to them, 'It was as if Teddie himself gave the signal' to open fire. Bingham is killed and Merrick loses an arm and is badly burned in trying to pull him out of his jeep (intriguingly, he first saves the non-officer driver). Merrick tells the story to Sarah Layton when she visits him in hospital in Calcutta. He wants Sarah to see that all the Chillingborough and empire public-school stuff is nonsense, but Teddie is not diminished in Sarah's mind by the story. She thinks that Teddie's bravery in trying to win back the men to his regiment and Merrick's courage in trying to help him are both equally insane. While no one can doubt the wounded Merrick's stoicism, Sarah notes his blue eyes, which are like a doll's: 'a demanding but unseeing blue incapable either of acceptance or rejection'. Later, she tells her aunt: 'As a matter of fact he appals me.'

Paul Scott referred to the third volume, *The Towers of Silence*, as the 'slow movement'. Much of it is concerned with Barbie Bachelor, an elderly missionary who longs to find useful work, but is instead subject to humiliations and rejection. Her religious devotion is shaken by growing disillusionment; in one scene she is left sitting in the middle of the road with luggage showered about her after a cart has shed a wheel. In some ways she is an emblem of the expulsion the British face in India, but she is also the kind of unpromising character (like Miss Bates in *Emma*) who yield their inner gold only to the most patient novelist. At this point, it ought to be acknowledged that some critics of the 'based on' tendency have tried to explain the female characters of the Raj Quartet by reference to the nature of their creator. Daphne Manners, Barbie Bachelor and Sarah Layton are not, to them, three of the most successfully imagined female characters of mid-twentieth-century British fiction; they are instead 'based on' aspects of Paul Scott, because Scott himself was ... gay! To buy into this sort of thinking you would presumably need to believe that the psychological landscape of homosexual men and heterosexual women is so near to being identical as makes no difference. We know from every book written by these two groups of people that this is not true; but such a supposition remains irresistible to 'based on' critics because it means they do not then have to confront the possibility that the writer has invented: he has merely 'put himself in'.

Though Barbie is the focus of the third book, small pieces of the Merrick jigsaw continue to be put in place. While sharing a billet with him, Teddie Bingham notices both his trained physique – 'You could count the pads of muscle that made up his abdominal wall' – and the excessive neatness of his kit; it reminds us that Bronowsky (who has clearly read Freud since being exiled to the West) tells Merrick when he sees him picking up confetti at Teddie and Susan's wedding that tidy people are 'trying to wipe the slate clean'. Teddie thinks 'Merrick looked as though he had been made by a machine and was waiting for someone to come and disconnect him'. In a fever one night, Teddie thinks he has seen a Pathan standing in a long robe in his room. Much later we discover it was no dream, but that Merrick likes to dress up as a Pathan to go out at night, looking for information – and perhaps also for rough trade.

Hari's aunt prostrates herself at Merrick's feet at the railway station, begging for Hari's release, and we learn that it was persecution by his political enemies that drove Merrick from Mayapore and then from the police force itself. Harassment continues when a woman's bicycle – a reminder of Daphne's – is left on his verandah and chalk marks are scrawled on the floor. When he goes to Pankot, the hill station, to visit the Layton family, Merrick finds himself with Barbie, who senses 'something which made the air difficult to breathe'. Of modest background herself, Barbie is nevertheless impressed by Merrick, who mendaciously tells her that his transfer to the army was a 'reward for my handling of the Manners case'.

In the widowed Susan Layton, Merrick sees a final chance of being taken into the mainstream of the society that has rejected him. By means of a homosexual blackmail, he gains access to her psychiatric files, and, armed with what he finds there, is able to present himself to Susan as a man who 'really understands' her. In the closing sections of the book, married to Susan, Merrick becomes more reckless in his behaviour. Guy Perron, a young and independently minded staff officer under Merrick's command, believes that Merrick 'found it necessary to be close to someone whose antagonism he knew he could depend on', and that 'without this antagonism he had really nothing satisfactory by which to measure the effect of his behaviour'. At the same time, Merrick craves exposure. Perron thinks he was 'the kind of man who worked for preference within a very narrow margin of safety where his own reputation was concerned. He courted disaster. Deep down, I think, he had a death wish … He had a talent, one that amounted to genius, for seeing the key or the combination of keys that would open a situation up so that he could twist it to his purpose.'

Merrick's enemies begin to infiltrate rent boys into his marital home under the guise of gardeners and house servants, preying on his long-suppressed desires. For a time, Merrick retains control of his behaviour. Now a lieutenant colonel, and decorated with the DSO, he relishes the respectability of marriage. Paul Scott tells us that his stepson, Edward, a little boy frightened of everyone, does not fear Merrick – even with his one arm and his facial disfigurement. Whether Scott intends this as a small extenuation for Merrick or a signal that he has learned how to treat the child from his clandestine study of the mother's case notes is left satisfactorily unclear. The role Merrick allows Susan in nursing him and tending to his painful stump allows her to feel of some use again to other people. In another edgily balanced scene, Merrick uses his artificial hand as a lure to make a cobra strike, killing the snake with a kukri in his good hand. Physical courage and mental cruelty always find a nice balance in him.

The death of this grandly conceived and painstakingly analysed character is everything the reader craves. Dressed as a Pathan tribesman, he is strangled with his ceremonial sash and cut up with his ornamental axe by the rent boy with whom he has just enjoyed sex – perhaps, according to Count Bronowsky, for the first time in his life. The sexual act had brought him peace, but also contradicted all his theories of racial superiority; in death he meets the masochistic annihilation that his preening sadism and unresolved self-loathing have long courted.

Without men like Merrick, Paul Scott suggests, the Raj could not have run efficiently. Without Merrick, there would have been no tea exports, no profits for the occupier; but also no railways, no civil infrastructure and no mission schools for the occupied. Scott gives this view a full examination, through the eyes of Rowan in *A Division of the Spoils*:

Even the suspicion that Merrick had blundered was tempered by a determination not to allow it to be officially admitted. Uncorroborated and inadmissible evidence that in the case of Hari Kumar the blunder was one of a peculiarly unpleasant kind looked like having to remain a haunting burden on the consciences of a few. The irony of Merrick's act of bravery [with Teddie] and the recommendation for a decoration was not lost on Rowan. It would justify the opinion originally held by the rank and file of the administration, and never truly altered, that in the Manners rape case Merrick had acted with that forthright avenging speed which had once made the Raj feared and respected, and India a place where men did not merely operate a machine of law and order, but ruled and damned the consequences of ruling.

Ronald Merrick's crime is not that he cuts corners but that he allows personal feelings to override his civic and military duties. He persecutes Hari because he is sexually drawn to him. As well as beating him, or having him beaten, he fondles his genitals. Crucially, he plants Daphne's bike at Hari's house because he feels that if he can get Hari in prison for a good long time he may also get his own desires under lock and key. In this aim he fails. He carries the swagger stick with him everywhere – an odd little phallic symbol for a policeman and a strutting soldier, as it is perhaps the self-same stick he used to lift and examine Hari's genitals.

Merrick's insistence at various times that a white man would be degraded by contact with a 'black' woman, his stress on 'contempt', on class, caste, difference, hostility and so on are attempts to 'normalise' his own hankering after sadomasochistic fulfilment. If everyone is at it, his half-conscious thinking goes, then I am normal. The drama or the 'project' of Ronald Merrick lies in his crazed, almost heroic attempt to make the outer world of the Raj, with its repressive military and civil structures, both represent and validate his own sexual psychopathology.

In the Raj Quartet Paul Scott draws on what we might call the historical dividend. While Daphne Manners, Merrick, Barbie Bachelor and Sarah Layton have the authenticity of fully imagined characters, we also know that there were hundreds and thousands like them. This gives extra poignancy and resonance to their story. Steerpike stands or falls as a character by whether he 'works' in his created world, but Merrick is able to draw on our knowledge of history to discomfort us. Motivated by desires sometimes unclear to himself yet elegantly disclosed to the reader, fitted precisely into complex and developing social structures, he is a triumph of psychological realism – able to reveal to us not only the dark places of the human mind but the shadows of our real and painful history, so that, through his imagined life, our understanding of ourselves and who we are is thrillingly enriched.

'ISN'T THERE
A MAN HERE?'

JACK MERRIDEW

Jack Merridew, the bad boy in William Golding's novel *Lord of the Flies*, published in 1954, is a child-killer who does things that we now associate with blurred CCTV footage, Black Marias, screaming crowds and tabloid fury. The questions for the readers of such newspapers are when, if ever, such an individual should be released and whether he is entitled to a life of anonymity 'at the taxpayer's expense'. What the reader of the book has to ask, though, is whether Jack is really an individual at all.

It has been taken as read since its publication that while *Lord of the Flies* is an exciting story, its significance lies not in its characters or what they do, but in what they tell us about childhood and human nature. In other words, it is supposed to have an ulterior meaning, like a parable or an allegory. There are reasons for taking this view. To begin with, the book is set in a place and time that is not quite ours; it seems to begin after a nuclear

349

war that is not recorded in our history and to happen on an island that may not appear on our maps. It is as though the author is keen to shrug off some of the restraints of realism. Second, the boys who have survived the plane crash to be washed up, somewhat mysteriously, on the island, are not distinguished from one another in much detail. The differences between Ralph and Jack – the good boy and the bad boy – are given much less fully than, for instance, those between Barbie and Sarah, two good women in the Raj Quartet; and clearly this economy of detail is deliberate.

The logic, however, of viewing the book in this way is to say that because the setting is not exact and the characters have been to some extent depersonalised, it has liberated the author to exaggerate their actions. So that the 'lesson' of this cautionary tale is not that boys would literally turn into savages as these not-fully-realised characters do in their not-quite-actual world, but that all of us have violence close to the surface; that the veneer of 'civilisation' is a thin and fragile one. So, in the traditional way of fables, *Lord of the Flies* has first simplified things (in the characterisation) and then exaggerated them (in the action) to make its moral point.

In favour of this interpretation is its consistency. Against it is the simple fact that when you read the book it does not feel that this is what Golding is trying to do. On the contrary, it seems that the force of the novel lies in our believing that these are not the exaggerated events of fable, but are precisely and literally what boys – any boys – would do. The reason that their characters are somewhat underdeveloped is that Golding needed to remove the idea of individual psychological motivation from the equation; it cannot be an option for the reader to say that the boys are misled by a wicked leader and that with other individuals there would have been a different outcome. They behave as they do because that is what human beings are – all human beings. And twelve-year-old boys are probably the only human grouping in which a pack ethos is naturally dominant. It is therefore plausible for Golding to present his main characters with minimal psychological distinctions, because that fairly reflects the cross-section of humanity he is examining.

However, it is clear that distinctions are made. Simon, the fey, detached boy who faints in the heat is different from Roger, with his 'inner intensity of avoidance and secrecy' – a naturally aggressive child who goes on to become Jack's executive arm or henchman. Piggy, who remembers and clings to the English suburban world and all it stands for, is different from Ralph, who at once wants to make the most of their new island life. There is a whole group of younger boys, the fruit-eating 'Littluns', aged about six, 'who lived a quite distinct, and at the same time intense, life of their own'. I think the challenge of the characterisation for Golding was not to 'go fabular', but to show *limited* psychological motivation. These boys are properly different one from the other, but with two important provisos: difference is less important than similarity in a group of twelve-year-old boys, particularly boarders; and, second, even the most pronounced character trait of any individual is not enough to affect the overall outcome of the action, which would be the same with an entirely different group of individuals.

Jack in this scheme must therefore be a particular boy, but also any boy. And this mixed or partial characterisation undoubtedly represented a challenge for Golding.

Ralph has a 'mildness about his mouth and eyes that proclaimed no devil'. He is a good boy, but an unformed one. Jack, by contrast, is first seen as 'something dark' – part of an unidentified creature that reveals itself to be a group of black-clad choirboys; they all have a silver cross on the left breast and Jack alone has a gold cross on his cap. He vaults on to the platform, 'with his cloak flying' – part angel, part vampire. His first questions are all about the absence of adults: 'Isn't there a man here?' He presumes that the conch has been blown by a man. The absence of 'a man' is a problem for him in a way that it is not for Ralph or Piggy. Ralph is excited by the liberation from adult supervision; Piggy is anxious because his poor health has made him dependent on adult structures, but remains reasonably confident that he can carry the suburban world of opticians and aunties in his head; Jack, however, is simply frightened. Ralph wants to enjoy and Piggy wants to remember; but Jack needs to recreate. In the perturbing absence of the real thing, he sees it as his task to 'become' a man.

Adam Phillips, the writer and psychotherapist, put it to me like this: 'Jack behaves as he does because of all the boys he is the most frightened … Jack's a boy enacting the idea of adulthood … because he's trying to convince himself that he doesn't need parents.' When Ralph wins the first vote to be chief, the freckles on Jack's face disappear beneath a 'blush of mortification', but when he is allowed to keep control of the choir, for hunting, he and Ralph look at each other with 'shy liking'. The first time he is confronted with a pig to kill, however, Jack can't bring himself to do it, 'because of the enormity of the knife descending and cutting into living flesh'. His 'man' project needs work.

One of the best ways of imitating grown-ups in Jack's mind is to have rules. 'Lots of rules! And then when anyone breaks 'em—'. He is interrupted before he can finish, but it is clear that he thinks offenders should be punished. That's how adults behave: laws, police, courts, prison. Jack's path to 'manhood' turns out to have only an intermittent relationship with rules and a stronger affinity to force. He grabs the spectacles from Piggy's nose to use them to make fire; the need for fire comes from the 'rules' side of him, but ripping the glasses off the fat boy's face is an anarchic short cut. Rules become flexible to such a person. When Piggy asks to be heard because he has the conch, symbol of order, in his hand, Jack improvises: 'The conch doesn't count on top of the mountain, so you shut up!'

By the time Jack goes hunting for the second time, he has steeled himself to the task. He starts to use swear words; his eyes are 'bolting and nearly mad'. With Ralph, he 'tried to convey the compulsion to track down and kill that was swallowing him up'. Later, he confesses that when he is out hunting he sometimes feels as though he himself is the prey. Both he and Ralph are frightened of a snake, a thing, a 'beastie' – some nameless idea that the island might not be a good island. Simon gives voice to these fears – in what is later called 'his effort to express mankind's essential illness' – and by doing so marks himself down as dangerous and disposable. The small society had already generated a taboo – don't mention the Darkness – and Simon has broken it.

Piggy, meanwhile, is still living by the old rules of home. 'He wanted to explain how people were never quite how you thought they were' – and this goes as much for his auntie's house as it does for the island. But Ralph and Simon have diverged. 'They walked along, two continents of experience and feeling, unable to communicate.' Without defining their differences, Golding is insistent on them. There is a lovely passage on the self-absorbed innocence of Henry, one of the little boys, at play; yet while he becomes 'absorbed beyond mere happiness', Roger is starting to throw stones into the water round about him. Roger is testing the invisible limits – 'the protection of parents and policemen and the law' – that still surround the little boy at play. Jack displaces fear into practical grown-up action – swearing and hunting; Roger looks coolly and direct at the taboos of an absent civilisation.

For Jack, it is face-paint that provides liberation from shame and self-consciousness, and it's this disguise and the freedom it confers that finally enable him to kill. The dawn of shame in the Garden of Eden is the moment at which Adam and Eve become 'fallen' in religious language, or 'human' in evolutionary terms. Shame is the by-product of self-consciousness, and consciousness itself, so far as we know, is a key *Homo sapiens* attribute, still peculiar to the species. Jack sees his journey as an acquisition – of manly cruelty; but it can equally be viewed as a loss – the loss of inhibition, and a regression to the prelapsarian state.

Piggy rebukes Jack for having let the fire go out – and with it, perhaps, their chance of a rescue and return to England. At this moment, 'the bolting look came into his blue eyes'. Not 'a' bolting look, but 'the' bolting look, which suggests it is now habitual, or characteristic; another boy would not have it. Jack drives his fist into Piggy's abdomen and Piggy's glasses are broken in the scuffle. A fire is rebuilt, but something is different. 'Not even Ralph knew how a link between him and Jack had been snapped and fastened elsewhere.' Jack, as hunter-provider, is enraged that not all the others appreciate what he has done for them. He has, after all, been a 'man' for them. 'Jack looked round for understanding but found only respect.' This is a hard moment for Jack, and something that is perhaps the lot of public figures or leaders in all societies: the understanding that they have crossed a line and will no longer be judged by the same homely standards that non-leaders apply to themselves. The leader wants applause or even love, but can command only disengaged respect. Jack feels isolated; his rage is described as 'elemental and awe-inspiring', though it is still driven by fear. He rounds on the others to tell them that they are 'cry-babies and sissies' who contribute nothing – 'And as for the fear – you'll have to put up with that like the rest of us.'

Jack's way of defeating fear, through violence, is not necessarily a 'wrong' reaction to circumstances. When he says, 'If there's a beast, we'll hunt it down! We'll close in and beat and beat and beat!' he reminds us of the trials of early *Homo sapiens* and their attitude not only to gathering food, but to whole other species, such as the Neanderthals, they viewed as competition – and eliminated. In Darwinian terms the best way to deal with the unknown is to kill it. It is also the best way for Jack to deal with the frustration he feels about the fact that his considerable efforts to become a man have not been appreciated by the other boys; in fact, his striving seems simply to have isolated him – to have put him in a lonely place where he is more prey than ever to the fears he has set out to quell.

Golding's characterisation of Jack relies on Ralph as his counterpart; they are almost as interdependent as Fagin and Oliver Twist, though there is an odd little passage in which we are given a very specific glimpse of Ralph's home life – a naval father and an absent mother, modest but cosy Home Counties comfort, storybooks and a bowl of cornflakes with sugar and cream at bedtime – and there is nothing comparable for Jack. They seem to be drifting further apart, yet when a game of stick-the-pig, with one of the boys as the quarry, gets momentarily out of hand Ralph finds that the 'desire to squeeze and hurt was over-mastering'. Here is the moment at which Golding, having clearly differentiated Ralph from Jack, is having it both ways in his mixed or partial characterisation by stressing the underlying similarity. The success or otherwise of the novel depends on the effectiveness of these distinctions.

Jack presses for a second show of hands to see if he can now become leader, but no one votes for him. He departs in tears of shame and fury. The hunting goes on. Jack and Roger skewer a female pig, Roger driving a spear up the animal's rear. 'The sow collapsed under them and they were heavy and fulfilled upon her.' Golding does not have to use more than one suggestive word – 'fulfilled' – to make plain the force of this moment in the lives of boys coming up to puberty. The female is a significant absence in *Lord of the Flies*, or, as a true Freudian might perhaps have it, a significant presence.

Having failed to win support for his leadership by democracy, Jack finally prevails by offering more adventure to his followers, more 'fun' – and by withholding food from those who won't join his group of hunters. Ralph and Piggy are wrong-footed. By this time, Ralph, torn between individual personality and the tribal atavism he feels engulfing him, can barely remember what he is meant to be doing, though the mentally tougher Piggy still carries the world in his head and can remind him: build a fire, hope for rescue; get back to 'houses an' streets an' TV'.

And now, at last, Jack is triumphant. 'Power lay in the brown swell of his forearms; authority sat on his shoulder and chattered in his ear like an ape.' To some extent, you feel, he has earned it, because he has had to overcome more fear than the others. Now even Piggy and Ralph find themselves 'eager to take a place in this demented but partly secure society'. During a thunderstorm the boys surround and stab the 'pig' to death with sharpened sticks, but this time the pig is a child: Simon. Golding's editor at Faber, Charles Monteith, persuaded Golding not only to drop some opening chapters that explained how the boys had got to the island but to make Simon a much less obvious Christ-figure. To be effective, Monteith argued, allegorical intent should be invisible.

After this appalling climax, Jack finds himself removed into a strange realm of authority where others will carry out his wishes – out of fear, out of shame, out of truculence. A boundary has been crossed; now Jack is evil without having to do evil. Ralph, Piggy and the twins Sam and Eric were also present at the murder; they were accessories, though they deny it: 'Memory of the dance that none of them had attended shook all four boys convulsively.'

It is the isolation of Jack that seems so apt. At the end of the book he finds himself so revered by the other boys that he need no longer dirty his own hands: it is Roger who levers the large boulder off the top of the hill to kill Piggy. From this moment on, Golding refers to Jack in the narrative not by name but as 'the Chief'. It is his leadership and his example – the conquering of his own fears by violence – that has allowed more naturally violent children, such as Roger, to overcome the taboos of civilised society.

For the story to have universal force, I believe it was necessary for Golding to eliminate the idea that with other boys the outcome would have been different. To achieve this, he clearly had to limit the extent to which he individualised each child. The oddest passage in this very well-edited and meticulously written book is therefore the glimpse of Ralph's home life. It is strange that it was allowed to remain because it is so out of keeping with the rest of the novel; even for Ralph it seems to raise more questions than it answers. The most significant passage in the book, though, is one that isn't there – the equivalent snapshot of Jack's home life. To have given that would have risked normalising or explaining him as an individual; it would have made him too much Jack, too little Anyboy, and this would have lessened the impact of the novel.

However, the fact that the characterisation is limited does not mean to say it is non-existent. These are individual boys with real differences and real characteristics; the extremely delicate challenge to which Golding successfully rose was to give them their clear and touching identities, yet to make it plain – beyond any consolation – that with a cast of different boys, exactly the same events would have taken place. Jack is not a villain because he is Jack Merridew; he is a villain as well as being Jack Merridew.

'LONG-HAUL SOLITUDE'

BARBARA COVETT

Zoë Heller told me that she originally planned her admired 2003 novel *Notes on a Scandal* without the character of Barbara Covett. I felt like someone who had come across a notebook from Stratford-upon-Avon dated 1602 that read: 'Comedy. Old Danish courtier, windbag, and his two twenty-ish children. Boy despatched abroad on gap year. Girl moons about in love. Travails of single parenthood. First draft done. Perhaps needs another character. Maybe daughter boyfriend. Someone posh?'

Notes on a Scandal is Barbara's book as surely as *Hamlet* belongs to the prince. Zoë Heller may have begun with a Scandal, wanting to write about the affair between a woman teacher and a teenage pupil, but the Notes are Barbara's and her contribution quite rightly comes first in the title. This is a novel whose success depends on a tone of voice – Barbara's. First-person narration makes the obvious sacrifice of multiple viewpoints – we can learn what people think and feel through only one filter – and it is a sign of stress to have the narrator call out for other voices, to 'come across' a diary written by another character, for instance, as Graham Greene does with Bendrix in *The End of the Affair*, such reinforcements suggest that the singular voice has failed. Imagine Holden Caulfield enlisting help in such a way during *The Catcher in the Rye*. Barbara reconstructs some scenes between Sheba and the boy, Connolly, based on what Sheba has told her; but they are still narrated in Barbara's own voice, as though she is a voyeur in the corner. First-person narration requires self-discipline from the novelist and it helps if the voice you have found – or that has found you – is beguiling, clever and dangerous, as Barbara's is. It particularly helps if the reader can see the limitations of the narrator's understanding of events. Whether these limits are imposed by a lack of truthfulness or a lack of vision doesn't matter, so long as they are made visible.

The idea of the 'unreliable narrator', as well as being a cliché of modern journalism, is seldom, it seems to me, a helpful one. Anybody asked to tell a story will give a version of events shaped by their own experience and sensibility. Imagine Gertrude's account of the events in *Hamlet*. Or Merrick's of those in the Raj Quartet. All properly realised characters are therefore unreliable if asked to narrate; perhaps the only 'reliable' narrator the novel has ever produced is the authorial omniscience of Henry James. The success of Barbara Covett as a narrator lies, I think, in the fact that she is largely reliable. The acidic comedy of her phrasing simultaneously skewers her victims and reveals the limitations of her own perspective. This is the joy of a narrative voice that arrives in the author's head fully formed with its own tone and cadences; such a character pretty much writes the book for you.

Barbara is calm, self-critical and self-knowing. In her foreword, she compares herself to Sheba, the younger woman at the heart of the scandal, and says: 'It's not that Sheba is cleverer than me. Any objective comparison would have to rate me the more educated woman, I think. (Sheba knows a bit about art – I'll give her that; but for all her class advantages, she is woefully ill-read.)' This tells us quite a bit about both women, as does Barbara's talk of Sheba's 'insouciant frankness', which Barbara thinks is a 'class characteristic': Sheba is 'the only genuine upper-class person I've ever known. Her throwaway candour is exotic to me.' There is a comic antithesis throughout the book between Barbara, who tries so hard, thinks everything through, examines almost every nuance of her behaviour yet has ended up with nothing, and Sheba, whose careless abundance of money, sex and friends attracts more of the same.

It takes the reader a little while to get the hang of Barbara, to see which parts of her narrative are factual and which are her just 'being Barbara', as it were. Early on, she complains about the fact that every single newspaper reporter covering the court case has described her handbag – 'a perfectly unexceptional, wooden-handled object, with a needlepoint portrait of two kittens on it' – and one is not quite sure whether such a steely sixty-year-old would really be unaware of the signals sent out by pussycats on a bag. On the same page she confides that: 'My naïve hope, in acting as Sheba's spokeswoman, has been to counter some of the sanctimonious hostility towards my friend, and to shed a little light on the true nature of her complex personality.' We don't know at this stage if this is literally true or not. Later we learn that it is not; this is an example of Barbara persuading herself of something. Sheba's character is not really 'complex' at all – or certainly not in the eyes of Barbara, who largely considers her 'fey'. Of course anyone's personality is 'complex' when compared to a newspaper version of it, but as the story goes on we learn that such rationalisations are necessary to Barbara so that she can protect herself from guilt. She has done a single bad thing, and doesn't wish to be saddled with the ramifications of it, since that would dilute the joy that her misdeed has brought her.

The only weakness of Zoë Heller's very accomplished book lies in the feasibility of the central event. It is often – by no means all the time, but a little too often for comfort – hard to believe that Sheba, forty-two, a mother, privileged, arty and at ease with herself, would really have had an affair with an ordinary fifteen-year-old schoolboy. In the film version, with Sheba played by Cate Blanchett and lit as though in glowing Technicolor, it was frankly impossible. In the book, however, without Cate Blanchett's improbable beauty to distance us and with the cold lens of Barbara's narration to compel our complicity, it is usually possible to suspend disbelief.

Oddly enough, this credibility strain adds an extra level of tension. There is not only the slow-motion car crash of Sheba's life, there is the secondary anguish of wondering whether Barbara can make it credible to us; and this is what draws us most powerfully to her: she holds our entertainment in her hands. She must not only control the plot, she must make it believable. We sit at her feet like children, hoping to believe. The more ascetic her dried-up private life, the more factual and unfanciful, the more we can trust her as a storyteller. So when she says, 'To make sure I maintain maximum accuracy in this narrative, I have started putting together a timeline of Sheba's year at St George's. I store it – along with the manuscript – under my mattress at night', we give a little jump for joy. This is the sort of dotty pseudoscientific approach we want.

We trust Barbara because her accounts of other people have a strong internal conviction. The absurd maths teacher, Brian Bangs, who tries, embarrassingly, to flirt with Sheba, 'doing a twirl' in his hideous new shirt; Mr Pabblem, the go-ahead bureaucrat of a headmaster; the fat and desperate Sue Hodge, who becomes pregnant and is surprised that no one has 'noticed' how 'chunky' she has become (Barbara sees 'no discernible difference to Sue's Pantagruelian bulk'); Sheba's undistinguished yet arrogant husband Richard, who watches television sideways to let it know he's not interested in it; Richard's bitchy first wife, with whom he is on sickeningly good terms, and her annoying rheumatoid arthritis, vainly described as 'early-onset'... These and many other acid little etchings are not only funny but testify to a clear, if uncharitable, vision on Barbara's part. It is by the bright light of that intelligence that we understand her reluctance to give us all the details of why she left her first post in a school in Dumfries. If there was also a 'misunderstanding' with a previous woman teacher, Jennifer Dodd, that led to the threat of an injunction, well perhaps there were faults on both sides. And if Barbara was in the wrong, or even a bit crazy, that's still fine because it only adds a little more danger to the Sheba story she is telling now.

Barbara's personality – its malice, humour and truthfulness as well as its sliver of madness – really cohere only in her dealings with Sheba; only then does all of her come into focus. Her behaviour to Sheba is, to put it mildly, contradictory. She is proprietary yet dismissive; needy yet cruel. 'After half-term, I desisted from all the little genialities with which I had been attempting to semaphore my goodwill towards Sheba. I deliberately allowed my warm feelings to curdle into contempt.' She lets out mocking laughs at Sheba's vapid conversation in the staff room; she does stagey double-takes to show her disapproval of Sheba's outfits; she deliberately embarrasses

Sheba by offering a safety pin for a loose hem on her dress. Yet all of it is met with a 'perverse refusal to acknowledge my hostility'. How frustrating!

Barbara is lonely. There are precise, wince-inducing, itemisations of her solitude. It is her desire for company more than for sex that draws her to Sheba. Barbara is a woman who has discovered that she can't attract friendship by the attractiveness of her personality so, in her early sixties, has resorted to coercion. She has no specific plan for entrapping Sheba, she must simply wait for an opportunity. When she learns of the affair with Connolly, she sees it as a possible lever, but is too clever to opt for simple blackmail. In any case, how would that work? She can't say, 'Be my friend or I will tell the headmaster and the police.' She needs to manipulate the situation so that Sheba becomes her more or less willing friend – or captive.

The question of Barbara's sexuality is unclear. She is scornful of the way the newspapers deal with the Sheba–Connolly affair, of their neat categorisations and tabloid self-righteousness, beyond which all activity is unacceptable or 'kinky'. She suggests she is broad-minded; she admires only one report, which speculates that perhaps Connolly was not a virgin and asks what red-blooded teenage boy would not like to go to bed with Sheba. Barbara might enjoy it herself, just as she might have enjoyed sex with Jennifer Dodd, though what actually worried her about being seen out with Jennifer was not that people would think they were lesbians but that they'd laugh at them for being sad spinsters. In any event, sex is secondary to company in her list of needs, and it's not even clear that a woman would be her first choice of partner. When she talks of loneliness – which is the core of her – she reveals how the 'accidental brush of a bus conductor's hand on your shoulder sends a jolt of longing straight to your groin', and we assume that the word 'conductor' signifies a man. This all appeared too tricky for the film, which not only changed the ending of the story, but made Barbara into a predatory lesbian. Film-makers generally assume that their audience can't handle the same degree of complication as readers of a book, which seems a particularly odd assumption when the film in question is an adaptation of an existing novel and the producers hope, presumably, to attract a large number of the book's readers into the cinema. However, it's not an assumption that looks set to change at any time soon, and the film of *Notes on a Scandal* had plenty of good things about it. Some of Patrick Marber's acid lines for Barbara were almost as good as Zoë Heller's; I particularly liked the relish with which Judi Dench, as Barbara, recalled Sheba describing the beginnings of her affairs with Richard. 'After the initial fuck-fest ...' You could almost see the inverted commas that Dame Judi scorched on either side of the word.

The critical moment for Barbara comes at the end of an excruciating scene in which the risible Brian Bangs, the maths teacher, has asked her out on what Barbara believes is a 'date'. Back in his squalid bachelor flat after lunch, Bangs reveals his true intention, which is to confide in her that he has a 'crush' on Sheba. Barbara is stung by her own self-delusion as well as by the idiocy of Bangs; above all, she resents being used as a depository for other people's secrets. She sees her moment, and after she has humiliatingly assured Bangs that the entire staff room has been laughing at his idiotic 'crush' for weeks, she tells him Sheba is having an affair with a boy.

Bangs, in his humiliation, is sure to tell the headmaster. Barbara, feeling guilty at her betrayal, thinks quickly and, in a brilliant piece of pre-emption, warns Sheba soon afterwards that she had the impression that Bangs 'somehow' suspects the truth about her and Connolly. When the scandal breaks, the police are called and everything seems to be in meltdown, Barbara sees the wretched Bangs going into the Gents and hisses 'Little shit!' after him.

The unexpected charm of Barbara lies in the way that we identify so much with her. Although she is manipulative, cruel and dishonest, she is very funny. A great deal of what she says about the vanities and self-delusions of the other characters is not only accurate but seems to need saying. Life, we feel, needs more Barbaras; or at least more people with zero tolerance of bullshit. Our sneaky liking for her does not prevent the end of the book, when Sheba has become her flatmate, from being creepily unsettling. Barbara has convinced Sheba that she has nowhere else to go. And although Sheba has discovered (by reading exactly what we have just been reading: a very Richardsonian trick) that it was Barbara who told Bangs about the affair, she has somehow accepted the betrayal and, more importantly, has accepted that Barbara's friendship is not just a last resort, but her only resort. She is an all-but-willing captive; she has become institutionalised in the long-stay ward of Barbara's solitude. The eerie calm that hangs over the final page recalls Winston Smith in the Chestnut Tree café at the end of *Nineteen Eighty-Four*. Sheba has come to love Big Sister.

ACKNOWLEDGEMENTS

This book was originally conceived as an accompaniment to a television series of the same name. I was asked in 2008 by Basil Comely and Mary Sackville-West of the BBC if I would be interested in doing a series about books and I gave a tentative 'yes'. Basil and Mary assured me that we could develop something worthwhile for the programmes to be 'about' and that they would make sure I was all right on screen. They certainly did the former.

The initial idea was that the series should celebrate not novelists' lives but the books they had created; it was the suggestion of Janice Hadlow, the controller of BBC2, that we should talk not about novels but about individual characters. John Mullan of University College London started coming to meetings in a café in west London, where we discussed possible character types and individuals. The series was initiated by the then controller of BBC2, Roly Keating, and the commissioner for arts, Mark Bell. Mary had the toughest task as both point-person between many egos and as part-time medical officer in what sometimes resembled a casualty clearing station.

ACKNOWLEDGEMENTS

Originally, the four directors were Phil Cairney (The Hero), Kate Misrahi (The Lover), David Vincent (The Snob) and Adrian Sibley (The Villain). Unforeseen circumstances meant that David had to do the lion's share. This was not before Phil and I had had some adventures in Puerto Rico (Robinson Crusoe) and New York (John Self) or before Adrian and I had rendezvoused halfway up the Himalayas (Merrick). My thanks to all four directors, but especially to David Vincent, who showed heroic patience in dealing with a novice presenter. Judith Robson was the indefatigable editor.

The camera team was Justin Evans and Sam Al-Kadi. They were talented, hard-working and good company; we celebrated Justin's 40th birthday in Delhi and Sam's marriage in Shepherd's Bush. From Justin I learned a little of how television works, and from Sam I picked up some interesting new words.

The other people I would like to thank are:

The production co-ordinator Sara Cameron, without whose good cheer and thermal underwear some of the freezing early starts would have been unbearable; assistant producer Caroline Walsh, who battled through temperatures of minus ten degrees, flu and unfair teasing; and researcher Charlotte Gittins, with apologies for leaving the sloe gin in her glove compartment.

Thanks also to assistant producers Lucy Heathcoat Amory and Bex Palmer; researchers Toby Bentley and Simon Lloyd; archive researchers Kathy Manners and Peter Scott; and to Patrick Acum, who was behind the camera when Justin was unavailable. Jacmel Dent and Sarah Baxter kept things real back at White City.

Many work experience volunteers came and went – unpaid. I would particularly like to thank Anne Meadows, who had not only read *all* of

ACKNOWLEDGEMENTS

Clarissa, but was full of ideas about Lovelace; and Ben Masters and Bridie Bischoff, who wrote background notes on the historical reception of the characters and will doubtless both go on to much greater things.

The others were: Amelia Aspden, Fionnuala Barrett, Eleanor Burton, Alexandra Carruthers, Stephanie Cross, Alexandra Dewdney, Roma Foulds, Tom Garvey, Madeleine Gillies, Tom Goble, Marianne Gray, Emma Harrison, Jane Harrison, Oli Hazzard, Sarah Hunt, Charlotte Kelly, Kathleen Keown, Alexandra Lewis, Zeljka Marosevic, Alexander Moss, Katherine Newbigging, Lydia Nicholas, Alex Nicole, Carina Persson, Eleanor Priestman, Emma Pritchard, Polly Randall, Emily Ryder, Laura Shacham, Nick Tanner, Hugh Trimble, Lizzie Webster, Kathrynne West, Florence Wilkinson, Sarah Williams and Lottie Young. I only hope the 'experience' was worthwhile for them.

I would like also to thank the following, who kindly gave their time to be interviewed:

Monica Ali, Martin Amis, Simon Armitage, Melissa Benn, Bidisha, Alain de Botton, William Boyd, Joanna Briscoe, Michael Caines, John Carey, Jonathan Coe, Richard Dawkins, Omid Djalili, Helen Fielding, Aminatta Forna, Nick Frost, Bonnie Greer, Joanne Harris, Robert Harris, Ronald Harwood, John Hegarty, Zoë Heller, Charlie Higson, Alan Hollinghurst, John Hurt, Marina Hyde, P.D. James, Liz Jensen, Boris Johnson, Sadie Jones, Pratik Kanjilal, Brian Keenan, A.L. Kennedy, Hari Kunzru, Norman Lebrecht, Mike Leigh, Penelope Lively, Tim Lott, Blake Morrison, James Naughtie, Rowan Pelling, Adam Phillips, Tim Pigott-Smith, Ian Rankin, Ruth Rendell, Peggy Reynolds, Simon Schama, Matthew Scott, Elaine Showalter, Dan Stevens, Kate Summerscale, Matthew Sweet, Mark Tully, Jenny Uglow, Natasha Walter and Kate Williams.

ACKNOWLEDGEMENTS

In the preparation of this book, I would like to thank Gillon Aitken, my literary agent; Albert DePetrillo and Laura Higginson at BBC Books; and John Mullan, who made many helpful comments on the draft and spared me a couple of howlers – the remainder, of course, being all my own work. Thanks also to my wife, Veronica, for editorial and other kindnesses.

I was encouraged to include the story of my first reactions to some of these novels, since the idea of how great books seem different to you at different ages was thought to be interesting; some readers may prefer to skip these bits. Since these acknowledgements have already gone on a bit and since the book refers back so often to student days, perhaps I can also take three lines to thank those teachers who, all those years ago, first helped me to appreciate books: Mr and Mrs Sexton; Anne Sanderson; Alec Annand, Michael Curtis, Michael Fox, Philip Letts; and Professor Derek Brewer and Dr John Harvey. And since self-indulgence has now won the day, I would also like to thank my much-missed parents – my mother, who taught me how to read, then endured many lisping demonstrations of my new-found skill; and my father, who provided the books and the encouragement.

Finally, I would like to point out that the title of this book is not my fault. A high-up person at the BBC decreed that the series should be so called because this year's craze is for having the presenter's name in the title. My choice, and not just because it was my wife's idea, was for 'Novel People', and I hope it may be possible to reprint the book at some future date under that preferable title.

S.F. London, February 2011

BIBLIOGRAPHY

HEROES

Amis, Kingsley, *Lucky Jim* (Penguin Modern Classics, 2000).

Amis, Martin, *Money* (Vintage, 2005).

Conan Doyle, Arthur, *The Complete Sherlock Holmes* (Vintage Classics, 2009).

Defoe, Daniel, *Robinson Crusoe* (Penguin Classics, 2004).

Fielding, Henry, *The History of Tom Jones* (Vintage Classics, 2007).

Orwell, George, *Nineteen Eighty-Four* (Penguin Modern Classics, 2004).

Thackeray, William Makepeace, *Vanity Fair* (Vintage Classics, 2009).

LOVERS

Austen, Jane, *Pride and Prejudice* (Vintage Classics, 2007).

Brontë, Emily, *Wuthering Heights* (Vintage Classics, 2008).

Greene, Graham, *The End of the Affair* (Vintage Classics, 2009).

Hardy, Thomas, *Tess of the D'Urbervilles* (Vintage Classics, 2008).

BIBLIOGRAPHY

Hollinghurst, Alan, *The Line of Beauty* (Picador, 2004).

Lawrence, D. H., *Lady Chatterley's Lover* (Vintage Classics, 2011).

Lessing, Doris, *The Golden Notebook* (Harper Perennial Modern Classics, 2007).

SNOBS

Ali, Monica, *Brick Lane* (Black Swan, 2004).

Austen, Jane, *Emma* (Vintage Classics, 2007).

Dickens, Charles, *Great Expectations* (Vintage Classics, 2008).

Fleming, Ian, Complete novels and stories (Penguin Modern Classics)

Grossmith, George and Weedon, *The Diary of a Nobody* (Vintage Classics, 2010).

Spark, Muriel, *The Prime of Miss Jean Brodie* (Penguin Modern Classics, 2000).

Wodehouse, P. G., Various from the Jeeves and Wooster series (Arrow Books Ltd, 2008).

VILLAINS

Collins, Wilkie, *The Woman in White* (Vintage Classics, 2007).

Dickens, Charles, *Oliver Twist* (Vintage Classics, 2007).

Golding, William, *Lord of the Flies* (Faber, 2009).

Heller, Zoë, *Notes on a Scandal* (Penguin, 2009).

Peake, Mervyn, *The Gormenghast Trilogy* (Vintage Classics, 1999).

Richardson, Samuel, *Clarissa, or The History of the Young Lady* (Penguin Classics, 2004).

Scott, Paul, *The Raj Quartet Volumes 1 and 2* (Everyman, 2007).

INDEX

INDEX